WILD SEATTLE

WILD SEATTLE

Roddy Scheer

TIMBER PRESS • PORTLAND, OR

This page: Chestnut-backed chickadee, page 49

Photo and illustration credits appear on page 325.

Timber Press
Workman Publishing
Hachette Book Group, Inc.
1290 Avenue of the Americas
New York, New York 10104
timberpress.com

Timber Press is an imprint of Workman Publishing, a division of Hachette Book Group, Inc. The Timber Press name and logo are registered trademarks of Hachette Book Group, Inc.

Printed in Shenzhen, China (APO), on responsibly sourced paper

Text design by Kristi Pfeffer, based on a series design by Anna Eshelman
Cover design by Stevie Shao
Illustrations by Stevie Shao

The publisher is not responsible for websites (or their content) that are not owned by the publisher.

ISBN: 978-1-64326-544-5

A catalog record for this book is available from the Library of Congress.

CONTENTS

INTRODUCTION

Seattle is a city shaped by nature. Perched between Puget Sound and the Cascade Mountains, it's a place where forests press against skyscrapers, salmon swim through urban waterways, and bald eagles soar over morning commutes. Despite its reputation for tech and coffee culture, Seattle is also home to an astonishing variety of wildlife, from great blue herons stalking the shallows of Lake Washington to harbor seals basking on Elliott Bay's docks.

Wild Seattle is your guide to discovering the region's natural wonders, whether you're wandering through the old-growth trees of Seward Park, scanning the Sound for orcas, or watching a belted kingfisher plunge into the water along the Burke-Gilman Trail. This book highlights the diverse ecosystems in and around Seattle—from tide pools teeming with anemones at Golden Gardens to the secret wetlands of Magnuson Park—while also introducing the species that call these places home.

Nature in Seattle isn't limited to designated green spaces. It thrives in unexpected places: peregrine falcons nest on downtown high-rises, river otters slip through the Ship Canal, and coyotes roam the city's quieter neighborhoods. Even in the heart of the urban landscape, with a bit of patience and curiosity, you'll find wildlife adapting to city life in remarkable ways.

This book is broken down into three sections. In section 1, you'll learn about the past, present, and future of wild nature in and around Seattle. What was the city like before white settlement? What is it like now, some 175 years later? And what will the future bring regarding nature in this Northwest megalopolis?

Section 2 focuses on 106 Species to Know—the flora and fauna that make Seattle one of the wildest of America's major cities. You'll learn what makes all kinds of iconic local species—from fungi to trees and inverte-brates to megafauna—tick, and how their interactions with one another form the fabric of the region's ecosystems.

Section 3 guides readers through twenty-five Field Trips out into the wilds of Seattle, with details about parks and other open spaces where you can experience different types of natural habitats and see how the local flora and fauna make a living in the real world.

Seattle's wild heart beats in every tide pool, treetop, and tucked-away green space, waiting to be discovered. Whether you're a lifelong resident or a first-time visitor, *Wild Seattle* invites you to see the city through a new lens—one where nature isn't just a backdrop but an active, resilient force shaping urban life. As you turn the pages, you'll uncover the hidden stories of the plants and animals that share this landscape, the challenges they face, and the ways we can help them thrive. So grab your binoculars, lace up your walking shoes, and step outside—wild Seattle is all around you, ready to surprise and inspire.

WILD SEATTLE: PAST, PRESENT, AND FUTURE

From Wilderness to World City

Seattleites often refer to their home as the Emerald City, not because it gleams of gold like the fictional capital city of Oz, but because of the city's abundance of evergreen trees—towering Douglas firs, western red cedars, and hemlocks—that blanket the landscape, from its urban parks to the surrounding forests of the Puget Sound region. Unlike other cities that experience dramatic seasonal shifts, Seattle maintains a lush, verdant appearance throughout the year, with moss-covered trees, vibrant ferns, and deep green canopies dominating the scenery. The name also embodies Seattle's environmental consciousness and its commitment to preserving nature within the urban landscape, from vast green spaces like Discovery Park to the canopy of street trees lining sidewalks all over the city. For locals, calling Seattle the Emerald City is not just about the Northwest metropolis's natural beauty but also about a shared appreciation for the city's deep connection to the wild and its efforts to remain green—both in color and in sustainability.

And while the region has gone through substantial changes since the first white settlers started streaming in during the middle of the 19th century, the verdant scenery and green consciousness remain ever present, making the Emerald City moniker ring as true today as ever. Read on to find out more about what's changed regarding nature and Seattle over the past two centuries and what the future may bring to this truly Emerald City on the shores of Puget Sound.

▼ Arthur Denny is credited as the founder of modern Seattle, given his role leading a group of pioneers west from Illinois in 1851 and eventually settling on the shores of Puget Sound at Alki Point, which is now part of West Seattle.

Past

When the twenty-two white settlers comprising the Denny Party arrived at Alki Point on November 13, 1851, the city we now know as Seattle was little more than a Native American outpost amid a seemingly never-ending expanse of trees. While the group's first winter at Alki was marked by nonstop rain and cold temperatures— welcome to the Pacific Northwest!—soon enough they adapted to their new climate and lifestyle. The following spring most of the group set up shop across the bay on the land that is now Pioneer Square in downtown Seattle, where there was better access to the logs that they could sell to make a living and the deepwater port of Elliott Bay as a distribution hub.

But just what did it look like when those first settlers landed at Alki? Before white settlement, the landscape around Puget Sound was a vast, unbroken wilderness, part of the Pacific Northwest temperate rainforest ranging for 2500 miles between Southeast Alaska and Northern California. This region was characterized by towering old-growth forests, where trees like Douglas fir, western red cedar, and western hemlock reached in some cases 300 or more feet into the sky. These ancient giants, some over a thousand years old, formed a dense canopy, creating a world of perpetual twilight on the forest floor.

Beneath these colossal trees, the forest was alive with a rich understory of plants. Swordferns blanketed the ground, their fronds spreading out like giant green fans, while salal bushes, with their leathery leaves and dark purple berries, grew in thick, impenetrable thickets. Huckleberry and salmonberry shrubs added splashes of color with their delicate blossoms and juicy, edible fruits. The forest also supported Oregon grape, its holly-like leaves and yellow flowers providing a stark contrast to the deep greens of the ferns and mosses that carpeted the earth.

Fire, Ice, and Erosion Forged Seattle's Baseline Landscape

Seattle's landscape is a product of dramatic geological forces that have sculpted its dynamic topography over millions of years. The story begins in the depths of the last Ice Age, around 12,000 years ago, when massive glaciers advanced across the region. These colossal ice sheets, moving slowly but powerfully, carved deep valleys and sculpted the land with their immense weight and grinding force. As the glaciers retreated, they left behind a network of fjords and a rugged topography that defines much of the Seattle area today.

The glaciers' retreat revealed a transformed landscape, with valleys filled by the glacial meltwaters that formed the Puget Sound and its intricate system of bays and inlets. The glacial ice had also sculpted the region's hills, creating features like Capitol Hill, which stands as a testament to the enormous forces at work. The glacially smoothed and gouged terrain provided the foundation for the city's distinctive geography.

But the shaping of Seattle's landscape didn't stop with the retreat of the glaciers. The region is also part of the Pacific Ring of Fire, a region known for its volcanic activity. This volcanic influence added layers of volcanic rock to the landscape, further contributing to its complexity. Eruptions from nearby volcanoes, such as Mount Rainier and Mount St. Helens, spewed ash and lava that blanketed the region, adding to the geological diversity and creating a patchwork of volcanic and glacial features.

Over the millennia, erosion and sedimentation continued to play their part. Rivers and streams, fueled by rainfall and the melting of snow and ice, carved their own paths through the landscape, transporting sediment and reshaping the terrain. The relentless action of water eroded the land, cutting valleys deeper and smoothing hillsides, while also depositing sediments that filled in low-lying areas and contributed to the formation of fertile plains and delta regions.

Seattle's location on the boundary between the Juan de Fuca plate and the North American plate added yet another layer of complexity. The tectonic activity associated with this boundary caused the land to buckle and fold, creating the region's rugged topography. The ongoing tectonic forces continue to influence this dynamic and evolving landscape.

Together, these geological processes—glacial activity, volcanic eruptions, erosion, and tectonic forces—have created the diverse and striking landscape of greater Seattle, with its rolling hills, deep valleys, and scenic waterfront. The city's natural beauty is a testament to the powerful and continuous forces that have shaped it over eons.

The low-lying areas and riverbanks of Puget Sound were dotted with wetlands and marshes, teeming with life. Here, cattails and sedges thrived in the moist soil, providing habitat for countless birds and small animals. Willows and red-osier dogwood lined the streams, their roots stabilizing the banks and their branches offering shelter to wildlife. Skunk cabbage, with its large, bright green leaves and yellow flowers, emerged in spring, heralding the season's arrival.

The region was a haven for wildlife. Black bears roamed the forests, foraging for berries and fish, while Roosevelt elk and black-tailed deer moved in herds through the meadows and woodlands. Beavers were busy engineers of the landscape, building dams that created and maintained wetlands. Predators like cougars and wolves stalked the forests, playing a crucial role

▼ According to Native American folklore, you could walk across streams in Seattle on the backs of spawning salmon during summer and fall.

▲ A Duwamish chief named Chesheeahud lived on the shore of Lake Union, guiding and carving canoes for early white settlers.

► Camas flowers

in keeping the populations of prey animals in check. River otters and mink, sleek and agile, hunted along the waterways, their presence a sign of the health of the ecosystem.

The skies above were alive with the calls of birds. Bald eagles and ospreys soared high above the treetops, scanning the waters below for fish. In the depths of the forest, the drumming of pileated woodpeckers and northern flickers echoed, a constant reminder of the teeming life hidden in the trees. The elusive marbled murrelet, a seabird that nested in the ancient branches of the old-growth forests, exemplified the unique and interconnected nature of this environment.

The waters of Puget Sound itself were teeming with marine life. Salmon, the lifeblood of the region, migrated through the rivers, bringing with them nutrients from the ocean that fed the entire ecosystem. Resident orca pods, with their striking black-and-white coloring, were a common sight in the Sound, while seals, sea lions, and otters frolicked along the rocky shores, hunting fish and shellfish.

This landscape was not untouched by human hands, but rather shaped and nurtured by the Indigenous peoples of the region, particularly the Coast Salish tribes. These communities managed the land through practices like

controlled burns, which maintained open meadows and prairies where camas, a vital food plant, flourished. The relationship between the land and its people was one of balance and respect, creating a mosaic of habitats that supported an extraordinary diversity of life.

In this presettlement world, Puget Sound was a place of breathtaking beauty and ecological richness, where the towering trees, dense undergrowth, and abundant wildlife all played a role in a complex, interwoven tapestry of life.

Present

Seattle's transformation from a dense wilderness forest to a modern city is a story of exploration, industry, and urban development that spans more than a century. The tale begins in the mid-19th century when European-American settlers, led by the Denny Party, arrived in the Puget Sound region. At the time, the area was covered with thick forests and inhabited by Indigenous peoples, including the Duwamish and Suquamish tribes.

▲ Seattle's skyline is as modern as they get, yet the city still retains plenty of wild and natural charms.

Seattle's early growth was propelled by the timber industry. The city's vast tracts of old-growth forests attracted loggers and entrepreneurs eager to exploit the rich natural resources. Timber became the city's first major export, and Seattle quickly emerged as a key logging and milling center. As the forests were cleared, the wealth generated by the timber industry laid the groundwork for further development, transforming the landscape from a dense woodland to a burgeoning settlement.

THE IMPACT OF LOGGING ON EARLY SEATTLE

In the early days of Seattle, logging played a crucial role in transforming the city's landscape, economy, and society. The dense forests of western Washington, once dominated by towering Douglas firs, cedars, and hemlocks, were systematically clear-cut to fuel the burgeoning timber industry. As these ancient trees fell, the dense, forested terrain was replaced by open land, laying the foundation for urban development. The landscape, once characterized by its lush, towering trees, was quickly altered as the demand for timber grew.

The removal of the forests also allowed for significant changes in Seattle's topography. With the trees gone, the land could be leveled or reshaped to better suit the needs of a growing city. One of the most dramatic examples of this transformation was the Denny Regrade project, where entire hills were flattened to create more usable land. This drastic alteration of the landscape was a direct consequence of the extensive logging that had already cleared the area of its natural vegetation.

The economic impact of logging on Seattle was equally profound. Timber became the backbone of the city's early economy, with Seattle's strategic location near vast forests and its access to water routes making it an ideal hub for the timber trade. Lumber mills quickly sprang up along the waterfront, and the city's port became a critical point for shipping timber both nationally and internationally. The booming timber industry spurred the development of transportation infrastructure, including roads, railways, and shipping facilities, further accelerating the city's growth.

▼ Logs at the mill ready for processing.

However, the environmental consequences of this rapid deforestation were significant. The removal of trees led to widespread soil erosion, which in turn increased the risk of flooding. Rivers and waterways once stabilized by the thick forest cover began to change course and flow patterns, creating long-term environmental challenges for the region. The loss of the forests also meant the loss of habitats for countless species, leading to a dramatic reduction in biodiversity. The lush, vibrant ecosystem that had existed for centuries was replaced by a more barren, urbanized landscape.

The social and cultural impact of logging was also deeply felt in early Seattle. The booming industry attracted a large workforce, including many immigrants who arrived in the city seeking employment. This influx of workers contributed to the rapid growth of Seattle's population and the development of its diverse communities. At the same time, the expansion of the logging industry led to the displacement of Indigenous peoples who had lived in the region for millennia. As the forests were cleared and the land developed, these communities were forced to abandon their traditional ways of life and saw their access to natural resources diminish.

Logging, while instrumental in transforming Seattle from a small, forested settlement into a thriving urban center, brought with it significant environmental and social challenges. The city's early growth was fueled by the exploitation of its natural resources, a process that reshaped the landscape and left lasting scars on both the environment and the people who called the region home.

The Olmsted Brothers: Shaping Seattle's Green Spaces

In the early 20th century, Seattle was a city on the rise, with rapid population growth and urban expansion. But amid this development, the city's leaders recognized the importance of preserving its natural beauty. Enter the Olmsted Brothers, the renowned landscape-architecture firm founded by Frederick Law Olmsted Jr. and his brother John Charles Olmsted, who played a pivotal role in shaping Seattle's park system and green spaces.

The Olmsted Brothers, following in the footsteps of their father Frederick Law Olmsted Sr. (the designer of Central Park in New York City), became one of the most influential landscape-architecture firms in the United States. Their vision for urban spaces blended aesthetics with functionality, emphasizing the importance of nature in urban environments. The brothers believed that well-designed parks and public spaces could enhance public health, create community, and improve the overall quality of life in cities.

The firm's work in Seattle began in the early 1900s, when the city's park-planning was still in its infancy. The Olmsted Brothers' impact on Seattle's landscape started with their 1903 "Plan for Seattle Parks," which outlined a comprehensive vision for the city's public green spaces. The plan proposed a network of parks and boulevards that would connect different neighborhoods while preserving the city's scenic views and natural topography.

One of the most significant elements of their plan was the creation of a series of interconnected parks and parkways

▲ John C. Olmsted and colleagues from the Olmsted Brothers firm conduct a field survey at Green Lake in Seattle in May of 1903.

that would allow residents to experience nature without leaving the city. The firm envisioned a system where parks were not isolated, but instead part of a larger, cohesive network. This idea was revolutionary at the time, and it laid the foundation for the city's modern park system.

Perhaps the most visible legacy of the Olmsted Brothers in Seattle is the development of Volunteer Park in Capitol Hill, which remains one of the city's most cherished green spaces. Designed by the Olmsted firm in 1909, Volunteer Park combines sweeping views, open lawns, and naturalistic landscaping to create a serene environment amid the urban bustle. The park also features the iconic Volunteer Park Conservatory, a Victorian-style greenhouse that serves as a botanical oasis.

The Olmsted plan also guided the development of other notable green spaces, including Green Lake Park, Seward Park, and Ravenna Park, each with distinctive features that embody the firm's philosophy of creating parks that are not just functional but also beautiful and harmonious with the landscape.

Today, as the city grapples with urban growth and development, the Olmsted legacy remains ever relevant. The parks they designed continue to serve as vital public spaces that offer Seattleites respite, recreation, and connection to the natural world. And as Seattle continues to expand, the Olmsted vision offers a guiding principle: green spaces are not just luxuries, but essential to the health and vitality of urban life.

As the city grew, so did its need for modern infrastructure. The Great Seattle Fire of 1889, which devastated much of the downtown area, became a catalyst for a massive rebuilding effort. Streets were regraded, and new, more fire-resistant buildings were constructed. Public services like water, electricity, and public transportation were expanded, laying the foundation for modern urban life in Seattle.

A major turning point in Seattle's development came with the Klondike Gold Rush in the late 1890s. Seattle became the primary gateway for prospectors heading to the Yukon, causing a surge in both population and wealth. The city's infrastructure rapidly expanded to accommodate this growth, with new roads, railways, and ports being developed. This period marked the beginning of Seattle's transition from a small frontier town to a significant urban center.

REENGINEERING NATURE: THE LAKE WASHINGTON SHIP CANAL

The construction of the Lake Washington Ship Canal, which began in 1911 and took twenty-three years to complete, profoundly transformed Seattle's natural environment and ecosystems. Before the canal's creation, Lake Washington and Puget Sound were separate. The canal fundamentally altered this dynamic by linking these two bodies of water, which had far-reaching impacts on the region's ecology.

One of the most significant effects of the canal was on salmon migration. Salmon rely on specific migration routes to spawn. The canal disrupted these routes by introducing barriers and modifying natural streams and rivers. The shift in water-flow patterns had cascading effects on fish populations and other species that depend on them for food and habitat.

In addition to altering the flow of water, the canal's construction led to the loss of wetlands and other crucial natural habitats. These wetlands had previously provided essential breeding grounds for many species of birds, insects, and aquatic life. As the canal cut through the landscape, it displaced these habitats, contributing to a decline in biodiversity. The transformation of these natural areas into industrial and residential zones further exacerbated the loss of green spaces, changing the landscape from a largely natural environment to an urban one.

The construction process itself also had immediate environmental consequences. The excavation and alteration of the land increased erosion and sedimentation in nearby waterways. This not only degraded water quality but also affected the aquatic life that depended on clean, stable conditions. The introduction of sediment into the waterways can smother fish eggs and disrupt the growth of aquatic plants, further impacting the health of the ecosystem.

The canal's impact extended beyond just the immediate environmental effects. It spurred significant urban development along its banks, leading to a shift from natural landscapes to areas dominated by industrial and residential structures. This development pressure continued to reshape the environment, reducing the amount of available green space and altering local ecosystems even further.

Despite these challenges, there have been ongoing efforts to mitigate the canal's environmental impact. Restoration projects and habitat-management programs have been implemented to support the affected ecosystems, aiming to restore some of the natural functions and biodiversity that were lost during the canal's construction. These efforts highlight the complex interplay between development and conservation and the ongoing need to balance human activity with environmental stewardship.

The construction of the Lake Washington Ship Canal, completed in 1916, had significant effects on the Lake Washington shoreline ecosystems. When the canal was built, the water level in Lake Washington dropped by about 9 feet, causing widespread environmental changes.

The lowering of water levels drained large areas of wetlands around the lake, drastically altering habitats. Many native plant and animal species, particularly those reliant on shallow water and marshland environments, lost their homes. Wetland plants were replaced by species that could survive drier conditions, changing the local flora and fauna.

▼ The Montlake Cut as of 1914, two years before it was completed.

The decline in wetlands and shallow shorelines reduced spawning and rearing areas for fish, particularly salmon species. The drying of the shoreline likely decreased the availability of shelter and food sources for juvenile salmon and other fish species, contributing to declines in fish populations over time.

The new water-flow patterns caused by the canal construction changed how sediment was deposited around the shoreline. With the loss of wetlands, natural filtration systems were reduced, impacting water quality as pollutants were no longer being filtered out effectively.

The rapid drop in water level exposed areas of the shoreline that had previously been submerged. These areas, now unprotected by wetland vegetation, were more vulnerable to erosion, particularly during storms or periods of high water flow. This erosion further changed the shoreline structure.

Native species that had adapted to the original lake environment were displaced as their habitats were destroyed or altered. Some species adapted to the new conditions, but others, particularly wetland-dependent species, either died off locally or were forced to migrate.

• • • • • • •

The early 20th century saw Seattle's industrial base expand further, particularly with the rise of shipbuilding and airplane-manufacturing industries. The Boeing Company, founded in Seattle in 1916, became a cornerstone of the local economy, contributing to the city's growth. World War II further

▲ Even though houses and other construction seem to take up every square inch of land in Seattle, parks and other green spaces account for around 12 percent of the city's total acreage.

accelerated this industrial development, as Seattle became a major production center for the war effort.

In the years following World War II, Seattle experienced rapid suburbanization, a trend seen in many American cities during this period. The construction of interstate highways facilitated the movement of people and goods, leading to the growth of suburbs around the city. This era also witnessed the rise of modern architecture and the development of cultural institutions that further shaped Seattle's identity as a modern urban center.

THE IMPACT OF INDUSTRY ON SEATTLE'S ENVIRONMENT THROUGH THE YEARS

Seattle's industrial history is a story of growth, transformation, and the profound environmental impact that accompanies such development. In the late 19th and early 20th centuries, the city was a booming hub for the timber and logging industries. This growth led to widespread deforestation, which in turn caused erosion and sedimentation in rivers and streams, disrupting the natural habitats and affecting water quality. The city's expansion as a major port also contributed to environmental degradation, with shipping activities leading to water pollution from oil spills, chemical runoff, and waste dumping, all of which had lasting effects on the Puget Sound's marine environment.

The city's role in the aerospace industry, particularly with the rise of Boeing during and after World War II, brought significant economic prosperity

◀ Elliott Bay became a hub for the distribution of Pacific Northwest timber in the early 1900s and today remains a busy urban waterway plied by container ships, ferries, and plenty of pleasure crafts.

but also introduced new environmental challenges. The manufacturing processes at Boeing involved the use of hazardous chemicals, resulting in soil and groundwater contamination at several sites, including the infamous Boeing Plant 2. The Duwamish River, a critical waterway in Seattle, became heavily polluted with toxic substances like heavy metals and PCBs, leading to its designation as a Superfund site—a stark reminder of the environmental toll of industrial progress.

As Seattle continued to urbanize, the environmental impacts became more pronounced. Air quality deteriorated in the 1960s and 1970s, with pollution from vehicles and factories leading to health concerns for the city's residents. The spread of urbanization also contributed to significant stormwater runoff, as the increase in impervious surfaces like roads and buildings allowed pollutants to flow unchecked into water bodies, further degrading the water quality in Puget Sound and local rivers.

However, the environmental movement of the 1970s brought about a shift in how the city approached its industrial legacy. The introduction of stricter regulations through the Clean Water and Air Acts marked the beginning of efforts to mitigate some of the damage. Cleanup initiatives targeting the Duwamish River and other contaminated sites were launched, and the air and water quality gradually improved. In more recent years, Seattle has emerged as a leader in sustainability, embracing green building practices, renewable-energy initiatives, and efforts to reduce carbon emissions. These actions represent a significant departure from the environmental negligence of the past, signaling a commitment to a more sustainable future.

Despite these improvements, the city's rapid growth, fueled in part by the tech industry, has introduced new environmental challenges. The expansion of urban areas has contributed to the urban heat-island effect, where densely developed areas become significantly warmer than their surroundings. Additionally, the rise of the tech industry has raised concerns about electronic waste and the energy consumption of data centers, with companies like Microsoft and Amazon coming under scrutiny for their environmental footprints.

Looking ahead, Seattle faces the looming threat of climate change. As a coastal city, it is particularly vulnerable to rising sea levels and more frequent and intense storms, which pose risks to the city's industrial waterfront. Although the city has made strides in addressing the environmental impacts of its industrial past, ongoing pollution from industry, urban runoff, and transportation remains a persistent challenge. The story of Seattle's industrial growth is thus one of both environmental degradation and the ongoing struggle to reconcile economic development with the need for environmental stewardship.

• • • • • • •

By the latter part of the 20th century, Seattle had evolved into a hub for the technology industry, with companies like Microsoft and Amazon establishing their headquarters in the region. This tech boom brought significant wealth, population growth, and further urban development, solidifying Seattle's status as a global city with a diverse and dynamic economy.

Seattle: One of the Greenest and Wildest Cities on the Planet

Seattle's reputation as one of the greenest and wildest cities in the world is a blend of its stunning natural landscape, robust environmental policies, and engaged community. Nestled between the majestic Olympic and Cascade mountain ranges and bordered by the sparkling waters of Puget Sound and Lake Washington, Seattle enjoys a breathtaking backdrop of mountains, forests, and waterways. This natural beauty is complemented by an extensive network of parks and green spaces, such as Discovery Park—the city's largest green area—and the Washington Park Arboretum, which showcases a diverse array of plant species.

The city's commitment to sustainability is evident in its progressive environmental policies. Seattle has implemented strong recycling programs, efforts to cut greenhouse-gas emissions, and green building practices that set a high standard for environmental stewardship. The urban forest plays a crucial role in maintaining the city's lush appearance, with numerous initiatives aimed at preserving and expanding green spaces within the urban environment.

Water conservation is another priority for Seattle, which has programs designed to protect local watersheds and ensure sustainable water use. The city also supports alternative transportation options, including an extensive network of bike lanes, a comprehensive public-transit system, and pedestrian-friendly infrastructure, all of which contribute to reduced pollution and a smaller carbon footprint.

Community involvement is a cornerstone of Seattle's environmental ethos. Residents actively participate in local activism, community garden projects, and conservation efforts, reflecting a collective dedication to preserving the city's green and wild character. Together, these elements weave a narrative of a city deeply intertwined with its natural surroundings and committed to a sustainable future.

Throughout this transformation, Seattle's environment and culture underwent significant changes. The once-dense forests were largely replaced by urban infrastructure, though efforts have been made in recent decades to restore green spaces and protect the environment. The city's cultural landscape also evolved, shaped by the influx of diverse populations and the rise of new industries.

In essence, Seattle's journey from a wilderness forest to a modern city was driven by a combination of industrialization, transportation infrastructure, economic booms, and strategic urban planning. Each phase of development contributed to the city's growth, ultimately turning it into the vibrant metropolis we know today.

Future

Seattle's journey toward returning to a more natural and wild environment hinges on a combination of sustainability efforts and legislative action. Imagine a city where urban green spaces are no longer mere patches of grass, but thriving ecosystems teeming with native plant and animal species. This vision is brought to life through the expansion and restoration of parks, green belts, and urban forests. Programs like the Green Seattle Partnership play a pivotal role, aiming to reintroduce the richness of native biodiversity into the cityscape. Meanwhile, the restoration of wetlands, riverbanks, and shorelines becomes a priority, with projects focused on improving water quality and reestablishing natural habitats. To wit, recent efforts to restore South Seattle's Duwamish River, the lifeblood of local Indigenous peoples prior to white settlement in the area but subsequently a channelized Superfund site, exemplify how these initiatives can create healthier environments for wildlife and bring a touch of the wild back to the urban landscape.

SEATTLE'S STREET TREES: ENHANCING ECOLOGY AND MITIGATING CLIMATE IMPACT

Street trees are a vital but often overlooked feature of the urban landscape in and around metro Seattle. These trees—found lining sidewalks, in medians, and on other public spaces—provide a range of ecological and climate benefits that are crucial to the region's environmental health and climate resilience.

First and foremost, street trees help mitigate the urban heat-island effect. Seattle's summers are growing warmer, and the dense concentration of buildings and pavement can exacerbate heat in urban areas. Trees provide shade, cool the air through evapotranspiration, and reduce the need for energy-intensive air conditioning. These cooling effects are particularly important in low-income neighborhoods, which often experience higher temperatures and lower access to green spaces.

Ecologically, street trees contribute to biodiversity by providing habitat and food sources for birds, insects, and other wildlife, helping support urban ecosystems. They also improve air quality by absorbing pollutants like carbon dioxide, nitrogen oxides, and particulate matter, while releasing oxygen and storing carbon—critical functions as Seattle works toward its climate goals. Over time, these trees can sequester significant amounts of carbon, helping counterbalance the region's greenhouse-gas emissions.

Beyond climate impact mitigation, street trees enhance stormwater management. Their root systems absorb rainwater, reducing runoff and the burden on Seattle's stormwater infrastructure, which is vital in preventing flooding and water-quality issues, especially as rainfall patterns become more erratic.

In an effort to get residents to plant more street trees, the City of Seattle launched its Trees for Neighborhoods program in 2009. To date, the program, which gives up to six trees per household for planting in sidewalk planting strips, along driveways and medians, and in backyards, has distributed more than 14,000 saplings for planting all over the city. The city also provides help

► This Pacific madrone tree occupying the "parking strip" between the sidewalk and street in Seattle's leafy Mount Baker neighborhood is one of 130,000 or so street trees contributing to the Emerald City's tree canopy while sequestering carbon and reducing the urban heat-island effect.

WILD SEATTLE

Seattleites and Conservation: A Long History

Seattle has been a pivotal player in several significant conservation victories, largely thanks to the dedication and activism of its residents. One notable example is the ongoing effort to protect Puget Sound, a vital marine ecosystem. Residents of Seattle have been at the forefront of advocating for the health of the Sound, leading to the creation of the Puget Sound Partnership in 2007. This initiative has focused on restoring and safeguarding the region's environmental quality, reflecting the city's deep commitment to its natural surroundings.

In the early 20th century, Seattle's conservationists were also key in the establishment of Olympic National Park. Their tireless advocacy was crucial in preserving the unique biodiversity and landscapes of the Olympic Peninsula, culminating in the park's official designation in 1938. Similarly, the creation of Mount Rainier National Park in 1899 owes much to the efforts of Seattle-based conservationists. This was one of the earliest national parks in the United States, and it has since become a symbol of the region's natural beauty and dedication to preservation.

Another significant achievement is the Green Seattle Partnership, launched in 2004. This program represents a collaborative effort between the city, local organizations, and volunteers, all working together to restore and maintain Seattle's urban forest. The partnership has made substantial progress in enhancing the health and sustainability of the city's green spaces.

Seattle's commitment to environmental issues extends to policy changes as well. In 2012, the city became one of the first major US cities to implement a ban on plastic shopping bags. This bold move aimed to reduce plastic pollution and has set a precedent that has inspired similar measures in other cities across the country.

These conservation victories highlight Seattle's strong tradition of environmental activism and its unwavering commitment to protecting and enhancing the natural world.

▲ A western gull eats a sea star on Pier 62 in downtown Seattle.

selecting the right trees and planting locations, planting assistance, and a watering bag and mulch for each tree. Homeowners can apply for their free trees on the city's Trees for Neighborhoods web page (seattle.gov/trees/trees-for-neighborhoods). If approved, homeowners must attend a virtual workshop for planting and care training, after which the trees are delivered to their door for planting.

Street trees are a key tool in Seattle's efforts to build a sustainable, resilient, and livable city, benefiting both people and the planet. As the region continues to grow, investing in the planting and maintenance of these trees will be essential for reducing environmental stress and combating climate change.

• • • • • • •

Urban planning in Seattle embraces sustainability at its core. Green infrastructure, including green roofs, rain gardens, and permeable pavements, helps the city mimic natural water cycles while reducing urban runoff. These green solutions not only contribute to ecological health but also provide havens for urban wildlife. By promoting mixed-use development, Seattle minimizes the need for sprawling transportation networks, preserving surrounding natural areas and reducing its carbon footprint. The city's zoning regulations evolve, favoring higher-density developments that limit urban sprawl and protect precious natural landscapes from being consumed by commercial or residential projects.

Legislation becomes a powerful tool in Seattle's sustainability efforts. Strong environmental protection laws safeguard existing natural areas, preventing deforestation, restricting pollution, and mandating sustainable development practices. These regulations ensure that the city's growth aligns with environmental preservation, rather than coming at the expense of it. At the same time, Seattle's climate-action plans take center stage, focusing on reducing carbon emissions, promoting renewable energy, and increasing energy efficiency. These legislative moves are critical for combating climate change, which directly impacts the health of natural environments both within and beyond the city limits.

The transformation of Seattle also relies on the collective efforts of its residents. Public-awareness campaigns play a key role in educating the community about the importance of native species, biodiversity, and sustainable living. As people become more aware, they are more likely to participate in restoration projects and adopt sustainable practices in their daily lives. Volunteer programs flourish, with residents actively engaging in tree planting, invasive-species removal, and habitat restoration. This sense of ownership and responsibility for the local environment becomes a driving force in the city's return to a more natural state.

Seattle's economy aligns with its sustainability goals, offering support for businesses that adopt green practices. Incentives like tax breaks or grants encourage companies to implement eco-friendly technologies, reduce waste, and operate sustainably. The city also champions local agriculture, reducing the environmental impact of food production and transportation. Urban farming, community gardens, and farmers' markets become common sights, integrating nature more deeply into the urban fabric.

BATTLING INVASIVE SPECIES

In the greater Seattle area, the battle against invasive species is a continuous effort to protect native ecosystems and biodiversity. Invasive plants like English ivy and Himalayan blackberry are widespread in Seattle parks and yards, smothering trees and displacing native understory plants.

A notable recent concern is garlic mustard (*Alliaria petiolata*), a biennial herb native to Europe. Initially introduced in North America for culinary purposes, it has become a significant threat to natural areas in western Washington. Garlic mustard thrives in shady, moist environments, inhibiting nutrient uptake of native plants and disrupting local ecosystems.

To combat these invasions, the King County Noxious Weed Control program actively identifies and manages outbreaks of such species. Property owners are legally required to eradicate certain noxious weeds, including garlic mustard, to prevent their spread. The program offers assistance to residents, providing expertise in identifying and removing invasive plants.

Community involvement is crucial in this battle. Residents can contribute by removing invasive species from their properties and participating in local restoration efforts. The Green Seattle Partnership, for instance, organizes volunteer events to restore urban parks and natural areas by removing invasive plants and planting native species.

By staying vigilant and working together, Seattle's communities can protect their natural landscapes from the threats posed by invasive species.

To ensure wildlife thrives in this evolving urban environment, Seattle focuses on creating connectivity between natural areas. Wildlife corridors link parks, green spaces, and natural reserves, allowing animals to move freely and maintain healthy populations. The city also takes steps to reduce light and noise pollution, creating a more conducive environment for wildlife, particularly nocturnal species.

SEATTLE'S ENVIRONMENTAL COMMUNITY: ENGAGED AND COMMITTED

Seattle's environmental and conservation community is a dynamic and influential force within the city, weaving together grassroots activism, government policies, and community involvement into a rich tapestry of ecological stewardship. This vibrant network of individuals and organizations demonstrates an impressive dedication to sustainability and environmental protection.

At the heart of this movement are numerous local nonprofits and advocacy groups that champion a wide range of environmental causes. For instance, the Sierra Club's Washington State Chapter is deeply involved in efforts to promote clean energy and protect public lands. Their campaigns often focus on pressing issues such as defending Olympic National Park from threats and advocating for strong climate policies at the state level. Similarly, Earthjustice, a nonprofit environmental-law organization, tackles cases related to pollution and habitat destruction, working to enforce and expand environmental regulations.

The Puget Soundkeeper Alliance is another key player, dedicated to preserving the health of Puget Sound. They actively monitor water quality,

▲ Garlic mustard, an invasive plant species that crowds native plants out of their habitat, is a growing problem in and around Seattle.

conduct field investigations, and engage in legal action to address pollution sources. Their work is crucial in maintaining the ecological balance of one of Seattle's most vital natural resources.

Seattle's commitment to environmental sustainability is also reflected in its government initiatives. The City of Seattle has set ambitious goals through its Climate Action Plan, which aims to achieve carbon neutrality by 2050. This plan includes strategies for reducing greenhouse-gas emissions, increasing energy efficiency, and transitioning to renewable-energy sources. A notable example of these efforts is the city's investment in green infrastructure. Projects like the installation of green roofs on public buildings and the creation of extensive rain gardens throughout urban areas help manage stormwater runoff, mitigate heat-island effects, and enhance biodiversity.

The city's commitment to sustainability extends to its public transportation and urban planning as well. Seattle's light-rail system, with its expanding network, encourages the use of public transit over private vehicles, contributing to lower emissions and reduced traffic congestion. Additionally, Seattle's Land Use Code promotes dense, walkable neighborhoods that minimize the need for long commutes and support local businesses.

Community engagement plays a crucial role in Seattle's environmental efforts. Residents actively participate in events such as neighborhood clean-ups, tree-planting drives, and educational workshops. Community-driven events like these foster a sense of collective responsibility and encourage individual action toward a more sustainable future.

The city's emphasis on environmental education is evident in its support for programs that teach students and adults about sustainability practices. Programs like Seattle Public Schools' environmental-science curriculum help instill an early appreciation for nature and the importance of environmental stewardship. Moreover, Seattle's parks and recreation departments organize regular workshops and volunteer opportunities that engage citizens in conservation efforts, from maintaining trails to restoring native plant habitats.

Overall, Seattle's environmental and conservation community exemplifies a deep-rooted commitment to protecting the natural world. Through the combined efforts of advocacy groups, government policies, and active community participation, the city continually strives to balance growth with environmental responsibility, making it a model for sustainable urban living.

Water conservation and management have become pillars of Seattle's environmental strategy. By enforcing strict water-quality standards and investing in technologies to clean urban runoff, the city protects its aquatic ecosystems and promotes the return of native fish and other species. Sustainable water usage is encouraged through policies and incentives, helping maintain healthy water levels in natural habitats.

Through these combined efforts, Seattle can progressively restore its natural environment, fostering a harmonious coexistence between urban life and the surrounding ecosystems. The city's commitment to sustainability, supported by robust legislation and an engaged community, paves the way for a future where nature and urbanity flourish side by side.

▶ When Royal Dutch Shell's *Polar Pioneer* oil-drilling rig made a pit stop in Seattle on its way north back in spring of 2015, thousands of activists took to the waters of Elliott Bay in kayaks to show their antipathy toward the company's plans to expand offshore petroleum extraction in sensitive and climate-ravaged Arctic waters.

LEAVE THE ARCTIC ALONE
POLAR PIONEER
MAJURO

106 SPECIES TO KNOW

Greater Seattle, carved out of one of the world's largest temperate rainforests, may be one of the most biodiverse metropolitan areas at its latitude around the world. Choosing 106 wild species to represent this 6300-plus-square-mile Pacific Northwest metropolis is a daunting task indeed, given there are some 1249 types of vascular plants, 1500-plus invertebrates, 220 birds, more than 100 mammals, 13 amphibians, and 8 reptiles to choose from that each call the region home or at least like to visit. Here are 106 of the most iconic of the bunch, along with instructions for when and where to optimize your chances of spotting them right here in our urban wild.

Birds 34

Insects and Arachnids 81

Mammals 87

Birds

American Coot

Fulica americana

The American coot may look like a duck at first glance, but it actually belongs to the rail family, making it a unique sight on Seattle's ponds and lakes. With its round body, slate-gray feathers, and distinctive white bill, the coot is an unmistakable presence among waterfowl. At a distance, its robust frame and the contrast of the white bill against the darker plumage might mislead casual observers into thinking they are viewing an unusual type of duck. However, their unique characteristics set them apart from the typical duck silhouette.

One of the most striking features of the American coot is its fascinating foot structure. Unlike many waterbirds, coots lack webbed feet; instead, they have long toes with lobes of skin that allow them to swim efficiently and walk on soft surfaces. This adaptation makes them agile in the water, where they can navigate dense aquatic vegetation with ease, and surprisingly adept on land. Their toes function almost like flippers, providing a unique paddling motion that enhances their swimming speed. On land, they appear comical as they trot around, their lobed toes giving them a quirky gait.

Coots are highly social birds, often found in large flocks, which can sometimes number in the hundreds, during the nonbreeding season. These flocks can be quite a sight, with coots energetically swimming together, occasionally leaping over one another in a flurry of activity. They have a varied diet and are opportunistic feeders, consuming a mix

of aquatic vegetation, small fish, insects, and crustaceans. Their feeding behavior can be entertaining to observe; you can often see them diving for food or tipping forward like dabbling ducks to reach submerged plants. Their opportunistic nature extends to foraging, as they often steal food from other waterfowl, leading to amusing confrontations as they dart in to snatch morsels from unsuspecting ducks or geese.

During the breeding season, American coots build floating nests anchored to reeds or other vegetation, providing a safe spot for their eggs above the waterline. Both parents participate in raising the chicks, which are covered in black down and have bright orange-tipped feathers. The young coots are precocial—they can swim and dive shortly after hatching—though they still rely on their parents for guidance. Observing a family of coots, with fluffy chicks trailing behind, is a delightful experience; the adults lead the way, vigilant and protective.

Where to See Them

American coots are common in the Seattle area year-round, especially on freshwater lakes and ponds. You can easily spot them at Green Lake, where large flocks gather, or at Magnuson Park and the Union Bay Natural Area. They are also frequent sights at the Washington Park Arboretum and Seward Park. Keep an eye out for their distinctive swimming style and listen for their harsh, nasal calls, which sound like sharp "coot" sounds echoing across the water. Most American coots migrate south for winter, but given the relatively mild winters, a few stay in Seattle year-round.

American Crow

Corvus brachyrhynchos

The American crow is one of Seattle's most recognizable birds, with its glossy black feathers, sharp gaze, and loud, cawing calls. Known for its adaptability and intelligence, the American crow thrives in Seattle's urban, suburban, and rural environments, foraging for food in parks, garbage bins, and along roadsides. Crows are omnivorous, eating a variety of foods including insects, small mammals, fruits, and even carrion. Their remarkable intelligence has been well documented in studies, showing their abilities to use tools, recognize individual humans, and solve complex problems. These unique traits, along with their social nature, make crows one of the most intriguing birds in Seattle's urban landscape.

Crows exhibit quirky behaviors, such as "anting," where they rub ants or other insects onto their feathers. This behavior may help them control parasites, adding to their reputation as resourceful problem-solvers. But perhaps the most astonishing aspect of crow intelligence is their talent for recognizing individual human faces. A study led by Dr. John Marzluff, a wildlife biologist at the University of Washington, revealed that crows remember and react to human faces they associate with specific experiences—especially negative ones. In one experiment, researchers wearing

a distinctive "dangerous" mask trapped and tagged crows on the UW campus. When the same mask was worn later without any capture attempts, the crows still reacted aggressively, scolding and even mobbing the masked individual.

What's even more fascinating is how these crows communicate their experiences with others in their flock, teaching them to recognize the "dangerous" face even if they hadn't directly encountered it. Over time, more crows exhibited strong reactions to the mask, with nearly all the crows on campus recognizing and scolding the person wearing it. This ability to recognize faces and share information within their communities is a testament to the complex social intelligence that sets crows apart from other bird species.

Crows are also highly social, especially during the nonbreeding season when they gather in large communal roosts containing hundreds, sometimes thousands, of individuals. These roosts are a spectacular sight and sound at dusk, as crows from around the city congregate in one area to settle for the night. Within these roosts, crows not only find warmth and safety in numbers, but they may also share information about food sources or potential threats—adding to the cooperative and communal nature of their species.

The social bonds among crows are particularly strong within family groups. Offspring from previous years often stay with their parents to help raise new broods, a behavior known as cooperative breeding that is rare among birds. This cooperation and familial loyalty demonstrate the complex emotional and social structure of crows, furthering their reputation as one of the most intelligent bird species.

While American crows are considered resident birds in most of their range, including Seattle, some northern populations migrate south in winter. In the Pacific Northwest, they are typically year-round residents, taking advantage of the temperate climate and abundant food sources. Seattle's urban environment provides ample opportunities for crows to forage, roost, and thrive alongside humans.

Where to See Them

American crows are ubiquitous in Seattle, found in nearly every park, neighborhood, and even in downtown areas. They are especially active at dawn and dusk, when they fly to and from their communal roosts, creating an impressive spectacle. Discovery Park, Green Lake, Golden Gardens, and Seward Park are excellent places to observe crows, particularly in the evening when they gather in large numbers. Observing crows offers a unique glimpse into the lives of these intelligent birds and the surprisingly intricate social networks they build in Seattle's wild spaces.

▲ A crow contemplates its next moves on a sweet chestnut branch at Golden Gardens in Seattle.

American Goldfinch

Spinus tristis

The American goldfinch, designated as Washington's official state bird back in 1951, is known for its bright yellow plumage and joyful song and is a delightful sight in Seattle's parks and gardens. During the breeding season, males flaunt their vivid yellow feathers complemented by striking black wings and caps, making them one of the most visually stunning birds in the region. In contrast, females and nonbreeding males exhibit a more subdued olive-yellow hue, which helps them blend in with the surrounding foliage. This color difference not only aids in camouflage from predators but also influences social dynamics during the breeding season.

These small, acrobatic birds are often seen flitting between tall plants, particularly those adorned with seed-bearing flowers like coneflowers and sunflowers, where they forage for food. Their energetic movements and playful antics make them a joy to observe. They are known to hang upside down to reach elusive seeds, showcasing remarkable agility.

This unique foraging behavior allows them to access seeds often overlooked by other birds.

Goldfinches are primarily granivores, feeding almost exclusively on seeds, particularly from thistles, dandelions, and sunflowers. Their conical bills are perfectly adapted for extracting seeds from tough seed heads, allowing them to expertly navigate challenging seedpods. This feeding behavior benefits the plants, as goldfinches inadvertently help disperse seeds while foraging. In winter, their diet may also include small insects, especially aphids, which they hunt among the stems of shrubs and trees. This flexibility in diet helps them thrive year-round, even when seeds are scarce.

Interestingly, goldfinches breed later in summer than many other birds, timing their nesting to coincide with the peak abundance of seeds. This unique strategy ensures ample food for chicks when they hatch. Their nests, built high in trees or shrubs, are constructed from plant fibers and lined with soft materials such as feathers and down. This careful

construction provides a secure and comfortable environment for developing chicks. The nests are often well hidden among dense foliage, making them difficult for predators to spot.

One quirky behavior of American goldfinches is their social nature; they are often seen in small flocks, particularly during migration and winter months. These flocks engage in playful chases, creating a lively spectacle as they dart through the air in zigzagging flights. Their sweet, twittering calls resonate as they interact with one another, adding to their charm. The calls have a musical quality, reminiscent of cheerful phrases.

Where to See Them

American goldfinches thrive in open areas rich with wildflowers and shrubs. In the Seattle area, they can be spotted in locations like Discovery Park, Magnuson Park, and the Union Bay Natural Area. They are also frequent visitors to backyard bird feeders, particularly those stocked with nyjer (thistle) seeds, which they prefer due to their size and nutritional value. To observe these beautiful birds, watch for their distinctive bounding flight, characterized by rapid wingbeats followed by a short glide. Look for them around Seattle in summer, as they overwinter in the warmer climes of Mexico.

American Robin

Turdus migratorius

The American robin is one of the most familiar birds across North America, and Seattle is no exception. Easily recognized by its rusty red breast, gray-brown back, and orange-yellow bill, the robin is a common sight in gardens, parks, and woodlands throughout the city. These medium-sized songbirds are particularly noted for their distinctive and cheerful song, often heard at dawn and dusk, which adds to the vibrant soundscape of the urban environment.

American robins are ground foragers, frequently seen hopping across lawns and fields in search of earthworms, insects, and berries. Their keen eyesight and strong bills enable them to be efficient hunters. You can often spot them cocking their heads to one side, listening intently for the movement of worms just beneath the surface. This behavior is a hallmark of their foraging technique, allowing them to locate prey effectively.

One quirky trait of the American robin is its habit of "pursuing" other birds. When robins spot larger birds, they sometimes engage in playful chase flights, diving and darting to defend their territory or drive intruders away. This behavior can be quite entertaining to watch, as robins display impressive aerial agility and vocalizations during these encounters.

The breeding season for robins typically spans from early spring through summer. They construct cup-shaped nests in trees, shrubs, or even on man-made structures such as balconies or ledges. The female takes on the primary role in nest construction, using grasses, twigs, and mud to create a secure environment. She typically lays three to five eggs, which are a distinctive blue, and both parents assist in feeding the chicks, who fledge from the nest after about two weeks. Interestingly, during the feeding of their young, robins may engage in "food passes," where they quickly transfer worms or berries to each other mid-flight. This cooperative behavior highlights their strong partnership during the nurturing phase.

American robins also exhibit a playful side. They are known to bathe in puddles, hopping and splashing about, sometimes even rolling onto their backs in the water. This behavior not only helps them stay clean but can also be a form of social interaction as they share bathing spots with other robins.

Where to See Them

American robins are abundant throughout the Seattle area and can be found in nearly any park, garden, or open space. Some prime locations to spot them include Ravenna Park, Discovery Park, and Green Lake. In residential areas, robins are often seen in backyards, especially during the breeding season. They are most active during the early morning and late evening, making these times ideal for observation. Many robins remain in mild Seattle year-round, while others migrate south to the American Southwest and Mexico in winter.

▲ American robin males are unmistakable with their brightly colored breasts and beaks.

◄ The American robin is one of the most common birds seen around Seattle backyards and green spaces. Females like this one lack the rich coloration of their male partners.

Anna's Hummingbird

Calypte anna

Anna's hummingbird is a vibrant year-round resident of the Seattle area, celebrated for its iridescent green feathers and striking rose-pink throat patch, known as a *gorget*, seen most prominently in males. Females, while less showy, exhibit a green back and grayish underparts, but both sexes share the typical hummingbird trait of rapid, darting flight. These small birds are a delightful sight in gardens, parks, and woodlands, where they hover at flowers and feeders, showcasing their remarkable flying skills.

Unlike most hummingbirds that migrate, Anna's hummingbird remains in Seattle throughout winter, taking full advantage of nectar from flowering plants and hummingbird feeders. They also consume small insects and spiders, which provide essential protein in their diet. With their long, specialized tongues, Anna's hummingbirds can efficiently extract nectar from tubular flowers, often favoring plants like red-flowering currants and honeysuckles, which are abundant in the region.

One quirky behavior of Anna's hummingbirds is their territorial nature. Males can be fiercely protective of their feeding territories, often chasing off rivals and even larger birds that dare to approach. This aggressive behavior can include rapid dives and aerial displays to assert dominance, making for a dramatic spectacle. In addition, Anna's hummingbirds are known for their impressive vocalizations; their melodious chirps and whistles can be heard as they flit from flower to flower, contributing to the lively ambiance of their habitats.

During the breeding season, males perform impressive courtship displays, swooping high in the air before diving toward the ground in a dramatic arc to attract females. These displays can reach impressive heights, showcasing their agility and strength. Females take sole responsibility for nest-building and raising the young. Their tiny nests, constructed from plant fibers and spider silk, are often well hidden in shrubs or trees, providing safe havens for the developing chicks. Interestingly, female Anna's

◄ An Anna's hummingbird feeds chicks on the nest.

hummingbirds will sometimes build a second nest while still feeding their fledglings, maximizing their breeding success.

Anna's hummingbirds also display playful behavior; they may engage in aerial chases with one another, darting in and out of trees and shrubs in seemingly carefree frolics. They can often be seen "perching" on thin branches, which is unusual for hummingbirds, as they typically prefer to remain in constant motion. This behavior allows them to survey their territory, rest briefly, and prepare for their next feeding frenzy.

Where to See Them

Anna's hummingbirds are easy to spot year-round in Seattle's parks and residential gardens. Look for them at Discovery Park, the Washington Park Arboretum, or Seward Park, especially near flowering plants. Adding a hummingbird feeder filled with a sugar-water solution to your garden is a fantastic way to attract these energetic nonmigratory birds all throughout the year.

Bald Eagle

Haliaeetus leucocephalus

The bald eagle is a bird of immense cultural and ecological significance, symbolizing power, resilience, and national pride in the United States. One of the most recognizable raptors, the bald eagle stands out with its brilliant white head and tail, contrasted by a dark brown body and a bright yellow beak and feet. Although majestic in appearance, the bald eagle's behavior reveals a fascinating mix of power, opportunism, and resourcefulness.

Primarily fish-eaters, bald eagles are highly skilled hunters, often swooping down to snatch fish from the water with their sharp talons. However, they are not above scavenging carrion or stealing food from other birds, such as ospreys. This behavior, known as *kleptoparasitism*, is especially common in areas where food competition is high. Despite their predatory prowess, bald eagles demonstrate a practical side, conserving energy by taking advantage of easy meals when available.

Bald eagles are remarkable in flight, soaring effortlessly with their broad wings, often reaching altitudes of up to 10,000 feet. They can reach speeds of 30 to 35 miles per hour while gliding and can dive at speeds exceeding 100 miles per hour when attacking prey. Their

▲ The fact that this bald eagle hangs out in a tall tree in a backyard in Northeast Seattle is testament to the conservation efforts involved in bringing America's national symbol back from the brink of extinction in the Lower 48.

aerial displays during courtship, which include locking talons and tumbling through the sky, are both awe-inspiring and a testament to their strength and agility.

Another fascinating aspect of bald eagle behavior is their nesting habits. They build massive nests, called *aeries*, in tall trees or on cliff edges, and these nests can grow to enormous sizes—sometimes up to 10 feet in diameter and weighing over a ton—because they add new material to them each year. The dedication they show to nest-building is paralleled by their strong pair bonds. Bald eagles mate for life, and both partners share the duties of incubating their eggs and feeding their young. The chicks, or eaglets, are raised in these towering nests and fledge at around ten to twelve weeks old.

Bald eagle populations in the United States plummeted during the mid-20th century, primarily due to widespread use of the pesticide DDT, which caused eggshell thinning and led to reproductive failures. Habitat loss, illegal hunting, and contamination of their food sources also contributed to the decline.

By the early 1960s, the species was on the brink of extinction in the contiguous United States. Conservation efforts began in earnest after DDT was banned in 1972, along with strict legal protections under the Endangered Species Act (1973) and the Bald and Golden Eagle Protection Act. Breeding programs, habitat preservation, and public-awareness campaigns helped populations recover, leading to the bald eagle being removed from the Endangered Species list in 2007. Today, the species is a conservation success story with thriving populations across much of its range.

Where to See Them

In Seattle, bald eagles are often seen near large bodies of water such as at Lake Washington, Discovery Park, and Union Bay, where they perch on tall trees or soar over the water in search of fish. Winter months may bring even higher numbers as eagles gather near rivers and lakes to hunt. Most bald eagles in the Pacific Northwest do not migrate given the mild temps and an abundance of fish and other prey in the region's teeming waterways.

Barn Swallow

Hirundo rustica

Barn swallows are among the most graceful fliers you'll encounter in the Seattle area, characterized by their long, forked tails and sleek bodies that are expertly designed for aerial acrobatics. These small birds sport a stunning dark blue coloration on their upperparts, contrasting beautifully with their reddish brown throats and buff-colored bellies. Their swift, darting flight and habit of skimming low over fields and water make them a familiar sight during the warmer months. They can often be seen in the late afternoon, performing intricate aerial maneuvers as they hunt for insects.

As insectivores, barn swallows primarily feed on flying insects such as flies, beetles, and mosquitoes, which they catch mid-flight with remarkable precision. This diet not only benefits them but also plays a crucial role in pest control, as their feeding habits help reduce the populations of nuisance insects. They have been observed engaging in impressive aerial displays, where they will fly in loops and dives to chase down their prey, showcasing their agility and speed.

During the breeding season, barn swallows display interesting behavior as they collect mud to construct their distinctive cup-shaped nests. These nests are often attached to man-made structures like barns, bridges, or overhangs, making them a common sight in rural and suburban areas. The male performs courtship displays, which include swooping

flights and vocalizations to attract females. Once paired, the female usually takes the lead in nest construction, using a mixture of mud and plant fibers to create a secure home for their young.

These birds are highly social creatures and are often seen in large groups. After breeding, barn swallows gather in huge flocks, sometimes numbering in the thousands, before heading south for winter. Their social interactions are lively, with frequent vocalizations and displays of unity as they prepare for migration.

In addition to their remarkable flying abilities, barn swallows exhibit strong fidelity to nesting sites. Many will return to the same locations year after year, often using the same nest or rebuilding nearby. This behavior not only emphasizes their attachment to familiar surroundings but also their adaptability in utilizing human-made structures for breeding.

Where to See Them

Barn swallows are common in open areas near water, fields, and farmland. In Seattle, they can be spotted at locations like Magnuson Park, Union Bay Natural Area, and along the shores of Lake Washington. Look for them swooping gracefully through the air, especially near bridges or other structures where they might nest. Catch them while you can, as they are only around for Seattle's summer before heading back on the long migratory trek to Central and South America, where they overwinter.

Belted Kingfisher

Megaceryle alcyon

The belted kingfisher is a striking bird with a large, crested head, a stocky build, and blue-gray plumage and is often spotted perched near water. Males have a single blue breast band, while females display an additional rusty band on their bellies, making them one of the few bird species where the female is more colorful than the male. This sexual dimorphism adds a layer of intrigue to their behavior, as females can often be seen

engaging in more assertive displays during courtship. These birds are well known for their rattling call, a series of sharp, mechanical sounds that can often be heard before the bird itself is seen, providing an audio cue to their presence.

Belted kingfishers are skilled hunters, diving headfirst into the water to catch small fish, amphibians, and aquatic invertebrates. Their hunting technique is precise; they often hover over the water, scanning the surface for movement before plunging down. With sharp, powerful bills designed for gripping slippery prey, they grab their catch and return to a perch to eat it. Observing their hunting dives is a thrilling experience, as they can reach speeds of up to 25 miles per hour.

In addition to their hunting prowess, belted kingfishers are highly territorial, especially during breeding season. Males will aggressively defend their nesting territories, often engaging in aerial displays and vocalizations to ward off rivals. Their preferred habitats include lakes, rivers, and wetlands, where they can find abundant food and suitable nesting sites.

Belted kingfishers excavate burrows in sandy or earthen banks near water, where they lay their eggs. Both parents take part in digging these long tunnels, which can be several feet deep and help protect their chicks from predators. Interestingly, after hatching, the chicks are altricial, meaning they are born helpless and require parental care for survival. Parents tirelessly provide food for their young, often bringing them a variety of small fish and invertebrates.

Where to See Them

Look for belted kingfishers along Seattle's lakes and rivers. They're often spotted at the Washington Park Arboretum, Magnuson Park, and along the shores of Lake Union and Lake Washington. Their loud, rattling call is a give-away that one is nearby, perched on a branch or swooping over the water in search of fish. Most belted kingfishers stick around Seattle, although some of the birds overwinter as far south as Venezuela and Colombia.

Bewick's Wren

Thryomanes bewickii

Bewick's wrens are small, active birds characterized by a long, expressive tail and a bold white eyebrow stripe. Mostly brown with lighter underparts, these wrens are often seen flitting through dense undergrowth, where their inquisitive nature keeps them constantly on the move. Their distinctive tail, which they frequently flick, serves as a key identification marker, drawing attention to their lively antics.

Despite their small size, Bewick's wrens have powerful voices, and their melodious songs can often be heard emanating from the underbrush. Their song consists of a complex series of trills, buzzes, and whistles, which they use to defend their territory and attract mates. In addition to their vocal prowess, these wrens engage in fascinating behaviors; they are known to perform short, energetic flights from perch to perch, sometimes even hopping along the ground in search of food.

As insectivores, Bewick's wrens feed on spiders, beetles, caterpillars, and other small invertebrates, which they glean from foliage. They are adept foragers, using their quick movements and sharp eyesight to spot hidden prey. They often use their strong bills to probe into crevices and under leaves, showcasing their resourcefulness and agility.

When it comes to nesting, Bewick's wrens are cavity dwellers. They often utilize natural holes in trees, rock crevices, or even human-made structures like nest boxes or garden sheds. The nests are crafted from twigs and grass and lined with softer materials like feathers or plant down to cushion the eggs. The female typically lays a clutch of four to seven eggs, which she incubates alone, although the male may help guard the territory during this time.

Interestingly, Bewick's wrens exhibit social behaviors, especially outside the breeding season. They are often seen in small groups, foraging together and communicating with

a series of soft chirps. This social structure can be particularly beneficial in areas with abundant food resources, allowing them to exploit their environment more effectively.

Where to See Them

Bewick's wrens thrive in Seattle's gardens, parks, and woodland edges, particularly in areas with dense vegetation. Look for them at Seward Park, Discovery Park, or the Washington Park Arboretum. They are also common visitors to backyards with thick shrubs and brush piles, where they forage for insects and build their nests. These nonmigratory birds live year-round in the Seattle area.

Black-capped Chickadee

Poecile atricapillus

The black-capped chickadee is a small yet charismatic bird, easily recognized by its black cap and bib, white cheeks, and soft gray body. These lively and inquisitive birds are a common sight in Seattle's woodlands and urban green spaces, where they flit through trees and shrubs in search of food. Their playful nature and distinctive calls—particularly their cheerful "chick-a-dee-dee-dee" song—make them one of the most beloved birds in the region.

Social creatures by nature, black-capped chickadees often form mixed flocks with other small songbirds, especially during the nonbreeding season. These flocks provide safety in numbers, allowing them to forage more effectively and avoid predators. They are known for their curious behavior, often approaching humans and other animals out of curiosity rather than fear. This inquisitiveness makes them a joy to observe, as they hop from branch to branch, investigating their surroundings with keen interest.

As omnivores, black-capped chickadees have a varied diet that includes insects, seeds, and berries. In winter, they frequently visit bird feeders, showcasing their unique feeding behavior. They often grab a single seed, then fly to a nearby branch to crack it open and enjoy their meal. This habit is a testament to their remarkable memory, as they can cache food in various locations throughout their territory and later retrieve it when needed. This skill is especially crucial during the colder months, when food sources are limited.

During the breeding season, black-capped chickadees are equally fascinating. They typically nest in cavities, often choosing decaying trees or snags for their homes. When artificial nest boxes are available, they readily adopt them, making them a favorite among

birdwatchers and nature enthusiasts. Both parents take an active role in raising their young, diligently feeding the chicks, which fledge after about two weeks in the nest.

These birds also engage in interesting social behaviors, especially during the breeding season. They communicate with a variety of calls, with the "chick-a-dee-dee-dee" call serving different purposes depending on the level of threat from predators. The number of "dee" notes can indicate the degree of danger, allowing other birds to assess their environment and respond accordingly.

Where to See Them

Black-capped chickadees can be found in Seattle's parks, gardens, and wooded areas. They are commonly spotted at places like Discovery Park, Ravenna Park, and the Washington Park Arboretum. Additionally, they are frequent visitors to backyard feeders, particularly those stocked with sunflower seeds or suet. They live year-round in Seattle.

Bushtit

Psaltriparus minimus

Bushtits are tiny, energetic birds that are often seen moving through trees and shrubs in noisy, chattering flocks. They are easily recognized by their small, round bodies, long tails, and overall grayish brown plumage. Their diminutive size, only about 4.5 inches in length, allows them to flit through foliage with remarkable agility. In Seattle, bushtits are common in gardens, parks, and woodlands, where they forage primarily for insects and spiders.

One of the most charming behaviors of bushtits is their highly social nature. They often travel in large groups, which can number from a few individuals to more than a dozen, creating a delightful cacophony of soft, high-pitched calls that make them easy to locate. As they flit through branches, they are frequently seen hanging upside down, a trait that allows them to glean small insects and arachnids from the undersides of leaves and bark. Their energetic foraging style and playful interactions can be captivating to watch, especially as they chase each other in short bursts of flight.

During the breeding season, bushtits exhibit fascinating nesting behaviors. They construct elaborate, hanging nests that can resemble large, fuzzy balls. Made from materials like moss, lichen, and spiderwebs, these nests are often camouflaged within dense shrubs or trees, providing excellent protection from predators. Both males and females contribute to the nest-building process, which can take up to two weeks. Once the nest is complete, both parents share the responsibility of incubating the eggs and feeding the chicks. The chicks are altricial, meaning they are born helpless and rely on their parents for nourishment and protection.

Another interesting behavior trait of bushtits is their propensity for communal roosting. During the colder months, they often gather in small groups to roost together at night, which helps them conserve warmth and provides safety in numbers. This social behavior can be a delightful sight during fall and winter, as flocks settle into dense vegetation for the night, often producing a chorus of soft calls as they find their spots.

Where to See Them

Bushtits are most commonly found in areas with dense vegetation. Look for them in the Washington Park Arboretum, Ravenna Park, and even residential gardens, where they forage for insects in shrubs and trees. Birdwatchers in Seattle will appreciate bushtits' presence year-round, as they are nonmigratory.

Canada Goose

Branta canadensis

With its iconic black head and neck, white chinstrap, and brown, robust body, the Canada goose is one of Seattle's most recognizable birds. Known for their honking calls and graceful, V-shaped migratory formations, Canada geese are a common sight in Seattle's parks, wetlands, and along shorelines. Their bold presence, sociable nature, and adaptability to urban spaces have made them a memorable and sometimes divisive resident of the city's landscapes.

These birds are large and heavy-bodied, weighing up to 14 pounds, with wingspans reaching up to 6 feet. Their strong wings enable them to cover hundreds of miles in a single day, making them impressive long-distance travelers. However, in places like Seattle, many geese have adapted to urban environments and have become year-round residents, choosing not to migrate due to abundant food sources and mild winter temperatures. Their honking calls, which vary in pitch and rhythm, are not only a method of communication but also a way for geese to maintain flock cohesion, especially in flight.

Canada geese are herbivores, feeding primarily on grasses, seeds, and aquatic vegetation. Their diet often includes manicured lawns, which provide ideal grazing grounds in urban parks and golf courses. Although their diet is largely plant-based, these adaptable birds can shift to feeding on waste grain in agricultural fields or leftover food scraps in public spaces. Their foraging habits make them highly adaptable and opportunistic, enabling them to thrive in human-altered landscapes.

They form strong bonds with their mates, often mating for life. During the breeding season, the pair build a large nest, usually near water, using plant materials and lining it with soft down feathers for insulation. Both parents are involved in raising their goslings, and the family unit remains close even after the young are capable of flying. Canada geese are protective of their young, and parents will aggressively defend their nest and offspring against perceived threats, often hissing or charging to ward off intruders. Goslings stay with their parents until they are ready to join the larger flock, learning essential survival skills along the way.

Canada geese have a unique history in Seattle. In the 1970s, researchers from the University of Washington brought Canada geese to Seattle as part of a study on behavior and population dynamics. Many of these geese escaped, establishing a breeding population that quickly expanded. Over time, they became a permanent part of Seattle's wildlife, adapting to the city's parks, golf courses, and shoreline areas. Their proliferation has led to various

wildlife-management discussions due to concerns about overpopulation, droppings, and impacts on native species and vegetation.

Where to See Them

Canada geese are abundant in Seattle's urban parks, particularly around Green Lake, Lake Union, and the shores of Lake Washington, where they are often seen grazing or swimming in large flocks. Discovery Park, Magnuson Park, and the Washington Park Arboretum are also popular spots to observe these birds, especially during spring and summer, when families with young goslings are active.

Chestnut-backed Chickadee

Poecile rufescens

The chestnut-backed chickadee is a lively and charismatic bird that brightens the dense coniferous forests of the Pacific Northwest with its energetic antics and cheerful calls. With its signature chestnut-brown back and flanks, black cap, and white cheeks, this tiny bird may seem delicate, but it is surprisingly hardy and adaptable, thriving in the damp, cool forests that define much of its range.

One of the most endearing and interesting behaviors of chestnut-backed chickadees is their foraging technique. Like many chickadees, they are agile acrobats, often seen hanging upside down from branches or twigs as they search for insects, spiders, and other small invertebrates. This nimbleness allows them to explore crevices in bark or the undersides of leaves, where prey might be hiding. In addition to insects, they also eat seeds and berries, and during the colder months, they rely more heavily on seeds, which they readily gather from feeders stocked with sunflower seeds and suet. They are known to cache food items in hidden spots, such as under bark or in small cavities, to eat later when resources are scarce.

A particularly quirky aspect of their behavior is their social nature during winter. Chestnut-backed chickadees often form mixed-species foraging flocks, joining other small birds like kinglets, nuthatches, or bushtits. These flocks provide safety in numbers, with many eyes watching for predators, while also making foraging more efficient.

Chestnut-backed chickadees are cavity nesters. They typically nest in old woodpecker holes, natural tree cavities, or nest boxes, where they construct their nests using soft materials such as moss, feathers, animal fur, and even spider silk to insulate and cushion their eggs. Both the male and female participate in building the nest, and once the eggs are laid, the female incubates them while the male brings food. After the eggs hatch, both parents share the responsibility of feeding the chicks.

Though small, these chickadees are tough and well adapted to the cold, wet climates of the Pacific Northwest. Unlike many bird species, they do not migrate, staying in their territories year-round. Their ability to find and store food, along with their flocking behavior, helps them survive winter.

Where to See Them

Chestnut-backed chickadees are a year-round fixture in Seattle's wooded parks, including Discovery Park, Seward Park, and the Washington Park Arboretum. They are frequent visitors to backyard feeders, especially those offering sunflower seeds or suet, and their distinctive "chick-a-dee-dee-dee" calls can be heard as they move through the trees in energetic, chattering flocks.

Double-crested Cormorant

Nannopterum auritum

The double-crested cormorant is a large, black waterbird characterized by its long neck, hooked bill, and distinctive habit of spreading its wings to dry after diving. These birds are excellent swimmers, using their webbed feet to propel themselves underwater in search of fish, which make up the bulk of their diet. Their unique swimming technique involves a combination of deep dives and surface gliding, allowing them to cover significant distances as they pursue prey.

In Seattle, double-crested cormorants are commonly seen along the waterfront, perching on docks, pilings, and rocks. Their plumage appears dark and often glossy in sunlight, especially when they emerge from the water. During the breeding season, they develop two small tufts, or "crests," of feathers on their heads, which become particularly pronounced when they are excited or displaying. These crests are more prominent in males, who use them during courtship rituals and to establish dominance over other cormorants.

Cormorants are colonial nesters, often building large nests of sticks and vegetation in trees or on man-made structures like rooftops and bridges near water. Nesting typically begins in early spring, with pairs working together to construct their homes. The female usually lays three to five eggs, which both parents incubate for about twenty-eight to thirty days. After hatching, the chicks are altricial, meaning they are born helpless and dependent on their parents for food and protection. During the first few weeks, the adults take turns hunting and feeding the chicks regurgitated fish. As the young cormorants grow, they develop their swimming and diving skills, which are essential for their survival.

The behavior of double-crested cormorants extends beyond just foraging and nesting. These social birds are often seen engaged in communal activities, such as preening and vocalizing with their mates and neighbors. Their communication includes a range of low grunts and croaks, particularly during the breeding season, when establishing territories is crucial. These vocalizations play a key role in maintaining group dynamics within colonies.

In addition to their impressive fishing skills, double-crested cormorants also play a role in maintaining healthy aquatic ecosystems. By controlling fish populations, they contribute to the balance of marine life in their habitats. Their adaptability to urban environments allows them to thrive in various settings, from natural lakes to coastal cities.

Where to See Them

Double-crested cormorants are often seen along Lake Washington, the Puget Sound, and other bodies of water. Popular spots to observe them include the shores of Green Lake, Union Bay, and Discovery Park. Look for them perched on pilings, drying their wings in the sun, or diving gracefully beneath the surface in search of their next meal. Most double-crested cormorants are happy with the mild temps and seafood offerings in the Seattle area and stick around throughout the year.

▲ Double-crested cormorants are often seen drying their wing feathers, which become waterlogged when they dive for prey—an adaptation that allows them to dive deeper and access fish that other birds can't.

► This immature double-crested cormorant won't develop its darker adult coloration until it reaches its breeding age of about three years old.

Downy Woodpecker

Dryobates pubescens

The downy woodpecker is the smallest wood-pecker in North America, yet it is a familiar and hardy presence in Seattle's parks, woodlands, and backyards. These tiny black-and-white birds are easy to recognize by their checkered wing pattern and the white stripe that runs down their backs. Males can be identified by the small, vibrant red patch on the back of their heads, while females lack this colorful marking.

A quintessential behavior of the downy woodpecker is its methodical pecking as it forages. They tap their short but sturdy bills into tree trunks and branches to uncover insects, larvae, and other small invertebrates hiding under the bark. Their bill is proportionately smaller compared to larger woodpeckers, making their pecking softer and less forceful. This size difference allows them to exploit smaller branches and twigs that larger species might bypass. In addition to foraging on trees, downy woodpeckers are common visitors to bird feeders, particularly those stocked with suet and sunflower seeds. They are quite bold and will often feed in the company of other small birds like chickadees, nuthatches, and finches.

Downy woodpeckers exhibit fascinating behavior when it comes to nesting. They are cavity nesters, and both males and females participate in the excavation process, choosing dead trees or branches in which to drill their nest holes. This joint effort strengthens their pair bond, and once the eggs are laid (usually four to five), both parents share incubation duties. After about twelve days, the eggs hatch, and the chicks are altricial—born without feathers and completely dependent on their parents. For the next three weeks, the adults tirelessly forage for insects to feed their growing young, continuing to care for them even after they leave the nest.

One quirky behavior of downy woodpeckers is their "drumming" during the breeding season. Instead of singing like many other birds, males drum loudly on resonant surfaces like dead tree trunks, metal gutters, or even wooden fences to attract mates and proclaim territory. This drumming is distinct from their regular pecking, being faster and more rhythmic. In some cases, these woodpeckers will continue to drum throughout the year to communicate with their mates or defend their territory from other woodpeckers.

Another intriguing trait is their ability to adapt to urban environments. While they are naturally forest birds, downy woodpeckers are quite at home in residential areas, parks, and gardens, where they find plenty of trees and even human-made structures for foraging and nesting. Their adaptability and inquisitive nature make them a common yet always delightful sight in Seattle's green spaces.

Where to See Them

Downy woodpeckers are year-round residents in Seattle and can be found in woodlands, parks, and backyards. Ideal spots to look for them include Seward Park, Discovery Park, and the Washington Park Arboretum. Their distinctive drumming on tree trunks often gives away their location, and their small size makes them surprisingly nimble as they move along branches in search of food.

European Starling

Sturnus vulgaris

The European starling is one of the most ubiquitous and successful bird species in North America, thriving in Seattle's urban and suburban environments. Despite their non-native status—they were introduced from Europe in the late 19th century—starlings have adapted remarkably well to a variety of habitats. Most birders consider them an invasive species given the starlings' success at taking over habitat once occupied by less aggressive native birds. Their iridescent black feathers shimmer with purple and green in the sunlight, and their plumage becomes speckled with white in the winter months, giving them a striking appearance. During the breeding season, their bills turn a bright yellow, contrasting sharply with their dark plumage, while in winter, their bills darken.

One of the most fascinating aspects of starlings is their vocal ability. These birds are renowned mimics and can imitate the calls of other birds as well as a wide array of man-made sounds, including car alarms, ringing phones, and even human speech. This vocal versatility makes them excellent communicators, and they use a range of sounds to defend their territory, attract mates, and coordinate with their flock. The song of a starling is a complex mix of whistles, clicks, and gurgling sounds, which can vary from one bird to another.

European starlings are omnivores, with a varied diet that includes insects, fruits, and seeds. Their foraging behavior is often a noisy, social affair, as they move across lawns, parks, and fields in search of food. They use their strong bills to probe the soil for worms, grubs, and other invertebrates, often leaving small holes in the ground as evidence of

their feeding. In urban areas, they are known to forage near dumpsters and picnic areas, making them a common sight in parking lots and parks.

Starlings are highly social birds and are often observed in large flocks, especially outside the breeding season. One of the most breathtaking behaviors they exhibit is called a "murmuration," where thousands of star-lings move in coordinated, fluid formations in the sky. These mesmerizing aerial displays are thought to confuse predators and help the flock maintain cohesion during flight. Although murmurations are more commonly seen in larger starling populations, smaller groups can still be seen engaging in intricate flight patterns over Seattle.

In terms of nesting, starlings are oppor-tunistic and adaptable, often competing with native bird species for cavities in trees, buildings, and other structures. They build messy nests using grass, twigs, and discarded materials. A pair will typically raise two broods per year, with both parents involved in feeding the chicks, which fledge after about three weeks.

Where to See Them

European starlings are a common sight across Seattle, especially in urban areas, parks, and open fields. Some prime locations to observe their busy foraging and social behaviors include Discovery Park, Green Lake, and the Union Bay Natural Area. They are often seen perched on power lines, fences, or buildings, chattering away as they survey their surround-ings. Once the starlings got to Seattle, they had no intention of leaving, and as such are year-rounders.

Gadwall

Mareca strepera

The gadwall is a medium-sized dabbling duck that often gets overshadowed by its more colorful cousins but is fascinating for those who take a closer look. Male gadwalls, with their grayish brown feathers, may seem drab at first glance, but a closer inspection reveals intricate patterns, a subtle patch of white on the wings, and a distinctive black rear. Females

resemble female mallards, featuring mottled brown feathers that provide excellent camouflage within their wetland surroundings. Both sexes possess a rounded head and a slightly smaller bill compared to other duck species, making them easier to spot for experienced birdwatchers.

One quirky behavior that sets gadwalls apart is their unique feeding technique. While dabbling, they often tip forward in the water, submerging their heads while their rear ends remain up in the air—a behavior known as "tipping." This can make them quite comical to observe. Gadwalls primarily consume plant matter such as algae, grasses, and seeds, though they occasionally eat small invertebrates. Their preference for plant-based foods makes them important contributors to the health of wetland ecosystems, as they help control the growth of aquatic plants and promote biodiversity. Unlike some of their flashier relatives, gadwalls often forage in more secluded areas, appearing somewhat shy.

Gadwalls are generally more solitary than many other duck species, often seen in pairs or small groups. During the breeding season, males engage in subtle courtship displays, including gentle bobbing motions and soft calls. Once paired, gadwalls are known to be monogamous for the breeding season, with a strong bond between partners.

Breeding pairs typically form in late winter or early spring, and females build nests in thick vegetation near water. These well-hidden nests protect eggs from predators, showcasing the female's intelligence in selecting safe locations. Ducklings are precocial, meaning they can swim and forage shortly after leaving the nest, but they still rely on their mother for guidance and protection during their early days.

One unusual behavior observed in gadwalls is their communal resting. When not foraging, gadwalls can be seen resting in small groups, grooming and preening their feathers, helping maintain their plumage. This social grooming can strengthen bonds between individuals and provide safety in numbers.

Where to See Them

Gadwalls are commonly found in wetlands and ponds around the Seattle area during the winter and migration seasons. You can spot them in large numbers at locations like the Union Bay Natural Area, Magnuson Park's wetlands, and the restored ponds at Seward Park. The freshwater marshes of the Washington Park Arboretum are also prime spots for observing gadwalls up close. During the colder months, they often mingle with other duck species, creating excellent opportunities for birdwatching and photography enthusiasts. Some gadwalls migrate to the southern United States and Mexico, while others spend the whole year in and around Seattle.

Glaucous-winged Gull

Larus glaucescens

The glaucous-winged gull is a large, robust bird commonly seen along Seattle's waterfronts, piers, and beaches. These gulls are easily recognizable by their pale gray wings and wingtips, white bodies, and pink legs. Adults also have a hefty yellow beak with a distinct red spot near the tip, a common feature among large gulls. While they might look similar to other gull species, their pale wingtips, as opposed to black, help set them apart.

Glaucous-winged gulls are opportunistic omnivores, and their diet reflects their adaptability to a wide variety of environments. They primarily eat fish and marine invertebrates but are not picky, often scavenging garbage or hunting small birds, mammals, and even insects when necessary. Their resourcefulness allows them to thrive in urban areas, where they can be seen rummaging through trash bins or patrolling parking lots in search of discarded food. They're also known to hover near fishing boats or docks, hoping to snag an easy meal.

Breeding for glaucous-winged gulls takes place in colonies on rocky cliffs or isolated islands, usually along the Pacific coast. Their nests are made from grass, moss, seaweed, and other soft materials to protect their eggs. Both parents participate in nest-building, incubation, and feeding the chicks, demonstrating a high degree of parental care. The young are born altricial, meaning they hatch in a relatively helpless state, relying on their parents for food and protection. Once fledged, the juvenile gulls are distinguishable by their brownish plumage, which gradually changes over several years as they mature.

Glaucous-winged gulls are also known for their loud, raucous calls, which are used to communicate within the flock and establish territory. Their vocalizations are a familiar sound along Seattle's coastlines, particularly near busy docks or ferry terminals.

Where to See Them

You can find glaucous-winged gulls year-round along Seattle's coastline, particularly at places like Alki Beach, Pier 62, and Discovery Park. They are often spotted hovering near fishing boats or ferries, patrolling shorelines, or perched on pilings, ever-watchful for their next meal. Their ability to adapt to both wild and urban settings makes them a constant presence in the city's waterfront areas. They live in the region year-round, but many of the birds survey a large range up and down the coast and into the sounds and inlets along it in search of sustenance.

▼ Glaucous-winged gulls are a fixture of Seattle's Puget Sound waterfront.

Great Blue Heron

Ardea herodias

The great blue heron is the largest and most widespread heron in North America, easily recognized by its long legs, elongated neck, and striking blue-gray plumage. In Seattle's wetlands and lakeshores, this graceful bird is a common sight, often seen wading slowly in search of fish, amphibians, or small mammals. Known for their solitary hunting style, great blue herons stand motionless in shallow water, waiting patiently to spear prey with their sharp bills. Despite their height—up to 4 feet—their lightweight bodies allow for elegant, steady flight, with their necks pulled into a distinctive S shape and slow, deep wingbeats.

While typically solitary hunters, great blue herons gather in colonies, or rookeries, during the breeding season. In the Seattle area, these rookeries are often found in tall trees near water. Herons build large stick nests, sometimes reused and expanded each year, with both parents sharing responsibilities for nest-building, incubation, and feeding the chicks. The young fledge within two months but remain dependent on their parents for food.

Adaptable hunters, great blue herons primarily eat fish but will also prey on small birds, reptiles, and invertebrates when available. They thrive in a variety of wetland environments, from lakes and rivers to tidal marshes, making Seattle's waterways an ideal habitat. Although typically quiet, they become more vocal during breeding season, producing loud croaks and squawks, especially in competitive rookeries. Their patient hunting style and

It's no wonder that the great blue heron is Seattle's official bird—so declared by the city council in 2003—given that the iconic blue-gray wading bird species doesn't seem perturbed by a little rain.

graceful flight add to their dignified, almost prehistoric presence.

The great blue heron was officially named the city bird of Seattle in 2003, a decision that reflects the bird's deep connection to the city's natural landscapes and its iconic presence along Seattle's waterways. The designation was made by the Seattle City Council following a campaign led by environmental and bird-conservation groups, who highlighted the heron's role as a symbol of Seattle's abundant natural beauty and the city's commitment to preserving its wetlands and wildlife. The great blue heron was chosen not only for its majesty and grace but also because of its reliance on healthy ecosystems, particularly the region's aquatic environments. As a species that thrives in urban settings, from the shores of Puget Sound to the lakes and rivers that wind through Seattle, the heron serves as a reminder of the delicate balance between urban development and nature conservation. Its selection as the official bird of Seattle emphasizes the city's dedication to environmental stewardship and protecting the diverse habitats that support wildlife within and around its urban areas.

Where to See Them

Seattle is home to several large great blue heron rookeries where hundreds of the "old crankies" gather in spring and early summer in the canopies of tall waterside trees to birth and rear their young. The most well known of the rookeries can be found at Kiwanis Ravine near the southern edge of Discovery Park, Union Bay Natural Area in the Laurelhurst neighborhood near the University of Washington, Commodore Park near the Chittenden Locks in Ballard, Swamp Creek at the north end of Lake Washington, and Lake Sammamish State Park near the mouth of Issaquah Creek in Issaquah. Even if you can't make it out to a heron rookery in spring, chances are good you'll encounter these majestic birds if you spend any time at all around Seattle's wetlands and shorelines. Popular viewing spots include Discovery Park, Union Bay Natural Area, and Seward Park, where these birds can be seen wading through shallow waters, often standing motionless while hunting. They are also common along Lake Washington and near the Puget Sound shorelines. Keep an eye out for them perched in tall trees or flying slowly overhead. They live year-round in Seattle.

House Finch

Haemorhous mexicanus

The house finch, a small and colorful songbird, has become a familiar and beloved presence in Seattle's urban landscape. Known for its joyful warbling song and vibrant plumage, the house finch has adapted well to city life, thriving in parks, gardens, and residential areas. Originally native to the western United States and Mexico, house finches were introduced to the eastern United States in the 1940s and have since expanded their range, becoming a widespread and resilient species.

Male house finches are easily recognized by their striking red plumage on the head, throat, and chest, a feature that makes them particularly eye-catching. The red coloration varies from bird to bird and is actually a result of the pigments in their diet; males that consume more carotenoid-rich foods tend to have brighter red feathers. Females, on the other hand, have a more understated appearance, with streaky brown markings that help them blend into their surroundings. The male's bright coloring plays an important role in attracting mates, as females tend to prefer males with more vibrant plumage, a sign of health and good nutrition.

One of the house finch's unique traits is its adaptability to human environments. These birds are primarily seed-eaters and are especially fond of sunflower seeds, which makes them frequent visitors to backyard bird feeders. Their diet also includes fruits, buds, and flower seeds, allowing them to take advantage of the ornamental plants and shrubs commonly found in urban landscapes. House finches have even been known to forage in garden beds, dining on dandelion seeds and other weeds. Their ability to thrive on various plant materials and adapt their diet to what's available makes them one of the most successful songbirds in city settings.

House finches are nonmigratory, meaning they remain in Seattle year-round, enduring both the mild winters and the rainy season. During the breeding season, which lasts from spring to early fall, they are highly adaptable nesters, often choosing unusual locations close to human activity. Their nests can be found in a variety of places, from trees and shrubs to man-made structures like building eaves, porch lights, and hanging planters. This adaptability allows them to raise multiple broods each season, sometimes as many as three or four, with both parents sharing the responsibilities of feeding and protecting the young. Males are known for their attentive care, often bringing food to females during incubation and helping feed the chicks once they hatch.

In addition to their adaptability and bright appearance, house finches are known for their lively songs. Males produce a varied, bright warbling song that can be heard throughout neighborhoods, adding a pleasant soundtrack to urban life. These complex vocalizations serve to attract mates and establish territory, and each male's song is slightly different, adding a unique layer of charm to their presence in Seattle.

Where to See Them

House finches are abundant across Seattle's residential neighborhoods, parks, and open woodlands, particularly where bird feeders are present. They are easy to spot in places like the Washington Park Arboretum, Volunteer Park, and most neighborhoods with gardens. Their friendly demeanor, tolerance for human activity, and preference for backyard feeders make house finches one of the most approachable and observable birds in the city.

House Sparrow

Passer domesticus

The house sparrow, an introduced species originally from Europe, has become one of Seattle's most familiar and resilient urban birds. Though often considered invasive due to its competitive nature, the house sparrow has carved out a niche for itself in Seattle's cityscape, thriving in the human-modified landscapes of parks, neighborhoods, and

remarkable flexibility in selecting nesting sites. In cities like Seattle, where natural nesting sites may be scarce, house sparrows make use of almost any available cavity or nook, from building eaves to vents and the undersides of signs. They are even known to nest in hanging planters and crevices in busy shopping centers, schools, and residential buildings. This ability to use human-made structures for nesting has helped them become a constant presence in urban areas.

A highly social species, house sparrows are often seen in flocks, chattering and foraging together, especially around food sources. They are also communal nesters, frequently forming loose colonies in which nests are built close to one another. This gregarious behavior extends to their breeding habits, as house sparrows are prolific breeders, capable of raising multiple broods each year. Their adaptability in nesting sites and high reproductive rate contribute to their population's stability and growth, making them one of the most common birds in urban environments.

House sparrows also play a complex role in Seattle's urban ecosystem. While their abundance and adaptability make them strong competitors, they contribute to the city's biodiversity in ways that are sometimes overlooked. They help control insect populations by feeding on them, particularly during the breeding season when protein is needed for growing chicks. Their prolific nature also makes them an important prey species for urban raptors like hawks and owls, contributing to the food web and supporting urban predators.

Where to See Them

House sparrows are virtually everywhere in Seattle, especially in highly urbanized areas like public squares, parking lots, and around shopping centers. They are easy to spot in parks, residential neighborhoods, and busy streets, where they forage and nest close to human activity. Their nonmigratory nature means they remain in Seattle year-round, braving the cold and finding food even in winter.

bustling public spaces. These small, stocky birds—with males featuring gray heads, black bibs, and chestnut-brown backs, and females with more muted, streaky brown plumage—may be ubiquitous, but they have unique qualities that make them fascinating players in urban ecosystems.

One of the most striking traits of the house sparrow is its adaptability. This bird is an opportunistic feeder, eating an exceptionally wide range of foods that allows it to thrive in a variety of environments. While its primary diet consists of seeds and grains, it readily consumes scraps from human garbage, discarded fast food, and crumbs found in public spaces. In backyards, it's a frequent visitor to bird feeders, especially when sunflower seeds are available. House sparrows' omnivorous diet, combined with their willingness to forage in busy, human-populated areas, enables them to make the most of Seattle's urban resources and outcompete some native bird species.

House sparrows are not only adaptable in their diet but also in their nesting habits. These birds are cavity nesters and show a

Killdeer

Charadrius vociferus

Killdeer, a medium-sized member of the plover family, are a familiar sight in Seattle's open spaces, where their sharp "kill-deer" call echoes as they move across fields, lawns, and shorelines. With their distinctive brown upperparts, white underbelly, and bold black bands across the chest, killdeer are easily recognized. Though classified as shorebirds, they are highly adaptable and are often found far from water in dry, open habitats such as golf courses, parking lots, and even suburban lawns. Their versatility and intriguing behaviors make them an important and charismatic player in Seattle's ecosystems.

One of the most captivating behaviors of killdeer is their "broken-wing" act, a well-known display in the birding world. When a predator or human approaches their nest, the adult killdeer will pretend to be injured, fluttering along the ground and dragging a wing as though it's broken. This performance lures the predator away from the vulnerable nest, as the "injured" killdeer appears to be an easy target. Once the predator has been drawn far enough from the eggs or chicks, the bird miraculously "recovers" and flies off, leaving the intruder baffled. This remarkable display of deception shows both intelligence and instinct, highlighting the bird's dedication to protecting its young.

Killdeer typically nest in shallow scrapes on the ground, often in open, exposed areas with little to no vegetation. Their choice of nesting sites can seem counterintuitive—often right out in the open, where they appear vulnerable. However, killdeer rely on camouflage for protection. Their nests are usually lined with small pebbles or debris, blending seamlessly with their surroundings and making it difficult for predators to spot the eggs. In urban areas, killdeer have been known to nest on gravel rooftops and in parking lots, further showcasing their adaptability to human-altered environments.

As opportunistic foragers, killdeer primarily feed on insects, worms, and other small invertebrates, which they find by running in short bursts and pecking at the ground. Their quick, darting movements allow them to cover ground efficiently, and their sharp eyesight

helps them spot tiny prey in various terrains, whether in grassy fields, sandy shores, or gravelly lots. This diet of insects and other small creatures positions them as natural pest controllers, reducing populations of pests such as beetles, caterpillars, and other insects that can impact local vegetation and agriculture.

Killdeer play an important ecological role in Seattle by contributing to pest control and acting as a food source for local raptors and other predators. They also add a level of biodiversity to urban and suburban spaces, where their presence enriches the area's birdlife and offers unique opportunities for birdwatchers and residents to observe their interesting behaviors.

Where to See Them

In Seattle, killdeer can be spotted in a variety of open, flat habitats, including golf courses, ball fields, gravel lots, and natural shorelines. Magnuson Park, Discovery Park, and Union Bay Natural Area are excellent places to observe them, especially during the early morning or late afternoon when they are most active. In these open spaces, killdeer can be seen year-round, as Seattle's temperate climate allows them to avoid seasonal migration. However, their numbers do increase during migration periods in spring and fall, as other killdeer pass through Seattle on their way to or from overwintering grounds in the southern United States, Mexico, and Central America.

Mallard

Anas platyrhynchos

The mallard is one of the most easily recognizable and widespread ducks across the globe. Male mallards stand out with their striking, iridescent green heads, bright yellow bills, and distinctive curled black tail feathers. Females, while more subdued in appearance with their mottled brown plumage, are still notable with their orange bills and a blue wing patch bordered by white, visible both at rest and in flight. Both sexes have the same elegant blue speculum on their wings, a feature that often catches the light as they take to the air or glide on the water.

Mallards are "dabbling" ducks, a behavior that is both practical and comical to observe. When feeding, they tip forward, their heads submerged while their tails stick up in the air as they forage for aquatic plants, seeds, and small invertebrates in shallow water. They don't dive like some other waterfowl species but instead skim the surface or forage along the edges of ponds and lakes.

Aside from their feeding habits, mallards are known for their adaptability and are found in a wide range of habitats. They thrive in both urban and natural settings, ranging from large lakes and wetlands to small city ponds, rivers, and even drainage ditches. This adaptability makes them one of the most successful and ubiquitous duck species.

Mallards exhibit a variety of interesting behaviors. During courtship, males engage in elaborate displays, bobbing their heads, flicking water, and making soft vocalizations to attract a mate. These displays often involve multiple males vying for the attention of a single female. While their courtship rituals are fascinating, mallards can also be aggressive, particularly during the breeding season. Males will sometimes chase away rivals or even harass females.

Mallards are social ducks, often found in large groups, especially outside of the breeding season. You might notice them paddling together in loose flocks or gathering on land to preen and rest. One quirky behavior is their habit of "preening parties," where several ducks gather and meticulously groom their

► With its iridescent green head and yellow beak, the male mallard duck is one of the most recognizable birds in and around Seattle's freshwater lakes and streams.

▼ Mallard ducklings stay with their parents for about two months after hatching before they can fly away.

feathers for long periods, ensuring they remain waterproof and in top condition.

Where to See Them

Mallards are abundant around Seattle's many lakes, ponds, and wetlands. Excellent spots for observing these birds include Green Lake, Lake Union, and the Arboretum wetlands.

In urban parks, even small water features like fountains and ponds are frequented by mallards, making them an easy species to spot regardless of the season. In Seattle, mallards can be found throughout the year, though their numbers may increase in winter as migratory birds from colder regions join the local populations.

Northern Flicker

Colaptes auratus

The northern flicker is one of the more charismatic and unusual members of the woodpecker family. Unlike many of its relatives, which are often spotted high in the trees or drumming on trunks, the flicker is frequently seen foraging on the ground. Its striking plumage features a brown, barred back and a spotted chest with a dramatic black crescent-shaped patch on it. Depending on the region, flickers will have either bright yellow or red shafts along the undersides of their wings and tails, which are particularly noticeable in flight. In the Pacific Northwest, the red-shafted subspecies *Colaptes auratus cafer* is most commonly seen.

Northern flickers are well known for their quirky behavior, particularly their ground-feeding habits, which set them apart from most other woodpeckers. They use their long, barbed tongues to extract ants and beetles, a primary food source, from the soil, making them more likely to be spotted pecking at the ground than hammering on trees. Their preference for ants is so strong that they can consume thousands in a single day, using their specialized tongue to probe deep into anthills.

One of the flicker's most recognizable behaviors is their loud drumming, not just on trees but on metal surfaces like chimneys, gutters, or even street signs. This drumming serves two purposes: establishing territory and attracting a mate. While this behavior might frustrate homeowners, it's an essential part of flicker courtship and communication. Flickers are also known for their loud, repetitive "wick-a-wick-a-wick" calls, which are often heard before the bird is seen.

Northern flickers excavate their own nests in dead or decaying trees, creating a deep cavity where they will lay five to eight eggs. Both males and females participate in nest-building, incubation, and raising the chicks, which

▲ Unlike other species of woodpeckers, northern flickers derive most of their sustenance from ground-feeding, not burrowing into tree bark.

fledge after about four weeks. In urban areas, flickers have also been known to use nest boxes or even burrow into the sides of buildings, showcasing their adaptability.

One of the most fascinating traits of the northern flicker is their "anting" behavior, where they allow ants to crawl on their feathers. The ants release formic acid, which is thought to help control parasites on the flicker's body. This behavior is shared with a few other bird species, but it is particularly notable in flickers due to their reliance on ants as a food source.

In addition, flickers exhibit a form of aerial display during courtship. Males will fly in looping patterns, showing off their bright underwing and tail feathers to potential mates. This acrobatic flight is accompanied by calls and drumming, forming a multisensory performance.

Where to See Them

Northern flickers are common across Seattle, thriving in a variety of habitats, including wooded areas, parks, and even suburban neighborhoods. You can often spot them foraging on lawns or perched on fence posts, telephone poles, or large trees. Good places to observe flickers include Discovery Park, Seward Park, and the Washington Park Arboretum, particularly in open woodlands or near the edges of forests. Their distinct calls and drumming sounds are often the first clue that a flicker is nearby, so keep your ears open as you explore. Flickers in the Seattle region generally stay put year-round, taking advantage of the temperate climate and ample food sources in urban and suburban areas.

Peregrine Falcon

Falco peregrinus

Peregrine falcons are among the most remarkable birds of prey in the world, known for their incredible speed and adaptability. Once endangered due to pesticide use, these raptors have made a dramatic comeback, and Seattle has become a stronghold for them. These days they thrive in and around the city, using its towering buildings and bridges as substitutes for their traditional cliffside nesting sites.

Peregrine falcons hold the title of the fastest bird on the planet. When hunting, they perform breathtaking aerial dives, or "stoops," reaching speeds of over 200 miles per hour as they strike prey—primarily pigeons, starlings, and other medium-sized birds—out of the sky. Unlike hawks that soar while searching for food, peregrines rely on surprise attacks, often launching from high perches to ambush their prey mid-flight.

Their physical adaptations make them formidable hunters. Their long, pointed wings allow for rapid acceleration, while their keen eyesight, eight times sharper than a human's, helps them track prey from incredible distances. Their strong talons and notched beak are designed for swift, efficient kills.

Peregrine falcons nearly disappeared from North America in the mid-20th century due to widespread DDT pesticide use, which weakened their eggshells and led to reproductive failure. By the 1970s, they were almost extinct in the continental United States. However, after DDT was banned in 1972 and extensive conservation efforts were implemented, their populations rebounded.

Urban environments like Seattle have played a key role in the peregrine falcon's recovery. Tall buildings provide the perfect high-rise nesting spots, mirroring their natural cliffside habitats. Cities also offer an abundant food supply—feral pigeons, European starlings, and other urban birds make up a large portion of their diet. As a result, peregrines have become a common sight in many cities, including Seattle.

Peregrine falcons prefer to nest on tall structures, where they lay their eggs in simple scrapes on ledges rather than in traditional stick-built nests. In Seattle, falcons have established nests on several downtown high-rises, bridges, and even the University of Washington's campus. These birds are fiercely territorial during breeding season, which runs from March to June.

Chicks, known as *eyases*, hatch after about a month of incubation and grow quickly. By six weeks, they begin practicing flight and are often seen flapping awkwardly before making their first leaps. By fall, the young falcons disperse, sometimes traveling hundreds of miles to establish their own territories.

Despite their successful urban adaptation, peregrine falcons still face threats. Window collisions, habitat loss, and climate change can impact their populations. Conservationists work with the Washington Department of Fish and Wildlife to monitor nesting sites and install nest boxes and with building managers to protect breeding pairs, in a team effort to keep peregrine populations thriving in and around Seattle.

Where to See Them

Peregrine falcons can be seen throughout the year in Seattle, favoring the city's tallest structures as their hunting and nesting grounds. Skyscrapers in downtown Seattle serve as ideal perches, where these swift predators scan for pigeons before launching into breathtaking, high-speed dives. On the University of Washington campus, nesting pairs have been known to take up residence on the rooftops of academic buildings, their sharp cries occasionally cutting through the hum of student life.

Seattle's many bridges—especially the Ship Canal, West Seattle, and University Bridges—often attract peregrines as well, offering sturdy ledges and strategic vantage points for spotting prey. Along the Elliott Bay waterfront, these raptors sometimes appear near the piers and industrial buildings, patrolling the skies above the bustling shoreline.

Pied-billed Grebe

Podilymbus podiceps

The pied-billed grebe is a small, uniquely adaptable bird known for its remarkable swimming and diving abilities, perfectly suited to Seattle's wetlands and quiet water bodies. Though often overlooked due to its inconspicuous appearance, the pied-billed grebe plays a significant role in Seattle's ecosystems, particularly within its lakes, ponds, and marshes. With a compact body, brown plumage, and a distinctive thick bill marked by a dark band during the breeding season, the pied-billed grebe is easily identified by bird enthusiasts who seek it out in Seattle's waterways.

One of the most fascinating behaviors of the pied-billed grebe is its ability to control its buoyancy. While many waterbirds are skilled divers, the pied-billed grebe has the unique ability to adjust how much of its body remains visible above the water's surface. Often described as "submarining," this grebe can sink its entire body below the water, leaving just its head exposed or even disappearing completely. This behavior helps the bird remain stealthy, allowing it to hunt unsuspecting prey or avoid detection from predators like raptors and large fish. This submarining technique sets the pied-billed grebe apart from other waterfowl, enhancing its survival in Seattle's urban and natural wetlands.

The pied-billed grebe's diet is diverse and includes small fish, crustaceans, insects, and occasionally plant material. To aid in digesting this varied diet, the grebe consumes its own feathers, a quirky behavior shared by other grebe species but especially notable in the pied-billed grebe. By swallowing its feathers, the bird forms a protective layer in its stomach, which helps filter out and trap indigestible materials, such as sharp fish bones, preventing them from causing harm. The grebe later regurgitates these indigestible parts as pellets, keeping its digestive system healthy and efficient. This unique adaptation allows the grebe to consume tougher prey and thrive in diverse environments, from quiet urban lakes to secluded marshes.

During the breeding season, pied-billed grebes become fiercely territorial. Males perform elaborate displays on the water, including head bobbing and calling with a distinctive, throaty hoot to attract mates and warn rivals. These territorial displays and vocalizations create a lively atmosphere in Seattle's ponds and wetlands during the spring and summer months. Though pied-billed grebes are migratory, their migrations are often limited, with some individuals moving only short distances to avoid harsh winter conditions. Seattle's mild climate makes it a suitable year-round habitat, and many grebes can be seen in local wetlands throughout the year, though some may travel farther south when conditions are particularly harsh.

Where to See Them

In Seattle, pied-billed grebes are most commonly found in quiet, sheltered water bodies where they can dive and forage without strong disturbances. Green Lake, Union Bay Natural Area, and the wetlands of Magnuson Park are excellent places to observe these fascinating birds. Often, they can be seen floating low in the water or submarining as they hunt for food. Their preference for still or slow-moving water makes them a frequent sight in Seattle's smaller lakes, ponds, and protected coastal inlets.

◄ Surprise! A pied-billed grebe pops up out of the water amid the fragrant water lilies of Seattle's Duck Bay.

Pine Siskin

Spinus pinus

The pine siskin is a highly social and lively finch that is easily recognized by its streaky brown plumage and subtle flashes of yellow on its wings and tail, which become especially noticeable in flight. These small, energetic birds are common in Seattle's parks, gardens, and forests, particularly during the winter months when they travel in flocks to search for food. Known for their noisy and competitive nature, pine siskins bring life and activity to Seattle's green spaces, and they play an important role in the local ecosystem.

Pine siskins are highly social birds that often gather in large, chaotic flocks, creating lively scenes at bird feeders where they compete for seeds, sometimes aggressively displacing other birds. Their fast, undulating flight pattern is typical of finches, and they frequently travel with other finch species, such as goldfinches, during winter. These mixed-species flocks allow them to cover large areas in their search for food, and this gregarious behavior not only provides safety in numbers but also increases their chances of finding abundant food sources.

One of the unique behaviors of pine siskins is their habit of caching seeds. They will store seeds in crevices of bark or other hidden spots, creating small caches to rely on when food is scarce, especially during harsh winters. This behavior is particularly beneficial for survival in cold weather, as Seattle's winter food supplies can sometimes be unpredictable. By caching seeds, siskins ensure they have a backup source of nourishment during lean times. This caching behavior also benefits the ecosystem, as some stored seeds are never retrieved and may eventually germinate, contributing to plant growth in the area.

Pine siskins are primarily seed-eaters, with a diet that includes conifer seeds, buds, and small flowers. They are especially attracted to sunflower and thistle seeds at bird feeders, which is why they are frequent visitors in Seattle's backyards. Their fondness for coniferous forests makes Seattle, with its abundance of evergreens, an ideal habitat. In the wild, they forage by extracting seeds from pine and fir cones, a skill that allows them to make use of the conifer-rich forests in and around Seattle, such as those in Seward Park and the Washington Park Arboretum.

During the breeding season, pine siskins expand their diet to include insects, which provide the protein necessary for raising young. This seasonal diet shift helps control insect populations, contributing to the balance of Seattle's ecosystem. Pine siskins are partial migrants, meaning their migratory behavior is unpredictable. While some may remain in their breeding range year-round, others migrate south during harsh winters in search of food. This variability sometimes results in "irruptions," where large numbers of pine siskins move far beyond their typical wintering range, often reaching the southern United States and even Mexico. These irruptions, driven by food shortages, can result in sudden increases in their local population in places like Seattle, where they form large flocks around bird feeders and coniferous habitats during winter months.

Where to See Them

In Seattle, pine siskins are most commonly seen during the colder months, gathering in noisy flocks at bird feeders and in coniferous forests. Seward Park, Washington Park Arboretum, and Discovery Park are excellent places to spot them foraging in pine and fir trees, especially during irruption years when their populations surge. They are also frequent visitors in residential gardens, where they are drawn to feeders stocked with sunflower and thistle seeds. Their sociable and lively behavior, combined with their unique caching habit, makes them a captivating species to observe and a valuable contributor to Seattle's ecosystems.

Red-breasted Nuthatch

Sitta canadensis

The red-breasted nuthatch is a small but lively bird, often spotted darting up and down tree trunks in search of food. Its compact body, stubby tail, and distinctive head pattern—featuring a black cap and white eyebrow—make it easy to identify. What really sets this species apart is its warm, rusty red breast, which adds a splash of color to its otherwise gray-and-black plumage. Despite its small size, the red-breasted nuthatch has a big personality, known for being curious and bold, often approaching humans at bird feeders.

One of the most unique behaviors of the red-breasted nuthatch is its habit of moving headfirst down tree trunks, a behavior common to nuthatches but rarely seen in other bird species. This allows them to spot insects and seeds that other birds may miss while climbing up the tree. They have incredibly strong legs and sharp claws that help them cling to vertical surfaces with ease.

Red-breasted nuthatches are quite vocal, often giving a high-pitched, nasal "yank-yank" call that sounds a bit like a toy horn. This call is used to communicate with their mate or to ward off intruders in their territory. They are also known for being quite fearless around humans, regularly visiting bird feeders where they find suet and sunflower seeds. Unlike some birds that linger at the feeder, nuthatches tend to grab a seed and fly away to stash it in a nearby tree crevice for later consumption.

During the breeding season, red-breasted nuthatches excavate their own nest cavities, usually in dead or decaying trees. They use

their sharp bills to chip away at the wood, often lining the entrance with sticky resin, which may help deter predators or competitors from entering the nest. Inside, they create a cozy nest using soft materials like fur, feathers, and grass, ensuring a warm environment for their eggs and chicks.

One particularly quirky behavior of the red-breasted nuthatch is its practice of smearing sap around the entrance of its nest cavity. This sticky barrier may serve as a defense mechanism, discouraging predators such as squirrels or other birds from entering the nest. The nuthatches themselves are able to avoid the sticky substance by carefully maneuvering around it.

Additionally, red-breasted nuthatches exhibit food-caching behavior, meaning they hide seeds in tree bark or crevices for later retrieval. This helps them survive during times when food is scarce, such as in the winter months. They have an excellent memory, allowing them to locate their hidden food stores long after they've cached them.

Where to See Them

Their preferred habitat includes mature coniferous forests, particularly those with firs, pines, and spruces. During the winter months, red-breasted nuthatches may also venture into mixed forests and urban areas, where they can be found frequenting bird feeders. In Seattle, they can be seen year-round in areas like Discovery Park, the Washington Park Arboretum, and any local parks with a good mix of evergreen trees. Keep an ear out for their distinctive "yank-yank" calls, which will often lead you right to them. Seattle's red-breasted nuthatches are generally year-round residents. However, during irruption years, when food supplies in their northern breeding grounds are low, more nuthatches may migrate southward, sometimes reaching as far as the southern United States or even northern Mexico. These irruptions usually occur during fall and winter, from late September to November, as the birds move in search of better foraging opportunities.

Red-tailed Hawk

Buteo jamaicensis

The red-tailed hawk is one of the most common and widespread raptors in North America, and Seattle is no exception. These large birds of prey are easily recognized by their broad wings, reddish brown tail, and dark patagial marks on the leading edge of their wings. Adult red-tailed hawks exhibit a range of plumage variations, but their signature characteristics remain constant. You can often see them soaring high above open fields, utilizing thermal updrafts to glide effortlessly or perched prominently on poles, trees, and other vantage points, surveying their surroundings for potential prey.

Red-tailed hawks are versatile hunters, primarily feeding on small mammals like rabbits, rodents, and squirrels. However, their diet can also include birds, reptiles, and insects when available. Their incredible eyesight allows them to spot prey from great heights, making them efficient hunters. Once they identify a target, they dive down at remarkable speeds, using their powerful talons to capture their meal with precision. Interestingly, red-tailed hawks are known to adapt their hunting strategies based on their environment, employing techniques like ambush hunting or following other predators to scavenge leftovers.

These hawks are not just solitary hunters; they are also quite social outside of the breeding season, often seen in pairs or small groups. They communicate with a variety of calls, not only the familiar "kee-eeeee-arr" but also a series of chattering sounds used to convey excitement or alert others to potential threats. In urban areas, red-tailed hawks have shown remarkable adaptability, using man-made structures for perches and nesting sites, which can lead to interesting interactions with humans.

During the breeding season, red-tailed hawks build large stick nests, often situated in tall trees or on cliffs. These nests can reach impressive sizes and are frequently reused year after year. Both parents participate in incubating the eggs, which typically number between one and four, and share the responsibility of raising the young. The nestlings are altricial, meaning they are born helpless and require care until they fledge, usually around ten weeks after hatching. During this time, the parents work tirelessly to provide food, often bringing back large prey items to feed their growing chicks.

In addition to their remarkable hunting skills, red-tailed hawks play a vital role in their ecosystems as top predators, helping maintain the balance of prey populations. Their keen senses and adaptability ensure their success in diverse habitats, from forests to urban landscapes.

Where to See Them

In Seattle, red-tailed hawks are frequently spotted in open areas, including Discovery Park, Magnuson Park, and around the edges of Lake Washington. They are often seen perched on streetlights, fences, or the tops of tall trees, watching for signs of movement below. During warmer months, the sound of their calls echoes through the air, particularly in areas where they are nesting. These non-migratory hunters spend the entire year in and around Seattle.

Red-winged blackbird

Agelaius phoeniceus

The red-winged blackbird is one of the most easily recognized birds in the Seattle area, thanks to the striking red and yellow epaulettes on the wings of the males. Males are jet black, and these bold shoulder patches are prominently flashed during the breeding season as they defend their territory. Their vibrant plumage serves as both a warning and an attraction, drawing females while warding off rivals. In contrast, females possess streaked brown plumage that helps them blend into their wetland habitats, providing effective camouflage against predators. Both sexes feature strong, conical bills suited for a diet consisting mainly of seeds and insects, which they forage from the surrounding vegetation.

Red-winged blackbirds are typically associated with wetlands, where they nest in dense vegetation such as cattails, reeds, or shrubs. These birds are highly territorial, with males aggressively defending their nesting areas from rivals and predators alike. Their

distinctive call, a harsh "conk-la-ree," is a familiar sound in marshy areas during spring and summer, signaling their presence and establishing their territory. Males can often be seen perched prominently on tall grasses or reeds, using their calls to announce their dominance.

During the winter months, red-winged blackbirds primarily feed on seeds, particularly from grasses and weeds, but they also hunt insects, spiders, and small snails during the warmer seasons. Their adaptability to both wetland and drier upland areas has enabled them to thrive across the Seattle region, where they can be found in a variety of habitats. One quirky behavior of these birds is their tendency to engage in "mobbing" when threatened. They often join forces with other bird species to harass potential predators, such as hawks or raccoons, showcasing their cooperative nature.

Another interesting trait is their courtship display, where males perform elaborate flights, rising high in the air and then diving down while calling, creating a stunning aerial show that is both a display of strength and a way to attract females. These displays can be quite a spectacle, especially during the early morning or late evening when the light enhances their colors.

Where to See Them

Red-winged blackbirds can be spotted throughout the Seattle area, especially in wetland regions. Look for them at Magnuson Park, the Union Bay Natural Area, or along the shores of Green Lake. Other excellent locations to observe them include the marshy areas at Mercer Slough Nature Park and the Washington Park Arboretum. They are especially abundant during the breeding season, when their distinctive calls fill the air. For a striking display, visit a wetland at dawn or dusk, when the males are actively showing off their bright red wings. Some blackbirds remain locals year-round while others leave in August to September for the southern United States and Mexico.

Song Sparrow

Melospiza melodia

The song sparrow is one of Seattle's most familiar and resilient songbirds, often heard before it's seen. Known for its lilting, complex melodies that resonate through Seattle's parks and neighborhoods year-round, this small bird is a significant contributor to the region's avian

► Song sparrows are common across the United States, but local populations of the bird have distinct regional "dialects" that they use to defend territory and attract mates.

soundscape and a valuable player in local eco-systems. While the song sparrow's appearance may be modest—marked by brown streaks on a lighter background and a distinctive dark central chest spot—its vocal abilities and adaptive behaviors make it stand out.

One of the most unique features of the song sparrow is its varied and melodious song. Males develop an impressive repertoire of tunes, often with up to twenty different song variations. During the breeding season, these songs serve dual purposes: attracting mates and defending territory. Males sing from exposed perches to assert their pres-ence, broadcasting their complex melodies to neighboring sparrows and potential rivals. They are known to engage in "song duels," where two males sing back and forth in a competitive, almost conversational manner, each bird trying to outdo the other. This intri-cate communication underscores the song sparrow's intelligence and social complexity, as these "duels" are a sophisticated method of establishing dominance and reinforcing territorial boundaries.

In addition to their vocal prowess, song sparrows exhibit fierce territoriality and aggression, particularly during nesting season. Despite their small size, they are known to chase away much larger birds, such as crows or jays, that might threaten their nests. This defensive behavior helps protect their young and contributes to maintaining a balanced avian population in Seattle's green spaces. Their territorial nature ensures that food resources and nesting sites are defended from rivals, which benefits the stability of song sparrow populations in urban and sub-urban habitats.

The song sparrow's adaptability to diverse environments is another trait that has enabled it to thrive throughout Seattle. These birds are not limited to a single habitat type; they are equally at home in wetlands, gardens, forest edges, and even heavily urbanized areas. This versatility allows them to exploit a range of food sources, including seeds, insects, and small invertebrates. They are skilled ground foragers, often seen hopping through under-brush or along the edges of trails, scratching at the soil and leaf litter with both feet to uncover food. This foraging behavior not only helps control insect populations but also aids in seed dispersal, making song sparrows benefi-cial to the ecosystem as both pest managers and facilitators of plant growth.

Song sparrows are generally resident birds in Seattle, meaning they can be found in the area year-round. However, during winter, migra-tory populations from colder regions, such as Alaska and northern Canada, may join local residents. These visiting sparrows blend into the local flocks as they forage in Seattle's parks and wetlands, adding to the already robust song sparrow population during the colder months. This influx provides added biodiversity and enhances the resilience of Seattle's bird communities through the winter season.

Where to See Them

Song sparrows are abundant throughout Seattle's green spaces and are commonly observed in Discovery Park, Union Bay Natural Area, and the Washington Park Arboretum. In these areas, you'll find them flitting between shrubs, perching on low branches, or foraging on the ground near trails. Even in urban settings, their sweet, complex songs are easy to hear, a reminder that these adaptable birds are always nearby.

Spotted Towhee

Pipilo maculatus

The spotted towhee is one of the most distinctive birds of the Pacific Northwest, often recognized by its striking black, white, and rufous coloring. These medium-sized sparrows are a common sight in the Seattle area, where they thrive in the dense undergrowth and shrubby areas that characterize much of the city's green spaces. While the vibrant black plumage with white spots on the wings and back makes the male towhee especially eye-catching, the females display a subtler brown version of the same pattern. The white belly and rich rufous sides complete their bold look, making them easy to identify for birdwatchers.

One of the most notable features of the spotted towhee is its vocalization. These birds are often heard long before they are seen. Their calls include sharp, cat-like mews, and the males are known for their distinctive song, which sounds like a sharp introductory note followed by a trilling "drink-your-tea" melody. This song serves as a territorial claim during the breeding season and is a common sound in Seattle's brushy areas.

The spotted towhee's behavior is as distinctive as its appearance. These birds are ground foragers, using a unique double-scratch technique to uncover food. If you watch closely, you'll see them hop forward and then quickly scratch the ground with both feet to reveal insects, seeds, and berries hidden in the leaf litter. This foraging method is highly effective and is often accompanied by the rustling of leaves, signaling their presence before you spot them.

During the breeding season, female spotted towhees build their nests on or near the ground, hidden within dense shrubs or thick undergrowth. The nests are carefully constructed from twigs, leaves, and grasses, lined with softer materials like fine grass and hair. This low-profile nesting strategy helps protect the eggs and young from predators. Once the chicks hatch, both parents take an active role in feeding them, foraging for food throughout the surrounding area to ensure their survival.

Where to See Them

The spotted towhee's preferred habitat includes shrubby areas, dense thickets, and forest edges, making the Seattle area's many parks and natural spaces an ideal home. These birds thrive in places with a mix of open ground for foraging and dense cover for nesting and protection. Fortunately, Seattle is rich in such environments, and several parks offer excellent opportunities for observing these colorful birds up close. Discovery Park, with its mix of meadows, forests, and shorelines, is a favorite spot for birdwatchers. Seward Park, which features old-growth forest along Lake Washington, also provides a rich environment for these birds. Magnuson Park's restored wetlands, Ravenna Park's dense understory, and the lush plantings of the Washington Park Arboretum are other excellent places to observe towhees in their natural habitat. They live in Seattle year-round.

Steller's Jay

Cyanocitta stelleri

The Steller's jay, with its striking blue-and-black plumage and bold crest, is one of Seattle's most charismatic and eye-catching birds. Larger and more robust than other jays, this Pacific Northwest native stands out not only for its flashy appearance but also for its inquisitive and assertive nature. Known for their intelligence and adaptable behavior, Steller's jays play an important role in Seattle's ecosystems and are a favorite among birdwatchers and casual observers alike.

Steller's jays are intelligent and highly adaptable birds, often compared to crows for their problem-solving abilities. They are opportunistic feeders and readily take advantage of human food sources, often raiding bird feeders, campsites, and picnic areas with boldness. In natural settings, their diet is varied and includes insects, nuts, seeds, berries, and even small vertebrates like lizards and nestlings. This diverse diet makes them versatile foragers who contribute to the balance of local ecosystems by helping control insect populations and dispersing seeds through their feeding habits.

A fascinating trait of Steller's jays is their food-caching behavior. They often hide food in various caches, storing it for later consumption. This habit is especially useful during lean times and showcases their planning abilities, as they strategically hide seeds, nuts, and other food items to retrieve when resources are scarce. By caching seeds, Steller's jays also play a role in forest regeneration, as some of their hidden seeds are left untouched, eventually germinating and growing into new plants.

This inadvertent reforestation effort benefits Seattle's green spaces and contributes to the health of local ecosystems.

Another unique behavior of Steller's jays is their ability to mimic the calls of other birds, particularly raptors like hawks. They often use this mimicry as a tool to scare other birds away from food sources, creating the illusion of a nearby predator. This impressive mimicry skill also serves as a form of communication within their social groups, alerting others to potential threats. The jay's loud, raspy calls are a constant presence in Seattle's forests and parks, often serving as an alert system for other animals and establishing the Steller's jay as a vigilant and clever bird in the wild.

Steller's jays are social creatures, often seen in small groups or pairs. They are known for their dynamic courtship displays, during which they raise their crests, perform elaborate postures, and share food to strengthen pair bonds. Both mates participate in building their nest, usually located high in conifer trees, where they raise their young with attentive care. This teamwork and social bonding are part of what makes Steller's jays so adaptable and successful in various environments.

Where to See Them

In Seattle, Steller's jays are commonly found in forested parks and wooded areas, where they add a lively presence with their bold colors and loud calls. Discovery Park, Seward Park, and the forests around Lake Washington are excellent places to observe them. These birds are often seen hopping along trails, scouring the ground for food, or boldly approaching picnic areas in search of scraps. You're likely to hear their distinctive calls before spotting them, as their vocalizations echo through the trees, announcing their presence in the area.

Western Tanager

Piranga ludoviciana

The western tanager is one of the Pacific Northwest's most eye-catching songbirds, known for the striking colors that bring flashes of vibrant yellow and red to Seattle's forests each spring and summer. Male western tanagers are especially dazzling, with brilliant yellow bodies, black wings, and a flame-red head that sets them apart from any other bird in the region. Females, while less vivid, still display a lovely olive-yellow plumage, making them beautiful in their own right. For bird-watchers and nature enthusiasts in Seattle, the arrival of western tanagers each spring is a highlight, as these birds add a striking dash of color to local woodlands.

Western tanagers are primarily insectivorous, feeding on bees, wasps, and caterpillars, which they expertly catch while foraging in the upper canopy. Their unique ability to capture insects mid-flight showcases their agility and quick reflexes, traits that make them highly effective hunters in their forest habitats. In late summer, as insect availability declines, they shift their diet to include a variety of fruits, particularly berries. This dietary flexibility allows western tanagers to adapt to changing food sources as they prepare for their autumn migration, ensuring they have the necessary energy reserves for the journey.

These vibrant songbirds are migratory, arriving in the Pacific Northwest each spring from their wintering grounds in Central America and parts of Mexico. By late summer or early fall, they depart once again for their southern wintering habitats. Their seasonal presence in Seattle makes them a favorite target for birdwatchers who are eager to catch a glimpse of their colorful plumage before they leave. Their brief stay in the Seattle area underscores the importance of preserving local forests as a critical breeding habitat that supports their migratory life cycle.

During the breeding season, western tanagers establish territories in forests with tall coniferous trees, which offer both food sources and high nesting sites safe from ground predators. These birds prefer to build their nests high in the branches, using materials like twigs, grass, and moss to construct a secure platform where they can raise their

young. Males and females share nesting duties, with both parents contributing to building the nest, incubating the eggs, and feeding the chicks once they hatch. This cooperative behavior not only strengthens the pair bond but also increases the chances of survival for their offspring.

In Seattle's ecosystems, western tanagers play an important role as both insect controllers and seed dispersers. By consuming insects, they help maintain balanced insect populations, particularly by targeting pests that could otherwise damage trees and vegetation. Their late-summer diet of fruits and berries also contributes to seed dispersal, aiding in the growth and spread of various plant species. Through these behaviors, western tanagers support the health and diversity of Seattle's forests, making them an integral part of the region's ecological web.

Where to See Them

Western tanagers prefer forested areas with tall conifers, which makes Seattle's larger parks ideal for sightings. Discovery Park, Seward Park, and the Washington Park Arboretum are some of the best spots to catch a glimpse of these vibrant birds. Look for them in the upper branches of trees, where their bright yellow and red colors stand out against the green foliage, especially during spring and early summer. Because they often forage high in the canopy, binoculars can be helpful for spotting them.

White-crowned Sparrow

Zonotrichia leucophrys

The white-crowned sparrow is a distinctive songbird that brings charm and energy to Seattle's natural spaces, especially during migration and winter. Recognizable by its striking black-and-white-striped crown and clear, whistled song, the white-crowned sparrow is a favorite among birdwatchers. Its pale gray breast and bold head markings set it apart, while its ground-foraging behavior and cheerful presence make it a lively addition to Seattle's fields, parks, and gardens.

White-crowned sparrows are primarily ground foragers, often seen scratching through leaf litter or soft soil in search of seeds, berries, and insects. Their foraging method is systematic; they use both feet to scratch at the ground, kicking away leaves and dirt to uncover food hidden beneath. In the winter months, they typically forage in small groups, sometimes alongside other sparrow species. These sparrows are particularly fond of areas with dense underbrush, weedy fields, and brushy edges, where they can forage with some cover. Their feeding habits help control insect populations and facilitate seed dispersal, making them essential contributors to Seattle's ecosystem balance.

During the breeding season, white-crowned sparrows are highly territorial. Males are known for their continuous singing, which they use to establish and defend their territory from rivals. What makes their song especially interesting is that it varies by region, with each population developing unique "dialects" that are comparable to human accents. Young male white-crowned sparrows learn these dialects from older males in their community, which means that their songs are a learned behavior passed down within regional populations. This cultural transmission of song dialects is fascinating, as it highlights the social learning that plays a crucial role in the life of these birds.

One of the quirkiest behaviors exhibited by white-crowned sparrows is their "migratory restlessness," particularly in fall as they prepare to head south. Before migration, these sparrows often exhibit increased nocturnal

activity, becoming more vocal and restless in a phenomenon known as *zugunruhe* (migration restlessness). This premigration behavior indicates an innate readiness for their long journey southward, which typically takes them to wintering grounds in southern California and Mexico. White-crowned sparrows are strong, efficient migrators, traveling hundreds or even thousands of miles between breeding and wintering grounds. This annual migration is essential for the health of their populations, as it allows them to exploit seasonal food sources in both northern and southern habitats.

Where to See Them

In Seattle, white-crowned sparrows are most common during the fall and winter months, as they migrate between breeding grounds in Canada and Alaska and wintering areas to the south. They frequent parks, gardens, and open fields, particularly favoring places with dense vegetation and open ground for foraging. Union Bay Natural Area, Discovery Park, and Magnuson Park are excellent locations to spot these sparrows. You'll often hear their clear, whistled song before seeing them, as they sometimes remain hidden in underbrush or beneath shrubs.

Wood Duck

Aix sponsa

The wood duck is one of North America's most visually stunning waterfowl, with the males particularly admired for their iridescent green heads, striking red eyes, and elaborate patterns of white, chestnut, and black. These colors give them an almost ornamental appearance, making them one of the most photographed ducks by birdwatchers and nature lovers alike. Female wood ducks, while more subtly colored, are equally beautiful in their own right, with gray-brown plumage and a distinctive white eye-ring that gives them an expressive look.

Wood ducks are among the few waterfowl species that regularly nest in tree cavities, a trait that sets them apart from most other ducks. These cavities are often found in large, mature trees near water, sometimes up to 50 feet above the ground. Once hatched, the tiny ducklings must take a courageous leap from the nest, often tumbling to the forest floor before making their way to the water—one of the most endearing and heart-pounding spectacles in the bird world. Despite the fall, the ducklings are remarkably resilient and usually land unharmed due to their lightweight bodies.

Quirky behaviors like this make wood ducks fascinating to observe. Another unique characteristic is their exceptional agility in flight. Their strong, broad wings enable them to dart through dense forests with ease, navigating between trees with impressive precision, a skill not often seen in other ducks. Their alert and wary nature also adds to their elusiveness, as they will quickly take flight at the first sign of danger.

Wood ducks are also known for their vocalizations. While their calls are not as loud or as well known as those of some other waterfowl, males produce a soft, high-pitched whistle during courtship, and females emit a distinctive, sharp "oo-eek" when alarmed. These calls are especially common during the breeding season, when males engage in displays to attract mates.

Wood ducks have a varied diet that changes with the seasons. They are omnivorous, foraging on a combination of aquatic plants, seeds, fruits, and invertebrates. In spring and summer, they rely more heavily on insects and other small animals, while in fall, acorns and other seeds become a significant part of their diet. Their strong beaks allow them to forage on land, sifting through leaf litter for food or plucking seeds from vegetation.

Where to See Them

In Seattle, wood ducks can often be found in quiet, tree-lined ponds and wetlands. They prefer areas with plenty of vegetation where they can forage and find nesting sites. Prime locations for spotting wood ducks include the Washington Park Arboretum, Union Bay Natural Area, and Magnuson Park. They are most active early in the morning and near dusk, making these times ideal for observation. Their elusive nature means you'll need patience to spot them, but their striking beauty is well worth the effort. The wood ducks of Seattle tend to be year-round residents, although their numbers swell in winter as migratory individuals come south escaping the freezing temps of Canada and points north.

◄ The wood duck is an arrestingly beautiful species of waterfowl that frequents the shoreline habitat of Seattle's freshwater "inland waterways."

Insects and Arachnids

Blue Dragonfly

Pachydiplax longipennis

The blue dragonfly (or blue dasher), often spotted gliding over Seattle's ponds, lakes, and marshes, is one of the most captivating and agile insect residents in the region. Known for their vivid blue color, large eyes, and long, slender bodies, these dragonflies are a striking sight against the lush green backdrop of the Pacific Northwest. These dazzling fliers play an essential role in their ecosystems as both predators and indicators of environmental health, making them an important species to observe and protect in Seattle.

Blue dragonflies have large, multifaceted eyes that allow for nearly 360-degree vision, which they use to detect even the slightest movement. This keen eyesight, combined with their exceptional flying ability, makes them highly effective hunters. Dragonflies are carnivorous, and adults feed primarily on other insects, including mosquitoes, gnats, and flies. They hunt with incredible precision, catching prey mid-flight and consuming it on the go. By controlling mosquito populations, they help keep local ecosystems in balance and provide a natural form of pest control, making them beneficial to human communities.

One of the most unique and quirky aspects of these dragonflies is their life cycle, which begins underwater. They lay their eggs in freshwater ponds, lakes, or streams, and the eggs hatch into aquatic larvae, known as nymphs. These nymphs can spend up to several years underwater, where they are voracious hunters, feeding on small fish, tadpoles, and other aquatic insects. This prolonged nymph stage allows them to develop in a relatively safe environment before emerging as adults. When the time comes, nymphs climb out of the water,

shed their skins, and take their first flights as adults—a dramatic transformation that showcases the dragonfly's adaptability.

Blue dragonflies are also sensitive to environmental changes, making them valuable bioindicators. Because they rely on clean, unpolluted water for breeding and development, the presence of dragonflies is often a sign of a healthy aquatic ecosystem. When water quality declines due to pollution or habitat degradation, dragonfly populations are typically among the first to dwindle, signaling ecological issues that may affect other species. Conservation efforts to protect Seattle's freshwater habitats, therefore, benefit not only dragonflies but also the broader array of wildlife that shares these spaces.

Where to See Them

Seattle's parks and wetlands are ideal for dragonfly-watching, particularly in the warmer months. Green Lake, Discovery Park, and Magnuson Park are popular spots where blue dragonflies can be seen darting over ponds and marshes. Washington Park Arboretum is another excellent location, offering a mix of wetlands and open water where dragonflies can hunt and breed. Additionally, the Arboretum's ponds and canals provide verdant sheltered areas that are perfect for spotting nymphs and adult dragonflies.

For those willing to venture a bit farther, Mercer Slough Nature Park in Bellevue and Juanita Bay Park in Kirkland offer extensive wetland areas where dragonflies thrive. Late spring through early autumn is the best time to observe blue dragonflies in Seattle, as this is when adults are most active, mating and hunting above the water.

Cross Orbweaver Spider

Araneus diadematus

The cross orbweaver, with its striking web designs and distinctive appearance, is one of Seattle's most fascinating and beneficial arachnids. Known for the cross-like markings on its back, this spider can be found in Seattle's gardens, forests, and even on porches, spinning intricate webs that glisten with dew in the early morning. Though they may look intimidating, these spiders are harmless to humans and play an essential role in controlling insect populations, making them a quiet ally in Seattle's ecosystem.

Cross orbweavers are medium-sized spiders, usually measuring around half an inch, with color variations from orange and brown to gray. Their backs display a characteristic white cross pattern, formed by small, pale markings, which gives them their common name. Unlike many spider species that hide from view, cross

orbweavers can often be found sitting right in the center of their large, wheel-shaped webs, awaiting their next meal. These webs are architectural marvels, designed to ensnare flying insects like flies, mosquitoes, and moths. The spider's silky web is not only an effective trap but also a form of camouflage, blending with the background and making it less visible to both predators and prey.

Each evening, the cross orbweaver constructs or repairs its web, a process that can take up to an hour. The webs are typically placed in well-lit, open spaces, such as between branches or across pathways, where insects are likely to fly into them. Cross orbweavers have a unique habit of eating their web each night before building a new one, recycling the proteins in the silk to produce fresh webbing. This efficiency showcases the spider's adaptability and resourcefulness in conserving energy and materials, especially in Seattle's variable weather.

As skilled hunters, cross orbweavers play a vital role in Seattle's natural pest control. By consuming flies, gnats, and other common pests, they help keep local insect populations in balance. This makes them valuable to both city residents and the broader ecosystem.

Despite their often-visible presence, cross orbweavers are shy creatures, and if disturbed, they quickly retreat to a safe corner of their web or drop to the ground to avoid confrontation.

Where to See Them

Cross orbweavers are most commonly seen in Seattle from late summer through early fall, when they reach maturity and their webs become more noticeable. Look for them in gardens, parks, and wooded areas where they can build their webs in peace. Discovery Park, Washington Park Arboretum, Seward Park, and Magnuson Park are all excellent spots for observing these spiders in action. In more residential areas, cross orbweavers often make their homes in eaves, garden trellises, and window frames, offering close-up encounters for those willing to take a closer look.

In the early morning, their dew-covered webs are often visible in open spaces, creating a delicate, shimmering display that highlights their craftsmanship. For the best chance to spot them, take a quiet morning walk or evening stroll in areas with dense foliage or garden structures.

Honeybee

Apis mellifera

Honeybees, with their busy hum and cooperative social structure, are essential residents of Seattle's gardens, parks, and urban farms. Known for their distinctive yellow-and-black-striped bodies and industrious work ethic, these pollinators are vital to the health of Seattle's ecosystem, supporting both native flora and the city's food systems. While their sweet honey may make them popular with humans, it's their role as pollinators that truly makes honeybees indispensable in Seattle and beyond.

Honeybees are social insects, living in colonies that can contain thousands of individuals, each with a specific role. A single hive typically consists of one queen, drones, and worker bees. The queen's primary task is laying eggs, while drones are responsible for mating, and worker bees, the most numerous members, perform a variety of tasks from gathering nectar and pollen to defending the hive. Worker bees are particularly important to Seattle's green spaces, as they are the ones who travel from flower to flower, collecting pollen and

nectar to sustain the colony. In the process, they transfer pollen between flowers, enabling plants to produce seeds and fruits.

As pollinators, honeybees are key to maintaining Seattle's biodiversity. They support local ecosystems by pollinating flowering plants, including wildflowers, fruit trees, and vegetable gardens. In Seattle, where urban agriculture and community gardening are popular, honeybees are a common sight in places like the UW Farm, P-Patch community gardens, and in neighborhood backyards. Without honeybees, many of the fruits, vegetables, and flowers that thrive in Seattle would be at risk, as these plants depend on pollinators to reproduce and bear fruit.

Honeybees' unique communication system also sets them apart in the insect world. Worker bees perform a "waggle dance" inside the hive to share information about the location of food sources, using specific movements to indicate direction and distance. This sophisticated behavior demonstrates their high level of social organization and teamwork, allowing the hive to efficiently gather resources. Seattle's flowering plants benefit from this coordinated effort, as honeybees maximize their visits to local gardens and parks, spreading pollen and ensuring the growth of Seattle's greenery.

Despite their importance, honeybees face challenges in urban environments. Habitat loss, pesticide use, and disease have all impacted honeybee populations worldwide, and Seattle is no exception. However, local initiatives aim to support bee health, including "bee-friendly" gardening practices and the use of native plants that provide natural nectar sources. Urban beekeeping has also gained popularity, with hives maintained at local farms and community gardens across the city. Seattle's public spaces, like the Washington Park Arboretum and the Seattle Pollinator Pathway, offer bee-friendly habitats with diverse plantings that encourage healthy bee populations.

Where to See Them

Honeybees are active from spring through fall, and you can find them almost anywhere flowers are in bloom. Seattle's community gardens, such as those in Ballard, Capitol Hill, and Beacon Hill, are buzzing with bees during peak flower season. Discovery Park, Union Bay Natural Area, and Volunteer Park are also excellent places to spot honeybees as they forage among native plants and flowering trees.

Seattle residents can also create a haven for honeybees by planting bee-friendly flowers like lavender, sunflowers, and wildflowers in their own gardens or balconies. For those interested in learning more, the West Seattle Bee Garden offers educational programs and an observational hive that allows visitors to see honeybees at work.

Western Tiger Swallowtail

Papilio rutulus

The western tiger swallowtail is one of Seattle's most vibrant and eye-catching butterflies, bringing a splash of yellow and black to the city's parks and gardens during the warmer months. With wings spanning up to four inches and distinct tiger-like stripes, this butterfly is both visually stunning and essential to Seattle's ecosystem, playing a vital role as a pollinator. Encountering one of these elegant creatures flitting from flower to flower is a delightful reminder of the biodiversity that thrives even within Seattle's urban environment.

Western tiger swallowtails are easily recognized by their bright yellow wings marked with bold black stripes and a row of blue and orange spots near their tails. This striking coloration not only makes them a pleasure to observe but also serves as a defense mechanism. The vibrant colors can deter potential predators by signaling that the butterfly may be toxic or unpleasant to eat, though in reality, swallowtails are harmless. Their tails, which extend from their hindwings, resemble antennae and may confuse predators, allowing the butterfly a chance to escape if attacked.

These butterflies are highly adaptable, flourishing in various habitats throughout the Pacific Northwest, including woodlands, river valleys, urban parks, and residential gardens. Seattle's mild climate and diverse vegetation make it an ideal environment for the western tiger swallowtail, which feeds on the nectar of many flowering plants, including lilacs, thistles, and honeysuckle. As they feed, they play a crucial role in pollination, transferring pollen from flower to flower and supporting the health of Seattle's local flora. This relationship between swallowtails and plants is symbiotic, as the butterflies rely on the flowers for food, while the plants benefit from the pollination services these busy butterflies provide.

The western tiger swallowtail's life cycle is a fascinating journey: it begins as a small, green egg laid on the leaves of host plants such as willow, alder, and cottonwood trees. After hatching, the caterpillars are a bright green with yellow and blue spots, a coloration that helps them blend in with leaves to avoid detection. As the caterpillar grows, it becomes more conspicuous, developing large, eye-like spots near its head to mimic a snake and ward off predators. Eventually, the caterpillar forms a chrysalis, from which it emerges as an adult butterfly after undergoing metamorphosis—a transformation that allows it to fulfill its role as a pollinator in Seattle's ecosystem.

Where to See Them

Western tiger swallowtails are most active during Seattle's summer months, from late spring through early autumn. They can often be seen in places where flowering plants are abundant. Popular spots include the Washington Park Arboretum, Green Lake, Discovery Park, and Kubota Garden, where the mix of wildflowers, shrubs, and trees provides ample feeding grounds for these butterflies.

Even within urban gardens and residential neighborhoods, western tiger swallowtails make frequent appearances, especially in areas with flowering trees and shrubs. Seattle gardeners can attract these butterflies by planting nectar-rich flowers such as zinnias, asters, and butterfly bushes, providing a reliable food source and encouraging these beautiful pollinators to visit.

▲ A western tiger swallowtail alights on a Pacific rhododendron flower.

Mammals

American Beaver

Castor canadensis

Beavers, renowned as nature's master architects, are exceptional ecosystem engineers with a remarkable ability to transform landscapes. These semiaquatic rodents, native to North America, are common in the Seattle area, where they thrive in slow-moving rivers and wetlands. Beavers have several distinctive adaptations that equip them for an aquatic lifestyle and enable them to construct intricate dam and lodge systems. Their large, flat tails serve multiple purposes: acting as rudders when swimming, providing balance on land, and functioning as a signaling device through loud slaps on the water surface to warn other beavers of danger. Their webbed hind feet make them strong, agile swimmers, while their thick, waterproof fur insulates them in chilly waters, allowing them to remain active even in winter.

One of the beaver's most intriguing features is its continuously growing front teeth, which are orange due to an iron-rich enamel that hardens and strengthens them. These powerful chisel-like teeth are indispensable for felling trees, a task at which beavers excel. Their preferred trees include willows, aspens, and birches, which they use both as a food source and as building material for their dams. Beavers chew trees into manageable pieces, strategically placing them in streams to slow

▼ An American beaver works on some downed logs in Duck Bay near Seattle's Arboretum to fortify its lodge.

water flow and create ponds. This not only provides a safe, stable environment for their underwater lodges but also significantly alters local hydrology. Their lodges—constructed from sticks, mud, and vegetation—are fortified structures with underwater entrances, offering protection against predators and insulation during the winter months.

Ecologically, beavers are a keystone species, meaning their presence has a profound impact on biodiversity and ecosystem health. The ponds and wetlands formed by their dams create critical habitats for numerous species, including fish, amphibians, and waterfowl, which depend on these wetlands for breeding, feeding, and shelter. Beaver ponds support a wide array of plant life, which in turn attracts insects and smaller animals that provide food for birds and other wildlife. In this way, beavers indirectly boost biodiversity and enhance the overall health of wetland ecosystems.

Beaver dams also improve water quality by trapping sediments, which help filter out pollutants. This sedimentation process is particularly beneficial for downstream environments, reducing soil erosion and improving habitat conditions for fish populations. Additionally, beaver dams help mitigate flooding by controlling water flow during heavy rains and promoting groundwater recharge, making beavers vital to the health and resilience of water systems.

Where to See Them

In the Seattle area, beavers are commonly found in parks and natural areas with slow-moving streams and wetlands. Magnuson Park, Discovery Park, the Washington Park Arboretum, and Carkeek Park are excellent locations for spotting beaver activity. Although beavers are nocturnal, visitors might see signs of their presence, such as partially chewed trees, stripped bark, or the iconic beaver dams themselves. Evening outings may increase the chances of encountering these industrious builders as they go about their nightly routines.

American Black Bear

Ursus americanus

Black bears are among the most iconic species of North American wildlife, and they inhabit forested and semi-open areas around the greater Seattle area, particularly in the Cascade foothills. Despite their name, American black bears come in a surprising range of colors, including shades of cinnamon-brown, blond, and even blue-gray. These color variations, while not as common as the classic black, help individuals blend into different environments, from dense forests to more open landscapes. Adult black bears are large mammals, with males typically weighing between 200 to 600 pounds and females generally weighing less. Their thick, insulating fur and large paws allow them to withstand cooler, wetter climates typical of the Pacific Northwest, while their strong, curved claws enable them to climb trees and dig for food with ease.

As omnivores, American black bears have a varied diet that consists mostly of plant material. In the wild, they feast on berries, nuts, grasses, roots, and mushrooms, which are abundant in the Northwest's forests. This plant-heavy diet is complemented by insects, small mammals, and carrion. When possible, they'll also eat salmon during spawning season, which provides a rich protein source to help them build fat reserves for winter. In urban and suburban areas, however, black bears are often drawn to human food sources like garbage, compost bins, and bird feeders, which can lead to potentially dangerous

conflicts with humans. To limit encounters, communities near bear habitats encourage residents to use bear-proof garbage cans and avoid leaving food outside.

American black bears play an essential role in their ecosystem as seed dispersers and soil aerators. By consuming fruits and berries and then depositing seeds throughout their range, they help maintain plant diversity in the forest. As they dig for roots and insects, their foraging activity also aerates the soil, which enhances nutrient cycling and supports plant growth. Interestingly, black bears have a curious, problem-solving nature and are quick to adapt to changes in their environment. They are excellent swimmers and climbers and will often be found near water sources such as rivers, lakes, and wetlands, where they can drink, cool off, and forage. During autumn, black bears go through a process called *hyperphagia*, where they consume thousands of calories daily to build up fat reserves for hibernation in winter.

Where to See Them

In the Seattle area, American black bears are commonly found in the forested foothills of the Cascades, particularly around communities like Redmond, Bellevue, and Bothell, where greenbelts and wooded neighborhoods provide ample habitat. Although rare within Seattle city limits, black bears have occasionally wandered into urban areas in search of food, with sightings making headlines in neighborhoods such as Ballard and Ravenna. For those looking to spot black bears in their natural habitat, state parks and greenbelts on the outskirts of Seattle offer the best opportunities, particularly at dawn or dusk, when bears are most active.

California Sea Lion

Zalophus californianus

The California sea lion is a lively and charismatic resident of Seattle's coastal waters, known for its playful antics, curious nature, and social behavior. Smaller than the Steller sea lion but no less impressive, these sleek marine mammals are a common sight along Seattle's waterfront and nearby islands. Adult males can reach up to 8 feet in length and weigh up to 800 pounds, while females are typically smaller, making them easier to distinguish from their Steller counterparts. Recognizable by their brown or dark tan fur, California sea lions are agile swimmers and skilled divers, perfectly adapted to the cold waters of the Pacific Northwest.

Unlike their larger cousins, California sea lions are often more vocal and social, gathering in noisy, bustling groups on docks, piers,

and rocky outcroppings. Their loud barks and honks can frequently be heard along the waterfront, where they engage in social displays and playfully interact with each other. These gatherings, known as *haul-outs*, are particularly common in the cooler months when the sea lions come closer to shore, using Seattle's rocky shores and man-made structures for resting and socializing.

California sea lions are highly intelligent animals, known for their curiosity and adaptability. They are often observed investigating fishing boats and occasionally even trying to steal fish from nets or lines, much to the chagrin of local fishermen. These clever sea lions are known to learn and mimic behaviors quickly, and their intelligence has made them popular in marine parks and research centers, though in the wild, they remain resourceful and opportunistic hunters.

Diet plays a key role in the ecological impact of California sea lions. They are opportunistic feeders, preying on a wide variety of fish, including anchovies, sardines, mackerel, and Pacific herring. During salmon runs, sea lions can also be seen chasing salmon through Seattle's waterways, adding a dramatic element to the city's iconic salmon migrations. Their foraging helps keep fish populations balanced and contributes to the overall health of Puget Sound. As predators, they play an important role in controlling the populations of smaller fish and squid, making them an integral part of Seattle's marine ecosystem.

While generally tolerant of each other, male California sea lions can be territorial, especially during the breeding season. Unlike Steller sea lions, however, they do not breed in Seattle's waters, instead migrating south to California for mating and pupping. During winter, many individuals head north, making Seattle's shores a seasonal home and creating opportunities for local residents to observe their playful and engaging behaviors.

Where to See Them

Seattle's waterfront provides several excellent spots for observing California sea lions. West Seattle's Alki Beach, Shilshole Bay Marina, and the piers around Elliott Bay are all prime locations where these sea lions haul out and play along the shore. A ferry ride to the nearby San Juan Islands also offers a chance to see them on rocky outcrops or lounging on buoys. Visitors can often hear their distinctive barks before spotting them, adding a lively soundtrack to Seattle's coastal areas. Winter through early spring is the best time to view California sea lions around Seattle, as they gather in larger numbers near shore before heading back south for the breeding season.

Columbian Black-tailed Deer

Odocoileus hemionus columbianus

The Columbian black-tailed deer is well-suited to the varied ecosystems of the Pacific Northwest and is one of the most commonly seen large mammals in the forests and woodlands around Seattle. These deer are smaller and more compact than their mule deer relatives, with adults typically weighing between 90 and 250 pounds. Males, also known as bucks, are larger than females and grow large, branching antlers each year, which they shed and regrow annually. A distinctive black-tipped tail sets them apart from other deer species, while their reddish brown summer coats turn a muted grayish brown in winter, providing them with seasonal camouflage against the forest floor.

Black-tailed deer are herbivorous, browsing on a wide variety of vegetation, including grasses, shrubs, berries, and the young shoots of trees. They are selective feeders, carefully choosing plants that meet their nutritional needs, and their foraging behavior often shapes the growth patterns of local vegetation. As browsers, they can influence the distribution and abundance of plants, making them a key species in their ecosystem. By browsing on shrubs and young trees, black-tailed deer help maintain open spaces in forested areas, which supports habitat diversity for other wildlife. In turn, they are a vital food source for large carnivores such as cougars and bobcats, making them an important part of the regional food web.

Black-tailed deer are crepuscular, meaning they are most active at dawn and dusk. This behavior helps them avoid the hottest parts of the day as well as some predators, while allowing them to feed on vegetation when visibility is lower. They are also highly alert animals with excellent hearing and a keen sense of smell, helping them detect potential threats. When alarmed, black-tailed deer exhibit a "stotting" behavior, bounding high into the air to quickly cover ground while showing off their white undersides, a visual cue that can signal danger to other deer.

Where to See Them

Black-tailed deer are commonly found in the forests, woodlands, and even some urban green spaces around Seattle. While you probably won't get through a visit to Olympic National Park, Mount Rainier National Park, or the trails near Snoqualmie Pass without seeing one of these all-too-common deer, sightings are much more rare in and around Seattle itself. That said, urban parks such as Discovery Park, Seward Park, Volunteer Park, and the Washington Park Arboretum provide refuge for them. Sightings are most likely in the early morning or late evening hours, especially during spring and fall when the deer are more actively foraging. Observing them at a distance and respecting their space helps ensure a safe, positive encounter with these remarkable animals.

Coyote

Canis latrans

Coyotes are some of the most adaptable and resilient mammals in North America, thriving in a wide range of ecosystems, from deserts and forests to the hearts of cities like Seattle. Their intelligence and adaptability make them highly successful in urban environments, where they learn quickly to navigate human activities, traffic, and new food sources. Unlike wolves, which tend to avoid human-populated areas, coyotes have evolved to coexist with people, exploiting suburban neighborhoods, parks, and even urban streets for food and shelter.

A typical coyote is slender, with grayish brown fur and a bushy tail, which gives it a natural camouflage against the brushy backdrops of the Pacific Northwest. Weighing between 24 and 46 pounds, they are smaller than wolves but incredibly agile and fast, reaching speeds of up to 40 miles per hour in short bursts when chasing prey. Their pointed ears and narrow snout contribute to their distinct appearance—a blend of both fox and wolf traits. These features are not only defining but help them excel as stealthy hunters and foragers in varied terrains.

Coyotes have an omnivorous diet that plays a significant role in their ability to adapt and thrive in diverse environments. In the wild, they consume small mammals, birds, fruits, and plants, which helps maintain ecological balance by controlling rodent and rabbit populations. In urban settings, they often scavenge, feeding on human garbage, pet food, and other available food sources. Coyotes hunt both alone and in pairs or small family groups, employing sophisticated strategies to catch

▼ A coyote chases prey at the Union Bay Natural Area in Northeast Seattle near the University of Washington.

prey. They may work together to distract and ambush larger animals, showing an unusual level of cooperation for solitary hunters.

One of their most fascinating behaviors is their vocalization, which includes a range of sounds—howls, yips, barks, and whines—that are often misunderstood by humans as evidence of a large population. In reality, a few coyotes can create a chorus that sounds like dozens, as they use these calls to communicate with each other, coordinate pack activities, and mark territory. A lone coyote's howl may simply announce its presence or call to family members rather than indicate a dense population. This vocal versatility highlights the coyote's highly social nature and complex family structure.

Coyotes generally form loose family groups rather than tightly knit packs, showing strong loyalty and cooperation, especially during the pup-rearing season. Both parents care for the young, teaching them survival skills and protecting them fiercely. Coyote parents are attentive and nurturing, and older siblings sometimes help with the rearing of new pups, showing a familial loyalty that is rare among other canines.

Where to See Them

In Seattle, coyotes are most active at dawn and dusk. They're frequently spotted in large parks such as Ravenna Park, Discovery Park, and Seward Park. They prefer wooded or brushy areas where they can hunt and avoid human disturbances, but sightings near trails and suburban neighborhoods are becoming more common as they grow increasingly comfortable in human-dominated landscapes. Though they tend to avoid direct contact with humans, keen observers might hear their calls at night or see their tracks along trails—a reminder of the wildlife thriving in urban settings.

Eastern Cottontail Rabbit

Sylvilagus floridanus

The eastern cottontail rabbit is a familiar sight in the greater Seattle area, thriving in suburban gardens, open fields, and woodlands. With its soft, brown fur and distinctive white, fluffy tail that resembles a cotton ball, the eastern cottontail is one of the most easily recognized rabbit species in North America. Adults weigh between 2 and 4 pounds, with a compact body, large eyes, and long ears that make them highly attuned to potential threats. These rabbits rely heavily on their acute hearing and sense of smell to detect predators, and they have powerful hind legs that allow them to make rapid, bounding escapes—capable of reaching speeds up to 18 miles per hour in short bursts. Their signature zigzagging hop helps them evade predators, as it makes their movement unpredictable.

As strict herbivores, eastern cottontails consume a diet that varies with the seasons. In the warmer months, they feed on grasses, clover, dandelions, and other flowering plants. Their diet shifts in winter to bark, twigs, and buds from woody plants, allowing them to adapt to limited food availability during colder months. Cottontails are selective feeders; they prefer young, tender vegetation but will graze on a wide array of plants when necessary. This adaptable diet often leads them to suburban gardens, where ornamental plants and vegetable patches offer an enticing source of food. Though they can be a nuisance to gardeners, cottontails are also beneficial as seed dispersers. As they forage, they unintentionally transport seeds that contribute to plant growth and biodiversity in their habitats.

One quirky behavior of eastern cottontails is "coprophagy," or the re-ingestion of their own feces. This might sound unusual, but it's a critical process for these rabbits. Cottontails

produce two types of droppings: hard pellets and softer, nutrient-rich "cecotropes." By re-ingesting cecotropes, cottontails can absorb additional nutrients and vitamins that their digestive systems couldn't initially extract, which is especially valuable in winter when food is scarce.

Eastern cottontails are crepuscular, meaning they are most active during dawn and dusk. This behavior helps them avoid both the heat of the day and the peak activity times of many predators. Though primarily solitary, they use scent-marking to establish territories and communicate with other rabbits. Despite their preference for a solitary lifestyle, cottontails are prolific breeders, with females capable of producing several litters each year. This rapid reproductive cycle compensates for their high predation rates, as cottontails are preyed upon by a wide range of animals, including foxes, coyotes, hawks, owls, and domestic cats.

Where to See Them

Eastern cottontail rabbits are commonly found in suburban and rural areas around Seattle, where a mix of grassy fields, gardens, and wooded edges provides ample food and cover. The Washington Park Arboretum, Discovery Park, and other green spaces around the city are excellent places to spot them, especially in early mornings or at dusk, when they are more active. These rabbits are generally shy and will often freeze when they sense danger, relying on their brown-gray fur for camouflage. With patience, observers can spot cottontails grazing in open areas or nestled under shrubs and bushes, adding a touch of wildlife charm to Seattle's parks and neighborhoods.

Eastern Gray Squirrel

Sciurus carolinensis

The eastern gray squirrel, introduced to the Pacific Northwest from the eastern United States in the late 1800s, has become a common resident of Seattle's urban parks, neighborhoods, and forests. Known for their curious and playful nature, these squirrels are easily recognizable by their bushy, gray tails and agile movements. Adult eastern gray squirrels typically weigh around 1 to 1.5 pounds and measure 16 to 20 inches from nose to tail, with their tails making up a large portion of their overall length. The tail is not only a signature feature but also serves important functions: it provides balance as the squirrel leaps through trees, acts as a blanket in cold weather, and can even be used as a communication tool, with flicks and movements signaling alarm or territoriality.

Primarily herbivorous, eastern gray squirrels favor a diet of nuts, seeds, berries, and fruit. They are particularly fond of acorns and hazelnuts, which they gather in large quantities in fall. One of the most fascinating aspects of their behavior is their instinct to cache, or bury, nuts as a food source for winter. Squirrels often dig small holes, called caches, where they bury food that will sustain them through leaner months. Remarkably, they use spatial memory and scent to locate their caches months later, though they don't recover every buried nut. This behavior inadvertently aids in forest regeneration, as the forgotten nuts have a chance to sprout and grow into new trees.

Strong, nimble limbs and sharp claws enable them to climb trees and leap across branches with ease. Their front teeth grow continuously, an adaptation that helps them gnaw through tough seeds and tree bark, a necessity for accessing the inner nutrients. In urban environments, they have adapted

▲ A gray squirrel feeds on tree blossoms.

well to foraging around human activity, learning to raid bird feeders, scavenge crumbs, and even beg for food from park visitors. This adaptability has contributed to their success as an urban species, and they are often seen in Seattle's residential neighborhoods and parks.

Eastern gray squirrels play a vital role in their ecosystems by dispersing seeds and helping maintain the health of forested areas. They are also a food source for various predators, such as hawks, owls, and foxes, helping sustain the food web. While they may be considered nuisances when they invade attics or steal from bird feeders, their lively antics and bushy tails make them a favorite among wildlife watchers.

Where to See Them

Eastern gray squirrels are easy to spot in Seattle's urban parks, including Discovery Park, Green Lake Park, and Volunteer Park. They are also common in residential areas, particularly where large trees provide abundant food and shelter. In autumn, you may notice them darting across lawns or paths as they gather and cache nuts in preparation for winter. Their active, high-energy lifestyle and acrobatic leaps between branches make them a delightful sight for both children and adults.

Harbor Seal

Phoca vitulina

The harbor seal is one of Seattle's most endearing marine residents, bringing charm to the city's waterfronts and coastal parks. Known for their round, expressive eyes, sleek spotted coats, and inquisitive faces, these small, shy seals are some of the most common and adaptable marine mammals in Puget Sound. With an average size of around 5 feet and a weight of 150 to 300 pounds, harbor seals are Seattle's smaller but charismatic coastal companions, often seen bobbing along the water or resting on rocks and docks.

Harbor seals are solitary by nature, but they gather in large numbers at haul-out sites (rocky areas or beaches where they can rest, molt, and warm up). Unlike sea lions, harbor

▲ Harbor seals are among the most frequently seen marine mammals in the nearshore waters of Puget Sound off Seattle.

seals don't have large flippers for moving on land, so they maneuver with a charming, undulating motion often compared to that of an inchworm. Their spotted coats, which vary from silver-gray to dark brown, help camouflage them from predators and add to their unique appearance. Unlike many marine mammals, harbor seals do not migrate, making Puget Sound their year-round home and providing Seattle residents with frequent opportunities to observe them.

These seals are known for being elusive and cautious, often keeping their distance from human activity. However, they occasionally display curious behaviors, such as "bottling," where they float vertically in the water with just their heads above the surface, appearing to keep an eye on their surroundings. This behavior may look playful, but it allows them to rest while still being alert to approaching predators, such as transient orcas that occasionally hunt seals in Seattle's waters.

Harbor seals are skilled hunters, using their sensitive whiskers to detect prey in the often-murky waters of Puget Sound. Their diet consists primarily of fish, squid, and crustaceans, and they have been observed diving up to 1500 feet in search of food. This ability to hunt in deep, dark waters is vital to their survival, as Puget Sound can be cloudy with limited visibility. By hunting smaller fish like herring and cod, harbor seals play a significant role in controlling local fish populations, contributing to the balance of Seattle's coastal ecosystem.

Where to See Them

Harbor seals are commonly sighted along Seattle's waterfront, especially near piers, marinas, and rocky outcrops. West Seattle's Alki Beach, Carkeek Park, and Discovery Park are popular spots to see these animals, particularly at low tide when they are more likely to haul out and rest. At certain times of year, they even appear on buoys or small floating platforms, providing a close-up view for onlookers.

Little Brown Bat

Myotis lucifugus

The little brown bat is one of the most common bat species across North America, including the Pacific Northwest, and plays a crucial role in controlling insect populations. Weighing just a few ounces, with a body length of 3 to 4 inches and a wingspan of up to 11 inches, these small, nimble flyers are expertly designed for nighttime hunting. Their fur is typically brown with lighter underparts, a coloring that helps them blend in with the bark of trees or the crevices of buildings where they roost during the day.

One of the little brown bat's most remarkable abilities is its use of echolocation, a sophisticated navigation system. These bats emit high-frequency sounds that bounce off objects, allowing them to detect insects and avoid obstacles in the dark. With large, rounded ears, they can "see" with sound, pinpointing even the smallest insects mid-flight. This adaptation is especially critical for survival, as they rely heavily on catching moths, beetles, and mosquitoes—often consuming up to half their body weight in insects each night. This makes them invaluable for natural pest control, helping keep insect populations in check, particularly around water bodies where insects breed.

Beyond their nightly hunts, little brown bats exhibit fascinating seasonal behaviors, including migration and hibernation. During warmer months, they are highly active near forests and water sources, where they find ample food and suitable locations for raising young.

As temperatures drop, these bats migrate to caves, abandoned mines, or even attics, where they enter hibernation to conserve energy. During hibernation, their metabolic rate drops significantly, allowing them to survive for months without food. However, this dormant state leaves them vulnerable to threats like white-nose syndrome, a fungal disease that has ravaged bat populations across North America. White-nose syndrome disrupts hibernation, causing bats to wake prematurely and deplete energy stores, often leading to starvation.

Little brown bats also exhibit intriguing social behaviors. While they are generally solitary hunters, they often roost in colonies, especially in hibernation sites, for warmth and protection. These colonies may include hundreds or thousands of individuals, and they communicate with each other using ultrasonic vocalizations. During the breeding season, males and females interact closely, but once young are born, mothers play a dominant role in caring for pups until they can fly and hunt independently.

Where to See Them

In Seattle, little brown bats are frequently seen near dusk, swooping and diving near water sources like the shores of Lake Washington, Discovery Park, and Green Lake. They roost during the day in tree cavities, under bark, or in man-made structures such as attics and bridges. People out in the parks at twilight may be treated to a display of these agile hunters darting through the air, contributing to the natural balance by controlling insect populations.

Norway Rat

Rattus norvegicus

The Norway rat, also known as the brown rat, is one of the world's most adaptable and widely distributed rodents. Originally from northern Asia and introduced to North America through European ships, these rats have become a permanent fixture in urban environments, including Seattle. Norway rats are robust animals, with adults typically measuring between 7 and 9 inches in body length, with a long, scaly tail that adds another 6 to 8 inches. They have coarse brown or gray fur, rounded ears, and a blunt snout. Known for their adaptability and resilience, Norway rats are often seen as pests, but their role in urban ecosystems is complex.

Norway rats are opportunistic feeders, able to consume almost anything they find, including garbage, pet food, grains, and even smaller animals when resources are scarce. This varied diet has allowed them to thrive in cities, where human waste and food sources are plentiful. Their strong survival skills include excellent swimming and climbing abilities, allowing them to navigate sewers, pipes, and buildings. Norway rats can chew through materials like wood and plastic to access food or shelter, making them challenging pests to control in urban areas. They are nocturnal and typically avoid human contact, emerging mostly at night to forage.

Despite their reputation, Norway rats play a significant role in the urban ecosystem. As scavengers, they help dispose of waste and organic debris, essentially acting as cleanup crews. This has indirect benefits, as their foraging helps decompose materials and break down food waste. However, they also compete with native species for resources and can disrupt local food webs. For example, they often prey on bird eggs and, if their numbers are high, can drive down populations of ground-nesting birds.

Norway rats are known for their intelligence and social behavior. They live in colonies with established hierarchies, often in burrows or hidden spaces where they feel secure. Rats communicate using ultrasonic vocalizations that are not audible to humans and display complex behaviors, such as grooming each other and caring for young within their social groups. These traits contribute to their success as a species, as rats are capable of learning from each other and avoiding dangers through social learning.

Where to See Them

Norway rats are common in Seattle's urban environments, especially in areas with high human activity. They are often found in alleys,

near dumpsters, and in basements or older buildings. Areas near restaurants, markets, or parks with accessible food sources are also hotspots for rat activity. While they are elusive during the day, signs of their presence, such as droppings, gnaw marks, or burrow entrances, are common. To avoid attracting them, it's important to secure trash and avoid leaving food outdoors overnight. Norway rats are not just resilient pests but an enduring part of the city's complex urban ecosystem.

Nutria

Myocastor coypus

Originally from South America, the nutria, or coypu, has become an invasive species in the Pacific Northwest, including Seattle's wetlands and marshes. These large, semiaquatic rodents closely resemble small beavers or large muskrats, with a few distinguishing features. Nutria have robust bodies, webbed hind feet for efficient swimming, and long, muscular tails. Their coarse fur ranges from brown to dark gray, and their distinctive orange teeth—similar to beavers'—are an adaptation to their diet and aquatic lifestyle. Nutria grow to over 20 pounds and can reach nearly 2 feet in length, making them one of the larger rodents in Seattle's ecosystems.

Nutria are herbivores with a particular taste for aquatic plants, grasses, and the roots of marsh vegetation. Their feeding habits, however, are highly destructive; they uproot large swathes of vegetation, often faster than the plants can regenerate. This behavior poses a serious threat to local ecosystems, as wetland plants play a crucial role in preventing erosion, stabilizing riverbanks, and providing shelter and food for native fish and bird species. As nutria populations grow, they displace native species and significantly alter the landscapes they inhabit, often to the detriment of ecosystem health.

Like beavers, nutria build dens in riverbanks and marshes, often burrowing into levees, embankments, and other structures. These burrowing habits can weaken flood-control structures, which increases the risk of flooding, particularly during heavy rains.

Nutria are known to cause significant damage to both natural and man-made water systems, making them a challenging species for conservation and water-management efforts. Furthermore, their large appetites and high reproduction rates exacerbate the environmental strain they place on wetland habitats.

Nutria are primarily nocturnal, often venturing out at night to forage. Although they are shy and tend to avoid direct encounters with humans, nutria populations in urban wetlands are growing, and their presence is increasingly noticeable in the Seattle area. Their social

behavior is another interesting aspect of their life cycle; they often live in family groups, sharing dens and foraging territories. Female nutria can reproduce multiple times a year, with each litter consisting of several young, leading to rapid population growth and further environmental impact.

Where to See Them

Nutria are commonly found in wetlands, marshes, and along riverbanks where aquatic vegetation is abundant. In Seattle, sightings are frequent in areas such as Duck Bay in the Washington Park Arboretum, the shores of Lake Washington, and the wetlands around Magnuson Park. Despite their increasing numbers, nutria can be difficult to spot due to their nocturnal habits. Visitors may instead see signs of their activity, such as tracks in muddy banks, burrow entrances, and areas of disturbed or destroyed vegetation. For those interested in wildlife tracking, learning to identify nutria signs can reveal the extent of their impact on local wetland ecosystems.

Orca Whale

Orcinus orca

The orca whale, or "killer whale" as it's often called, is not only the largest member of the dolphin family but also one of the most complex, charismatic, and mysterious marine mammals around the Seattle area. Known for their striking black-and-white markings, orcas inhabit the chilly waters of Puget Sound and are renowned for their intelligence, social structures, and the unique way they've adapted to their environment. Though often feared due to their name, these creatures are selective, highly skilled hunters that rarely pose a threat to humans.

Seattle's orca population is split into two primary groups: resident orcas, which predominantly feed on salmon, and transient orcas,

▲ Orcas occasionally make their way into Seattle's Elliott Bay, but people are more likely to see them when crossing over to Bainbridge Island or Vashon Island on a ferry or other boat.

also known as Bigg's orcas, which hunt seals, sea lions, and even other marine mammals. The resident orcas are incredibly loyal to family groups, known as pods, and each pod communicates with a unique set of vocalizations. This distinctive "language" helps pod members keep track of each other over vast distances and also serves as a fascinating marker of identity, as pods develop slightly different dialects over time.

Resident orcas are especially notable for their dietary preferences, showing a strong preference for Chinook salmon, the largest and most nutritionally dense salmon species in the Pacific Northwest. The health of resident orcas is deeply intertwined with salmon populations, and conservationists have voiced concerns over dwindling salmon numbers, highlighting the critical connection between orcas and their prey. Transient orcas, on the other hand, exhibit a unique hunting strategy that involves stalking and ambushing marine mammals, an approach they learned to minimize their vocalizations, which could alert prey. This adaptability has allowed transient orcas to thrive in various coastal waters and to extend their hunting range as they follow the populations of their preferred prey.

Orcas are highly intelligent and demonstrate advanced social behaviors. They are known to engage in play—breaching, tail-slapping, and even "spy-hopping" where they rise vertically out of the water to take a look around. These behaviors aren't just entertaining for onlookers but serve as methods for communication, environmental assessment, and even social bonding within pods. Young orcas, like human children, spend time learning skills from their mothers and other pod members, engaging in play to develop their hunting and social abilities.

Where to See Them

While orca sightings are more of a sure thing if you're out in a boat amid the San Juan Islands, you can occasionally spot them in and around Seattle proper, with the whales sometimes even venturing deep into Elliott Bay, Seattle's Puget Sound deepwater port. Grab some binoculars and perch yourself on Alki Beach, preferably early in the morning or late in the afternoon or evening, and hope for the best. An even better bet is to take a ferry ride from Seattle to Bainbridge Island—or Edmonds to Kingston farther north—and keep an eye out for orcas on the way.

Raccoon

Procyon lotor

Raccoons are known for their remarkable adaptability, cleverness, and iconic appearance, featuring a "masked" face and bushy, ringed tail. Medium-sized mammals that typically weigh between 8 and 20 pounds, raccoons have thick, grayish fur and expressive black facial markings, giving them a distinctive bandit-like look. One of their most remarkable physical features is their dexterous, hand-like front paws, which enable them to manipulate objects with surprising precision. These nimble paws allow raccoons to open containers, twist doorknobs, and even undo locks. This

dexterity, combined with their curiosity and intelligence, allows raccoons to exploit food sources and shelter in human environments, making them common urban inhabitants.

Raccoons are omnivores with a highly varied diet, eating fruits, vegetables, nuts, insects, small animals, and even garbage and pet food. They are adept foragers and have learned to hunt for eggs and small birds, making them quite resourceful in urban and natural settings alike. Unlike many mammals, raccoons have an excellent sense of touch and are known to "wash" their food in water before eating, although this behavior likely has more to do with tactile sensitivity than cleanliness. Raccoons also have strong memories and will return repeatedly to places where they've previously found food.

In the Seattle area, raccoons thrive in parks, neighborhoods, and near bodies of water. They are particularly drawn to areas where human refuse offers an easy meal, and they frequently rummage through garbage cans, compost bins, and outdoor pet-food containers. While raccoons are nocturnal and most active at night, it's not uncommon to see them during daylight, particularly if they're hungry or living near humans. Their inquisitive nature sometimes gets them into trouble, as they can raid chicken coops, steal food from campsites, and even enter attics or sheds in search of shelter or food.

Raccoons play an important role in the ecosystem as both predators and scavengers. By controlling populations of insects and small animals, they help maintain ecological balance. Additionally, their scavenging helps break down organic waste, contributing to natural recycling within urban and suburban landscapes. However, raccoons also have a role in disease transmission, as they are known carriers of parasites and diseases, such as rabies and raccoon roundworm, which can affect humans and pets.

Where to See Them

Raccoons are common in Seattle's urban and suburban areas, especially near parks, rivers, or other water sources. They are often spotted at night, rummaging through garbage cans or foraging near trails. Parks like Discovery Park, Carkeek Park, and the Washington Park Arboretum are prime locations for raccoon activity. Raccoon tracks, identifiable by their small, hand-like prints, can often be found along trails or near water, providing evidence of their nightly foraging adventures. Whether admired or considered a nuisance, raccoons are a fascinating example of a species that has adapted impressively to urban life.

River Otter

Lontra canadensis

River otters are playful, social mammals that thrive in both freshwater and coastal environments throughout the Seattle area. With their sleek, streamlined bodies, long tails, and thick, water-resistant fur, river otters are expertly adapted to an aquatic lifestyle. Their broad heads and small, rounded ears provide a low-profile shape that enhances their swimming efficiency, while webbed feet and powerful tails give them impressive speed and agility in the water. Known for their excellent swimming skills, river otters can dive as deep as 60 feet and hold their breath underwater for up to eight minutes, allowing them to catch fish, their primary food source, with ease.

River otters are opportunistic feeders and consume a wide variety of aquatic animals in addition to fish, including crayfish, frogs, and small invertebrates. Occasionally, they will also hunt on land for small mammals or birds, depending on food availability. River otters possess a highly developed sense of smell and vision, aiding them in detecting prey and evading potential predators. A particularly quirky behavior of river otters is their love for sliding. They often create mud or snow slides

▼ A jaunty river otter parades with his catch on a boat dock.

along riverbanks, repeatedly sliding down for the sheer fun of it. This behavior, along with playfully chasing each other through the water, is a hallmark of their social and energetic nature. Additionally, river otters are known to "raft" together, where multiple otters gather to rest or play as a group, which strengthens social bonds and helps protect individuals from potential predators.

River otters play a significant role in their ecosystems as top predators within the freshwater food chain. By preying on a variety of fish and amphibians, they help maintain healthy populations of these species, preventing any one type from dominating the ecosystem. This balance supports biodiversity and contributes to the overall health of aquatic habitats. Additionally, otters' foraging behaviors stir up sediment and redistribute nutrients, indirectly benefiting the plants and other organisms living in their habitat. River otters also serve as indicator species; because they require clean, unpolluted water to survive, the presence of river otters in an area often signals a healthy aquatic ecosystem.

Where to See Them

River otters are commonly found in habitats with ample water sources, such as rivers, lakes, wetlands, and coastal environments. In the Seattle area, they are frequently spotted at the Washington Park Arboretum, Seward Park, Discovery Park, and along the shores of Lake Washington. Early mornings and evenings are the best times to spot these otters, as they are most active around dawn and dusk. River otters are also known to leave distinctive tracks and scat near the water's edge, so keeping an eye out for signs of their presence can increase the chances of spotting them in the wild.

Virginia Opossum

Didelphis virginiana

Just because Virginia opossums are the only marsupials living in the United States and Canada doesn't make Seattle homeowners eager to see them fall into a window well or, even worse, make their way inside the house. Nevertheless, opossums are wondrous, flexible mammals well adapted to life not just in wooded areas and farmlands, but increasingly in the types of suburban environments that are so common in and around Seattle.

Like kangaroos and koalas, opossum young continue to develop even after birth in their mama's stomach pouch. Their long, pointed snouts, sharp teeth, and prehensile tails (used for grasping branches and balancing) give opossums a distinctive prehistoric appearance. Their fur is typically a mix of gray and white, and their faces have dark markings around the eyes, giving them a masked appearance. The opossum's feet are another unique trait; the hind feet have an opposable thumb, aiding in climbing and grasping. Known for their strength rather than agility, opossums are sometimes spotted climbing trees for various purposes such as escaping predators, searching for food, resting, or finding dens.

The diet of the Virginia opossum is omnivorous and highly varied, contributing to the species' adaptability. They consume fruits, vegetables, insects, small mammals, birds, and carrion. They are also known to scavenge from garbage cans and compost piles in urban areas. This opportunistic feeding behavior helps the opossum thrive in various environments and conditions. One interesting dietary habit is their consumption of ticks, which helps control tick populations and potentially reduce the spread of tick-borne diseases.

Perhaps the opossum's most notable behavioral trait is its ability to play dead, or

"play possum," when threatened. This involuntary response can last for several minutes to hours, during which the opossum becomes stiff and emits a foul odor to deter predators.

America's marsupial has a relatively short lifespan for a mammal of its size, typically living only two to four years in the wild. Despite this, they reproduce prolifically, with females giving birth to large litters of up to twenty young, although usually only about half survive to maturity due to the limitations of the pouch.

Where to See Them

Virginia opossums are native to Central America and the southeastern United States and didn't make it out to the Seattle area until the early 1900s as pets and novelties. Some of these animals and/or their offspring later escaped from captivity or were intentionally released into the wild. While plenty of opossums are around Seattle and its environs, chances are you won't see them, as they are nocturnal and avoid bright light. (Homeowners can keep this in mind: lighting up the exterior of the house and yard can help deter curious opossums.) That said, a nighttime walk along a path bordering a stream or wetland, or down an alley lined with trash cans, will occasionally turn up an opossum searching for food.

They prefer areas with access to water sources like streams or ponds, as they need to stay hydrated. Opossums den in hollow logs, tree cavities, or abandoned burrows and sometimes take up residence in human-made structures such as attics or garages. The Ravenna Ravine, Washington Park Arboretum, Union Bay Natural Area, Magnuson Park wetlands, Kubota Garden, Saint Edward State Park, Thornton Creek, and Mercer Slough are all excellent places to try to glimpse opossums, especially if you are willing to poke around at night.

Reptiles and Amphibians

Common Garter Snake

Thamnophis sirtalis

The common garter snake is one of the Pacific Northwest's most adaptable and resilient reptiles, thriving in diverse habitats, from wetlands and forests to suburban backyards. Their ability to live in various environments, even urban ones, has made them a familiar sight around Seattle. These slender, striped snakes typically grow between 18 and 26 inches in length, though some reach up to 3 feet. With their characteristic stripes in shades of yellow, green, or blue running the length of their bodies, garter snakes blend effortlessly into their surroundings, camouflaging among grasses, marshes, and forested undergrowth. This camouflage helps them avoid predators such as birds of prey, raccoons, and larger snakes.

One of the common garter snake's most fascinating adaptations is its unusual tolerance for colder temperatures compared to other snake species. This trait allows garter snakes to remain active later in the year and occasionally even emerge on mild winter days, giving them access to food sources while other reptiles are dormant. Additionally, garter snakes possess a unique resistance to the toxins of certain prey, such as the rough-skinned newt. While many predators avoid these toxic amphibians, garter snakes can safely consume them without harm. This adaptation grants them access to a food source that other animals often avoid, giving them an edge in the Pacific Northwest's ecosystem, where amphibians are abundant.

Another intriguing behavior of common garter snakes is their breeding strategy. During the mating season, male garter snakes engage in an unusual display known as "mating balls." Dozens of males will gather around a single female, competing to mate with her and creating what appears to be a writhing mass of snakes. This behavior, while chaotic, is essential to the reproductive success of the species, increasing the odds of successful mating in the short breeding season. Unlike many other snake species that lay eggs, garter snakes give birth to live young. This live-bearing adaptation is especially beneficial in Seattle's cooler climate, as it allows the young to be born in a more developed state, better prepared to face the elements and survive.

In addition to their adaptability, common garter snakes play a critical role in Seattle's ecosystems. As carnivores, they help control populations of small mammals, insects, and amphibians, keeping these populations balanced within the ecosystem. Their diet includes frogs, fish, earthworms, slugs, and occasionally small rodents, making them natural pest controllers. By feeding on species that thrive in wetlands, gardens, and fields, garter snakes help regulate these populations and maintain ecological balance. At the same time, they serve as prey for local predators, supporting the food web and contributing to the health of Seattle's wildlife communities.

Where to See Them

Common garter snakes can be found in Seattle's moist, grassy areas near ponds, creeks, and wetlands, where they bask on rocks or logs to warm up in the sun. They are especially active on warm days, and their sleek bodies are often seen gliding through grassy or marshy areas. Great places to spot them include the wetlands of Magnuson Park, the marshy edges of Discovery Park, around Green Lake, and along the Meadowbrook Pond shoreline—all places chock-full of tasty amphibians and insects near the water's edge.

Ensatina

Ensatina eschscholtzii

The ensatina is a fascinating and distinctive lungless salamander, easily recognized by its vivid coloration and unique physical traits. Measuring between 3 to 6 inches in length, this species comes in a range of orange, red, and brown hues, often with darker markings on its back. The color pattern varies greatly depending on its geographic location and environmental conditions. Some individuals display vibrant orange and red tones, while others are more muted, blending seamlessly with the forest floor. One of the most remarkable features of the ensatina is the constriction at the base of its tail. This feature allows the salamander to "drop" its tail when threatened by predators, a defense mechanism known as *autotomy*. The detached tail continues to twitch, distracting the predator while the ensatina makes its escape. The tail eventually regenerates, but this survival tactic comes at an energetic cost, as the salamander must expend considerable resources to regrow it.

Ensatinas are nocturnal creatures, preferring to stay hidden during the day to avoid desiccation. Their smooth, moist skin, essential for respiration, makes them extremely sensitive to changes in moisture levels. During the night, they emerge from their hiding spots under rocks, logs, and leaf litter to hunt for small invertebrates, their primary food source. They use their long, sticky tongues to capture ants, beetles, spiders, and other small arthropods. Despite their small size, ensatinas play a crucial role in controlling insect populations within their ecosystems.

One of the most intriguing aspects of the ensatina's biology is its lungless nature. Instead of using lungs to breathe, these salamanders rely entirely on cutaneous respiration, meaning they absorb oxygen directly through their skin. This adaptation requires them to remain in moist environments to facilitate gas exchange. As a result, ensatinas are highly dependent on their surroundings and are particularly vulnerable to habitat changes such as deforestation or climate change, which can alter the moisture balance of their habitats.

Unlike many amphibians that require water for reproduction, ensatinas are fully terrestrial. They do not undergo an aquatic larval stage, which is rare among amphibians. Instead, after mating in spring, the females lay eggs in hidden, moist locations on land. These eggs develop directly into miniature versions of adult salamanders, bypassing the free-swimming larval stage typical of many other species. This direct development is a key adaptation for living in terrestrial environments and allows them to reproduce in areas away from standing water, giving them more flexibility in habitat choice.

Where to See Them

Ensatinas are most often found in damp, forested areas throughout the Pacific Northwest, including the Puget Sound region. Popular sites include Seward Park and Carkeek Park. To spot an ensatina, carefully search under logs, rocks, and leaf litter in shaded, moist areas, especially after rain.

Long-toed Salamander

Ambystoma macrodactylum

The long-toed salamander is one of the most distinctive amphibians in the Pacific Northwest, easily identifiable by the elongated fourth toe on its hind feet. This unique physical trait, combined with its striking yellow or greenish dorsal stripe running along a dark brown or black body, makes it stand out from other salamanders in the region. Adults range from 3 to 6 inches in length, and like other amphibians, they have smooth, moist skin that helps them retain moisture, especially in drier environments.

Long-toed salamanders are highly adaptable creatures, capable of thriving in a wide range of habitats. They can be found in lowland forests, alpine meadows, wetlands, and even temporary vernal pools. While they require aquatic environments for breeding, they spend much of their adult life in terrestrial habitats. During the day, these nocturnal amphibians stay hidden under logs, rocks, and leaf litter to avoid predators and prevent dehydration. At night, they emerge to hunt, preying on a variety of small invertebrates such as insects, slugs, and worms. Their ability to live in both aquatic and terrestrial environments is one reason for their success across such a broad range.

Reproduction in long-toed salamanders begins in early spring, often coinciding with the melting snow and the creation of temporary pools. Females lay their eggs in clusters

One of the most interesting behaviors of the long-toed salamander is its ability to survive in environments with extreme seasonal changes. In some habitats, the ponds and pools they rely on for breeding dry up during summer, while in alpine regions, the ponds may freeze over for extended periods. To cope with these fluctuations, long-toed salamanders can exhibit paedomorphosis, where some individuals retain their larval characteristics, such as gills, and remain in the water indefinitely, while others fully metamorphose and transition to land.

attached to underwater vegetation or other submerged surfaces. The larvae are fully aquatic and possess external gills, which allow them to absorb oxygen directly from the water. Depending on environmental conditions, the larvae may take several months to undergo metamorphosis, during which they lose their gills and transition to a terrestrial lifestyle. In colder, high-elevation areas, larval development may take an entire year or more.

Where to See Them

Long-toed salamanders are found in a variety of habitats throughout the Pacific Northwest. They are most commonly spotted near ponds, wetlands, and streams, especially during their spring breeding season. Good places to observe them include Union Bay Natural Area and Discovery Park in Seattle. Look for them in moist, shaded areas, particularly under logs or stones near water.

Northern Alligator Lizard

Elgaria coerulea

The northern alligator lizard is a fascinating native reptile of the Pacific Northwest, known for its robust, elongated body; short limbs; and distinctive, alligator-like appearance. While significantly smaller than an alligator, these lizards can grow up to 10 inches in length, with a textured, scaly exterior that often appears in varying shades of brown, gray, or greenish brown. Their scales are usually marked with dark bands running across the back and sides, which provide excellent camouflage in their natural habitat among rocks, fallen logs, and forest debris.

Northern alligator lizards are highly adaptable, thriving in a range of environments, from coastal forests and grassy meadows to rocky outcrops and suburban areas. Their semiarboreal nature means they are equally comfortable on the ground or climbing low shrubs and trees, particularly when hunting or avoiding predators. These lizards are often found basking on sunny rocks or hidden under logs, utilizing their excellent climbing skills and agility to navigate their environment.

In terms of diet, northern alligator lizards are opportunistic carnivores, primarily feeding on a variety of invertebrates like spiders, beetles, ants, and moths. However, they are also known to prey on small vertebrates such as baby mice, other small lizards, or amphibians when the opportunity arises. Their feeding behavior is influenced by their environment; they take advantage of whatever prey is most abundant in their territory. This adaptability plays a critical role in their survival, particularly in areas where food sources fluctuate with the seasons.

One of the most intriguing features of the northern alligator lizard is its remarkable defense mechanism. Like many lizards, they possess the ability to shed, or autotomize, their tails when threatened by predators. The detached tail continues to wriggle, distracting the predator and allowing the lizard to escape. While the tail eventually regrows, it is never quite the same size or shape, and the process can be energy-intensive for the lizard. This unique strategy significantly increases their chances of survival in the wild, especially given their small size and many natural predators, such as birds of prey, snakes, and larger mammals.

During the breeding season, which typically occurs in spring, northern alligator lizards engage in interesting courtship rituals. Males often engage in combat with other males over territory and females, biting and grappling with each other in fierce displays. Females give birth to live young in late summer, usually between five to fifteen offspring per clutch. This live-bearing trait, known as viviparity, is an adaptation to the cooler climates of the Pacific Northwest, allowing the lizards to reproduce successfully in environments where egg-laying might be less reliable due to variable temperatures or moisture levels.

In terms of longevity, northern alligator lizards can live for up to ten years in the wild, although this lifespan can be shortened by predation or habitat loss. These lizards are

considered a species of least concern by conservation standards, but they do face pressures from habitat destruction and urban development, which can reduce their available living and hunting spaces.

Where to See Them

Northern alligator lizards are widely distributed across the Pacific Northwest, from coastal areas to the edges of forests and even in suburban yards where suitable cover exists. In Seattle, they can be found in the more forested parts of the city, particularly in areas like the Washington Park Arboretum, Discovery Park, and Seward Park. They are also commonly seen in nearby natural areas like the Olympic National Park, where they bask on sunny rock faces or scurry under logs and leaf litter. Keep an eye out for them on warm, sunny days, when they are most likely to be active and visible.

Northern Red-legged Frog

Rana aurora

The northern red-legged frog is an amphibian of striking appearance, most notable for the vivid red coloration on the undersides of its legs. This bright red hue stands in contrast to the frog's more muted brown, green, or reddish brown body, which provides camouflage as they rest among the leaf litter of the forest floor. Their reddish legs are thought to aid in this camouflage, blending into the natural hues of the forest's understory. These frogs also feature smooth skin and prominent dorso-lateral folds running along their backs, giving them a sleek yet well-armored appearance.

Northern red-legged frogs typically range between 2 to 5 inches in length, making them one of the larger amphibians in their range. Their size, along with their vibrant legs, makes them relatively easy to distinguish from other native frog species. However, they are also highly secretive, spending much of their time hidden in moist, shaded environments where they can avoid predators like raccoons, herons, and snakes. Their primary defense is their ability to remain still and rely on camouflage, although they are also strong swimmers, capable of escaping quickly into water if threatened.

As for habitat, they prefer cool, moist, forested habitats and are often found near slow-moving streams, ponds, and wetlands, where they breed. These frogs are not adapted to climb like Pacific treefrogs, and thus they spend most of their time on the ground or in shallow water, avoiding open areas and remaining near dense vegetation. During the breeding season, which typically runs from late winter to early spring, females lay large masses of eggs in shallow water, attaching them to submerged vegetation. Each egg mass contains hundreds of eggs, which develop into tadpoles that will metamorphose into juvenile frogs within several months.

A fascinating aspect of the red-legged frog's life cycle is its reliance on clean, cool water bodies for breeding. Tadpoles require months of development in these aquatic environments, and as the water temperature and quality play a crucial role in their survival, these frogs are sensitive indicators of environmental health. Unfortunately, habitat loss, climate change, and the introduction of invasive species like bullfrogs and non-native fish have led to declines in red-legged frog populations across their range. Conservation efforts are underway in many areas to protect critical habitats and ensure the survival of this species.

Where to See Them

Look for northern red-legged frogs in cool, moist forested areas near ponds, wetlands, and slow-moving streams. Discovery Park is one Seattle hotspot for these frogs if you're trying to see them. Time your visit for the spring breeding season, as the frogs tend to gather in shallow water then and are easier to spot.

Northwestern Garter Snake

Thamnophis ordinoides

The northwestern garter snake is one of the most common and easily recognizable reptiles in the Pacific Northwest, known for its slender, agile body and vibrant color variations. While they may not grow as large as some other snake species, northwestern garter snakes typically reach lengths of 16 to 24 inches, with some individuals nearing 30 inches. Their coloration varies greatly, with some showing bold stripes of yellow, red, orange, or cream running the length of their dark bodies, while others may have a checkered or mottled pattern. This variety in color makes them particularly fascinating to spot in the wild.

These snakes are highly adaptable, thriving in a variety of habitats, including forests, grasslands, wetlands, and even suburban gardens. They are often seen basking in the sun on rocks or logs to regulate their body temperature, or slithering through grass and underbrush in search of food. Northwestern garter snakes are generally nonaggressive and pose no threat to humans. When threatened, they may emit a mild musk as a defense mechanism but are more likely to quickly flee into dense vegetation or water.

As carnivores, northwestern garter snakes play a crucial role in controlling populations of various small animals. Their diet primarily consists of earthworms, slugs, amphibians, and small fish, though they have also been known to eat insects and even small rodents on occasion. One unique feature of these snakes is their ability to consume toxic amphibians, such as rough-skinned newts, which produce potent toxins. Northwestern garter snakes are immune to these toxins, allowing them to prey on creatures that other predators avoid, giving them an ecological advantage.

One of the most interesting behaviors of northwestern garter snakes occurs during the breeding season in early spring. Much like other garter snakes, they participate in the "mating ball" phenomenon, where multiple

males coil around a single female in a competitive effort to mate. This communal breeding behavior can result in what appears to be a chaotic writhing mass of snakes, but it is essential for ensuring genetic diversity within the population. After mating, females give birth to live young in late summer, typically producing between five to twenty offspring. This viviparous reproduction strategy—where the young are born live rather than hatched from eggs—helps increase the survival rate of the young, especially in the cooler climates of the Pacific Northwest.

Though small and often overlooked, northwestern garter snakes are vital components of their ecosystems. Their presence helps regulate the populations of pests like slugs and insects, making them beneficial to gardeners and farmers alike. Additionally, they serve as prey for a variety of larger animals, including birds of prey, mammals, and even larger snakes.

Where to See Them

Northwestern garter snakes are commonly found in and around Seattle, particularly in areas with abundant ground cover and access to water. Parks such as Discovery Park, Seward Park, and the Washington Park Arboretum provide excellent opportunities for spotting these reptiles, especially on warm, sunny days when they are most likely to be out basking. They are also frequently encountered in more suburban settings, particularly in gardens or near wetland areas. Their adaptable nature and prevalence in the region make them a common sight for anyone exploring the Pacific Northwest's diverse natural landscapes.

Northwestern Salamander

Ambystoma gracile

The northwestern salamander is a fascinating amphibian, notable for its large size and robust body compared to other salamanders in the Pacific Northwest. Adults range from 6 to 8 inches long, making them one of the larger species in the region. Their dark brown or grayish coloration helps them blend in with the moist forest floors they inhabit. One of the most distinctive features of the northwestern salamander is its large parotid glands located behind the eyes. These glands secrete a milky, mildly toxic substance that serves as a defense mechanism against predators such as birds, mammals, and snakes. Although the toxin is not harmful to humans, it can cause mild irritation if handled, which is why care should be taken when observing these salamanders.

They are typically found in moist forested environments, especially near ponds, lakes,

or slow-moving streams, as they rely on these water sources for breeding. Northwestern salamanders are nocturnal and highly secretive, often hiding under logs, rocks, or deep within leaf litter during the day to avoid predators and desiccation. They are primarily terrestrial outside of the breeding season, spending most of their time in the damp underbrush of coniferous forests. During the breeding season, which occurs in early spring, they return to water to lay eggs, often in gelatinous clusters attached to submerged vegetation. Each egg cluster can contain up to 200 eggs, providing a relatively high level of protection to developing embryos.

One of the most remarkable traits of northwestern salamanders is the phenomenon of neoteny observed in some populations. Neoteny is the retention of larval characteristics, such as external gills, into adulthood. In some environments, particularly those at higher altitudes or with colder temperatures, these salamanders may remain fully aquatic throughout their lives and never undergo complete metamorphosis. This adaptation allows them to survive in conditions where transitioning to a terrestrial life would be more energetically costly or disadvantageous due to limited resources on land.

The larvae of northwestern salamanders are easily identifiable by their bushy, reddish gills, which protrude from either side of their heads. These larvae remain aquatic for several months, feeding on small invertebrates and even other amphibian larvae. Depending on environmental conditions, they can take several months to metamorphose into terrestrial adults, though in colder regions, this process may be significantly delayed. In such cases, some individuals may remain in their aquatic form throughout their lives, which can increase their chances of survival in those particular habitats.

Where to See Them

Northwestern salamanders are commonly found in moist, forested areas across western Washington, especially near ponds and streams during the breeding season. Good places to spot them include Seward Park in Seattle and other natural areas with access to slow-moving water bodies. Outside of breeding season, look for them hiding under logs or rocks in damp, shaded parts of the forest.

Pacific Giant Salamander

Dicamptodon tenebrosus

This remarkable Northwest native amphibian is one of the largest terrestrial salamanders in the world, growing up to 13 inches in length. Its mottled body-coloring with a mix of brown, black, and sometimes yellow or gray, provides excellent camouflage among the debris of the forest floor.

Pacific giant salamanders are opportunistic feeders with a varied diet. As both larvae and adults, they consume a wide range of prey. Aquatic larvae feed on small invertebrates like insect larvae and crustaceans, whereas terrestrial adults expand their diet to include insects, spiders, slugs, and even other smaller salamanders. In some instances, they have been known to exhibit cannibalistic behavior. Their diet reflects their adaptability and the diverse food sources available in their forest habitats.

Several notable facts further highlight the uniqueness of this species. Unlike many other salamanders, the Pacific giant salamander possesses vocal cords and can produce barking sounds, especially when threatened. This is a rare trait among salamanders and adds an intriguing dimension to their behavior. Additionally, these salamanders have the capability of neoteny, where some individuals retain their larval features and remain aquatic even into adulthood. This trait allows them to adapt to various environmental conditions, especially when terrestrial habitats become less hospitable.

Believe it or not, these salamanders can live up to twenty years or more in the wild, a relatively long lifespan for amphibians. Their reproductive strategy involves laying eggs in well-hidden, moist locations near water, where

the larvae can then hatch and develop in aquatic environments before some transition to a terrestrial life.

Conservation-wise, the species is considered of special concern due to habitat loss and degradation, primarily from logging and water pollution. Preserving their old-growth and second growth forest habitats is critical for their continued survival. Efforts to conserve these environments not only benefit the Pacific giant salamander, but also myriad other species that share the same ecosystems.

Where to See Them

Pacific giant salamanders can be found in and nearby temperate forests from northern California up to British Columbia, but don't be surprised to stumble upon one of them in the Seattle's more forested sections, especially near creeks and ponds where there's lots of access to water and humidity as well as plenty of leaf litter for cover. Look for them in Magnuson Park's wetlands and the Ravenna Ravine as well as along the edges of Green Lake, Thornton Creek, and Coal Creek.

Pacific Tree Frog

Pseudacris regilla

The Pacific tree frog, also known as the Pacific chorus frog, is one of the most widespread and iconic amphibians of the Pacific Northwest. Measuring between 1 to 2 inches in length, these small frogs are well known for their distinctive "ribbit" calls that can be heard echoing through the night during the breeding season. Their coloration varies widely, ranging from vibrant green to brown or even gray, depending on their environment. Remarkably, Pacific tree frogs possess the ability to change their color to better blend with their surroundings, a camouflage adaptation that helps them evade predators like snakes, birds, and small mammals.

While Pacific tree frogs are often thought of as arboreal due to their name, they spend more time on the ground than in trees. They

▲ Pacific tree frogs are great climbers, thanks in part to sticky pads on their toes.

are excellent climbers, though, thanks to the sticky pads on their toes, which enable them to cling to vertical surfaces like tree trunks, plant leaves, and even rocks. This gives them a versatile lifestyle, allowing them to move between various microhabitats. These frogs are highly adaptable and can be found in a wide range of environments, from lowland forests and meadows to suburban gardens, parks, and urban areas. Their adaptability to both natural and human-altered landscapes makes them one of the most common amphibians in the region.

During the breeding season, which generally occurs in late winter or early spring, male Pacific tree frogs gather at the edges of ponds, marshes, and slow-moving streams to call for females. Their loud, distinctive calls are often one of the first signs of spring in the Pacific Northwest. Females lay small clusters of eggs, which are attached to submerged vegetation just below the water's surface. The eggs hatch into aquatic tadpoles, which undergo metamorphosis into froglets over the course of several weeks. The timing of this transformation depends on water temperature and environmental conditions.

As nocturnal hunters, Pacific tree frogs primarily feed on small insects, spiders, and other invertebrates. They play a crucial role in controlling insect populations, making them an important component of the local ecosystem. In turn, they serve as prey for a variety of larger animals, including snakes, birds, and small mammals, thus playing a key role in the food web.

Where to See Them

Pacific tree frogs are commonly found throughout the Pacific Northwest. In the Seattle area, they can be spotted in wetlands, ponds, and urban parks, especially during the breeding season, when their calls are most noticeable. Good places to observe them include Discovery Park, Magnuson Park, and the Union Bay Natural Area.

Painted Turtle

Chrysemys picta

The painted turtle is one of North America's most striking and widespread freshwater turtles, renowned for its vibrant coloration and adaptable nature. Its smooth, dark carapace (upper shell) features bright red and yellow markings along the edges, while the head and limbs are adorned with yellow stripes, giving it a vivid and unmistakable appearance. Adult painted turtles generally reach between 4 to 10 inches in length, with females typically larger than males. The species' bright coloration serves not only as camouflage among aquatic vegetation but also as a key identifying feature for those lucky enough to spot one basking in the sun.

Painted turtles thrive in a variety of freshwater habitats, including ponds, lakes, marshes, and slow-moving rivers with soft, muddy bottoms. They are particularly fond of areas with abundant vegetation and plenty of basking spots, such as logs or rocks. One of their most iconic behaviors is basking in large groups, sometimes stacked on top of one another, to regulate their body temperature. As ectothermic reptiles, painted turtles rely on external heat sources to maintain their metabolism, making basking a crucial part of their daily routine.

These turtles are omnivorous, with a diet that shifts as they age. Juveniles are primarily carnivorous, feeding on small aquatic invertebrates like insects, snails, and worms, as well as tadpoles and small fish. As they mature, painted turtles adopt a more herbivorous diet, consuming algae, aquatic plants, and other vegetation. Their ability to adapt to different food sources is a testament to their resilience and their vital role in maintaining the health of freshwater ecosystems. By controlling populations of aquatic insects and plants, painted turtles help maintain a balance within their habitats.

Painted turtles also have an interesting reproductive strategy. Mating occurs in spring and fall, and females can store sperm for extended periods, allowing them to lay fertilized eggs later. They dig nests in sandy or soft soil near the water's edge, where they lay between four to fifteen eggs. The temperature of the nest determines the sex of the

▼ Painted turtles crowd onto a log when the sun is out because, like all cold-blooded reptiles, they rely on external heat sources to regulate their body temperature.

hatchlings, with warmer temperatures producing females and cooler temperatures producing males. After hatching, the young turtles make their way to the water, though many may overwinter in the nest before emerging the following spring.

Painted turtles are not currently considered threatened, though they do face pressures from habitat loss, pollution, and road mortality. Protecting their freshwater habitats, including wetlands and riparian zones, is essential for their continued survival. Efforts to conserve these habitats benefit not only painted turtles but countless other species that rely on clean, undisturbed aquatic environments.

Where to See Them

Painted turtles are common throughout the Pacific Northwest, including in and around Seattle. Look for them basking on logs or rocks in sunny areas around ponds, lakes, and wetlands. Discovery Park, Magnuson Park, and Green Lake offer great opportunities to observe these turtles in their natural habitat. Keep an eye out for their distinctive red and yellow markings as they glide gracefully through the water or soak up the sun.

Pond Slider

Trachemys scripta

The pond slider is one of the most widely recognized freshwater turtles in North America, known for its adaptability and bold coloration. Its carapace is dark green or brown, adorned with yellowish streaks or stripes, while the plastron (underside) features dark, irregular markings. A key identifying trait is the yellow or red stripe behind each eye, giving the red-eared slider, a subspecies, its name. Adults typically range from 5 to 12 inches in length, with females larger than males. The striking patterns and distinctive head markings make the pond slider a common sight in many freshwater habitats across the United States.

Pond sliders thrive in diverse aquatic environments, from ponds and lakes to marshes and slow-moving rivers. They prefer habitats with soft, muddy bottoms and abundant aquatic vegetation, which provides both food and cover. Like other freshwater turtles, pond sliders are known for their basking habits. They can often be seen piled on top of one another on logs, rocks, or even floating debris, soaking up the sun to regulate their body temperature. As ectotherms, they depend on external warmth to keep their metabolism active.

As omnivores, pond sliders exhibit a versatile diet that shifts as they mature. Juveniles are more carnivorous, feeding on small aquatic invertebrates such as insects, snails, and crustaceans, as well as tadpoles and small fish. Adult pond sliders, on the other hand, consume a larger proportion of plant material, including algae and aquatic plants, while still eating occasional animal matter. Their varied diet helps keep aquatic ecosystems balanced

► A red-eared slider suns itself on a log at Duck Bay along the shoreline of Seattle's Washington Park Arboretum.

by controlling insect populations and managing vegetation growth.

One of the pond slider's more curious behaviors involves their winter survival strategies. During colder months, pond sliders enter a state of brumation, a hibernation-like dormancy. They remain submerged, often buried in the mud, where they slow their metabolism and breathe through specialized tissues in their throat and cloaca, allowing them to absorb oxygen from the water.

Reproduction for pond sliders occurs primarily in spring and summer. After mating, females venture onto land to lay clutches of four to twenty eggs in sandy or soft soil near the water's edge. As with many other turtles, the temperature of the nest determines the sex of the hatchlings, with warmer conditions producing females. Once hatched, the young instinctively make their way to the water, though only a small percentage survive to adulthood due to predation.

Pond sliders are not currently threatened, but they face challenges from habitat loss, water pollution, and competition from invasive species. Additionally, the red-eared slider, often kept as a pet and later released into the wild, has become an invasive species in many regions, posing a threat to native turtle populations.

Where to See Them

Pond sliders, especially red-eared sliders, are commonly seen in urban parks and ponds around Seattle. Visit places like Green Lake, Discovery Park, and the Washington Park Arboretum, where you can often spot them basking on logs or gliding through calm waters.

Rough-skinned Newt

Taricha granulosa

The rough-skinned newt is one of the Pacific Northwest's most recognizable amphibians, thanks to its distinctive rough, brownish skin and its vivid orange or yellow belly. These newts measure between 6 to 8 inches in length, making them relatively large compared to other amphibians in the region. Their rough, grainy skin sets them apart from the smoother-skinned salamanders and frogs. However, their most remarkable feature is the potent neurotoxin they secrete from their skin—tetrodotoxin—which is powerful enough to make them unpalatable and potentially dangerous to most predators. In fact, tetrodotoxin is the same toxin found in pufferfish, making rough-skinned newts one of the most toxic

animals in North America. Despite this, some predators, like garter snakes, have developed resistance to the toxin, leading to an evolutionary arms race between the two species.

The rough-skinned newt's bold coloration—bright orange on the belly and dull brown on the back—serves as an aposematic warning to potential predators. When threatened, these newts often display their bright underside in a behavior known as the "unken reflex," which involves arching their backs and exposing their bellies to signal their toxicity. This visual deterrent, combined with their slow, deliberate movements, helps them avoid attacks. However, despite their toxicity, they can sometimes fall prey to garter snakes and, on rare occasions, birds.

Rough-skinned newts are both aquatic and terrestrial, spending the majority of their adult lives on land but returning to water to breed in spring. During the breeding season, males develop rough patches on their skin to help them grip females during mating. The females lay eggs individually, attaching them to submerged vegetation in ponds, lakes, or slow-moving streams. The larvae are fully aquatic, possessing external gills, and take several months to metamorphose into their terrestrial adult form.

These newts are slow-moving creatures that are most active at night or during wet conditions. They are often seen walking along the forest floor, particularly after rainfall, in search of food. Their diet primarily consists of small invertebrates such as insects, worms, and slugs. During the drier summer months, rough-skinned newts may venture far from water, seeking damp microhabitats under logs, rocks, or within leaf litter to avoid desiccation.

Where to See Them

Rough-skinned newts are commonly found in moist, forested habitats and around wetlands in western Washington. Look for them in places like Seward Park and Carkeek Park, or along the edges of ponds and streams, especially during the breeding season or after rainfall. Their slow, deliberate movements and vivid coloration make them easier to spot when they are active.

Western Fence Lizard

Sceloporus occidentalis

The western fence lizard, often called the "blue-belly" lizard due to the vibrant blue patches on its underside, is a familiar sight across the western United States. This small, fast-moving reptile is known for its rough, spiny scales and its adaptability to various environments. Typically ranging between 4 to 7 inches in length, western fence lizards are dark gray or brown with black markings along their back. When the lizard is startled or engaged in territorial displays, it reveals its striking blue belly, a trait that sets it apart from other species. Males, in particular, exhibit brighter blue patches than females or juveniles.

Western fence lizards thrive in a wide range of habitats, from arid deserts to grassy fields and open woodlands. They are especially fond of rocky outcrops, fallen logs, and, as their name suggests, fences, where they bask in the sun to regulate their body temperature. These lizards are primarily diurnal, meaning they are active during the day, often seen scurrying along rocks or basking in sunny patches to absorb warmth. Like all reptiles, they are ectothermic and rely on the environment to control their body temperature, making sunbathing an essential part of their daily routine.

As insectivores, western fence lizards play a vital role in controlling insect populations. Their diet consists of ants, beetles, grasshoppers, and spiders, which they capture using their sharp reflexes and quick movements.

This lizard's ability to thrive in a variety of environments and feed on a range of prey highlights its adaptability and importance in maintaining a balance within its ecosystem. A fascinating fact about western fence lizards is their connection to Lyme disease prevention: the blood of these lizards kills the bacteria that cause Lyme disease in ticks, reducing the spread of the disease in areas where these lizards are abundant.

Western fence lizards are also known for their unique mating displays and territorial behavior. During the breeding season, males perform a series of push-ups to display their blue bellies and establish dominance over rivals or to attract mates. This behavior, combined with head-bobbing and tail-waving, creates an impressive visual display that is unmistakable in their sunlit habitats.

Females lay between three to seventeen eggs in sandy or loose soil, typically in spring or early summer. The eggs hatch after a few months, with the young emerging fully independent and ready to hunt insects. These lizards are relatively short-lived, with a typical lifespan of five to seven years in the wild.

Western fence lizards are not currently threatened, thanks to their wide range and adaptability, but they do face risks from habitat loss and predation by domestic animals. Preserving their natural habitats ensures that these agile, insect-eating reptiles continue to thrive.

Where to See Them

Western fence lizards can be found in Seattle's more open spaces. Look for them basking on rocks, logs, and fences in sunny areas around parks and trails like Discovery Park, Seward Park, and the foothills of the Cascade Range. Keep an eye out for their distinctive quick movements and the bright blue flash of their bellies during territorial displays or mating season.

Western Redback Salamander

Plethodon vehiculum

The western redback salamander is a small, striking amphibian native to the Pacific Northwest, known for the reddish stripe running down the length of its back. This red or orange dorsal stripe is sharply contrasted by the salamander's darker, slate-gray or black sides, giving it an unmistakable appearance. In some individuals, the stripe is absent or faint, replaced by a more uniform dark coloration, but the redback form is by far the most common.

Measuring just 2 to 4 inches long, the western redback salamander may be small, but it is an important part of the forest ecosystem.

Unlike many amphibians that depend on water bodies for reproduction, the western redback salamander is fully terrestrial. It does not have an aquatic larval stage and instead lays its eggs in moist environments like rotting logs or beneath forest debris. The eggs hatch into fully formed miniature salamanders, bypassing the tadpole-like stage typical of other amphibians. This unique trait allows the species to inhabit a wide range of moist, forested environments, including old-growth and second-growth forests, as long as there is sufficient moisture in the soil.

Western redback salamanders are most commonly found in the leaf litter of forest floors, hiding beneath logs, stones, and other ground cover to avoid predators. They are nocturnal and secretive, emerging at night to hunt small invertebrates like ants, spiders, and beetles, which make up the bulk of their diet. Their slender bodies and moist skin allow them to squeeze into narrow crevices and remain hidden during the day, making them difficult to spot despite their relatively common presence in Pacific Northwest forests.

One of the western redback salamander's most fascinating characteristics is its ability to absorb moisture directly through its skin, as it lacks lungs and breathes entirely through its skin and the moist surfaces of its mouth. Because of this, they are extremely sensitive to environmental changes, particularly those that affect humidity levels. Prolonged dry periods or disturbances to the forest floor, such as logging or urban development, can dramatically reduce their numbers. In healthy habitats, however, western redback salamanders can be found in great abundance, sometimes exceeding populations of other vertebrates in the same area.

These salamanders play a crucial role in maintaining forest health by controlling insect populations and serving as prey for a variety of larger animals, including birds, snakes, and small mammals. While not currently considered endangered, they are vulnerable to habitat destruction, making the preservation of moist, shaded forest environments key to their survival.

Where to See Them

Western redback salamanders can be found in moist, forested environments across western Washington, especially in areas with dense leaf litter and decaying logs. Seward Park and the Mercer Slough are good places to look for them in the Seattle area. These salamanders are best spotted at night or after rainfall, when they are most active.

Western Toad

Anaxyrus boreas

The western toad is one of the more recognizable amphibians in the Pacific Northwest, distinguished by its dry, bumpy skin and prominent white or pale-colored stripe running down the center of its back. This large toad, which can grow to 3 to 5 inches in length, is usually a mottled combination of brown, green, or gray, helping it blend into its natural surroundings. The bumpy, warty appearance of the western toad provides camouflage as well as some level of protection against predators.

Western toads are found in a wide range of habitats, from forests and meadows to wetlands and alpine areas. Unlike many amphibians that are highly specialized in their habitat preferences, western toads are generalists and highly adaptable, capable of thriving in both lowland and mountain environments. They are often found near ponds, lakes, and slow-moving streams, where they breed during spring and early summer.

Breeding is one of the most impressive sights of the western toad's life cycle. During the breeding season, female toads lay long, gelatinous strings of eggs in shallow water, with each string containing thousands of eggs. Once hatched, the tadpoles swarm in large groups, developing into adult toads over the course of several months. Tadpoles are black and relatively easy to spot, often forming large aggregations in warm, shallow waters. Adult toads are less tied to water than other amphibians and will travel considerable distances to find suitable habitats, often moving far from their breeding sites into drier upland areas.

Western toads are nocturnal and most active during wet conditions, but they can sometimes be seen basking in the sun near water during the day. Their diet consists mainly of insects, spiders, and other small invertebrates, which they catch with their long, sticky tongues. Larger individuals may also consume small vertebrates, such as mice or smaller amphibians. Like other toads, western toads have parotid glands behind their eyes, which secrete a mild toxin that deters many predators.

Despite their adaptability, western toads have been experiencing significant population declines in some areas due to habitat loss, climate change, and the spread of diseases such as chytridiomycosis, which affects amphibians globally. These threats have prompted conservation efforts to protect the species, especially in regions where they have become rare.

Where to See Them

Western toads are found throughout Washington in a variety of habitats, from wetlands to forests and even urban areas. They are frequently spotted in the wetlands and ponds around Seattle, including areas like the Washington Park Arboretum and Discovery Park.

◄ A western toad blends right into its preferred wetlands habitat.

Dungeness Crab

Metacarcinus magister

The Dungeness crab is a true treasure of Seattle's coastal waters. Known for their delicious, delicate meat, these crabs are not only popular on the dinner plate but also play a crucial role in the ecosystems of Puget Sound. With their broad, hard shells and quick, agile movements, Dungeness crabs are perfectly suited for life on Seattle's sandy and muddy seabeds, and they contribute to the biodiversity of this region by balancing the populations of smaller marine organisms.

Named after the fishing town of Dungeness in Washington State, these crabs have a distinct, classic crab shape: a hard, reddish brown carapace with five pairs of legs, including one pair of powerful claws. Their shells can grow up to 10 inches across, making them one of the larger crabs in the Pacific Northwest.

They use their claws to catch prey and to defend themselves from predators, including larger fish, octopuses, and humans. Unlike some other marine species, Dungeness crabs are not particularly social; instead, they are solitary and often aggressive with each other, especially during the breeding season, when competition for mates is high.

Dungeness crabs are expert scavengers, feeding on a variety of organisms, including clams, fish, small shrimp, and plant material. They play a vital role as both predators and scavengers in Puget Sound, keeping populations of smaller creatures in check and contributing to the cleanliness of the ocean floor. Their feeding habits help maintain a balanced ecosystem, as they break down organic material and prevent the overpopulation of their prey. This balanced diet and their adaptability to various food sources allow Dungeness crabs to thrive in diverse coastal habitats around Seattle.

One of the quirkiest behaviors of the Dungeness crab is its molting process. Crabs must shed their old shells to grow, and this molting happens several times throughout their life. During this time, crabs are particularly vulnerable to predators, as their new shells take a few days to harden. For protection, they often bury themselves in the sand or mud and lie low until their new armor is ready. In addition to this molting behavior, Dungeness crabs are known to dig shallow pits in the seafloor, where they can hide from predators and wait for prey. These pits add to the diversity of the seafloor habitat, providing small shelters and contributing to the richness of Puget Sound's marine environment.

Where to See Them

Dungeness crabs are often spotted along Seattle's waterfront, especially near piers and marinas where they forage for food. During low tides, places like Golden Gardens and Alki Beach may reveal crabs in the shallow waters, though they're more often seen by those who enjoy crabbing or kayaking in deeper waters. For those interested in catching a glimpse or even trying their hand at crabbing, the piers at Edmonds and Shilshole Bay are popular spots for recreational crabbing, especially during summer and early fall when crabbing season opens.

Sea Anemone

Actiniaria

Seattle's tidal pools and rocky shores are home to some of the most enchanting and strange creatures in Puget Sound: sea anemones. Often mistaken for plants because of their bright colors and petal-like tentacles, sea anemones are actually carnivorous animals, closely related to jellyfish and corals. Their fascinating survival tactics, vibrant hues, and unique feeding behaviors make them some of the most memorable marine residents in Seattle's wild coastline.

With their tentacles waving gently in the water, sea anemones appear almost like underwater flowers, and their colors range from deep greens and rich purples to bright pinks and oranges. This vibrant coloration serves as both a lure and a warning to other marine creatures. The tentacles, though soft and delicate-looking, are covered with tiny stinging cells called *nematocysts*, which they use to capture prey. When a small fish or shrimp brushes against these tentacles, the anemone injects a paralyzing toxin, allowing it to slowly pull the prey into its central mouth. These stinging cells help sea anemones secure food and also deter potential predators, making them effective hunters in Seattle's intertidal ecosystem.

Anemones are highly adaptable, able to cling to rocks and other hard surfaces with a muscular "foot," or pedal disk, that allows them to stay anchored even when battered by waves. Some species, such as the giant green anemone, can survive in extreme conditions, from bright sunlight at low tide to the dark, cold depths of high tide. They are also resilient to changes in temperature and salinity, which makes them well suited to the fluctuating conditions of Puget Sound. This adaptability helps them thrive in Seattle's intertidal zones, where they often cluster in crevices and form colorful colonies.

One of the most intriguing behaviors of sea anemones is their ability to form symbiotic relationships. In Puget Sound, certain types of small fish and shrimp are immune to the anemone's sting, allowing them to live among the tentacles. This mutualistic arrangement provides protection for the smaller creatures, while the anemone benefits from the waste products of its "guests," which contain nutrients that can aid its growth. Additionally, some species of anemones will engage in "clone wars," where colonies of genetically identical anemones will fight neighboring colonies for territory, showcasing a surprisingly aggressive side to these otherwise stationary animals.

Where to See Them

Seattle's shores provide excellent viewing opportunities for these colorful creatures, especially during low tide. At places like Richmond Beach Saltwater Park, Discovery Park, and Alki Beach, anemones are often found tucked between rocks or nestled in tide pools, where they wait for small fish, crustaceans, or plankton to drift within reach. The Seattle Aquarium also features a variety of anemone species in its tide-pool exhibits, allowing visitors to get an up-close view of their unique feeding and movement behaviors.

For a more natural viewing experience, head to Carkeek Park or farther afield to

Deception Pass State Park, where the tidal pools are rich with anemones, sea stars, and other marine life. Summer is an ideal time for tide-pooling, as lower tides reveal a vibrant array of anemone species in the shallows.

Seattle's sea anemones are not only captivating to observe but also play a critical role in the marine ecosystem. By feeding on small fish and plankton, they contribute to the balance of Puget Sound's underwater community, and their symbiotic relationships highlight the intricate connections within the marine environment. Beautiful, resilient, and sometimes fierce, Seattle's sea anemones are a vivid reminder of the complex and colorful life just below the water's surface.

Sea Star

Asteroidea

Seattle's tide pools and rocky shorelines are home to a remarkable array of sea stars, also known as starfish. Though often overshadowed by flashier marine creatures, sea stars are fascinating and quirky residents of the Puget Sound, offering an up-close look at some of the ocean's more unusual behaviors and survival tactics. These slow-moving echinoderms are known for their striking colors, resilience, and unique anatomy, all of which play crucial roles in the delicate balance of Seattle's coastal ecosystem.

Sea stars are known for their vibrant hues—deep purples, vivid oranges, and rich reds—that stand out against the rocky backdrop of tide pools. This coloration serves as both a warning to predators and a camouflage, blending with coralline algae and anemones. Sea stars don't have a centralized brain or blood; instead, they move using a water

vascular system that powers tiny tube feet located on the underside of each arm. These tube feet allow sea stars to cling to rocks with a remarkable strength, holding steady against the powerful pull of tides.

One of the most remarkable traits of sea stars is their ability to regenerate lost arms—a skill that not only aids in escape from predators but also serves as a survival mechanism after injuries. This ability to regenerate extends to other parts of their body as well; certain species can regrow an entire new sea star from a single arm segment. The resilience of sea stars is further exemplified by their diverse diets. Many species, like the ochre sea star, are keystone predators that feed on mussels and barnacles, helping prevent these populations from monopolizing space on rocky surfaces. This predatory role makes sea stars essential for maintaining biodiversity in tide-pool habitats, allowing a variety of species to coexist.

Sea stars feed in a way that might seem strange to human observers. They use their tube feet to pry open the shells of mussels and clams, and then, in a fascinating process, extend their stomachs out through their mouths to digest the prey outside of their bodies. This unique adaptation allows sea stars to consume large prey despite their relatively small mouths, enabling them to impact the population dynamics of other intertidal species.

Where to See Them

Seattle offers many places to catch a glimpse of these vibrant tide-pool dwellers. Discovery Park, Lincoln Park, and Richmond Beach are all excellent locations for tide-pooling, especially during low tide, when sea stars are most visible. In these locations, look for rocky outcrops and tidal pools where sea stars cling to surfaces or tuck themselves into crevices to avoid drying out in the sun.

For a more guided experience, visit the Seattle Aquarium, where tide-pool exhibits allow visitors to interact with sea stars up close. Alternatively, farther afield, Deception Pass State Park and the shores of the San Juan Islands also provide rich tide-pool habitats with diverse sea star species visible among anemones, crabs, and other marine life.

Yellow Shore Crab

Hemigrapsus oregonensis

Small but mighty, the yellow shore crab is one of Seattle's most abundant and adaptable coastal creatures. Often overlooked due to its small size, this feisty crab thrives in the intertidal zones of Puget Sound, bringing a splash of color and activity to Seattle's beaches and rocky shorelines. Known for its resilience and agility, the yellow shore crab plays an important role in the marine ecosystem, making it a valuable, if understated, part of Seattle's wild shoreline.

Measuring only about an inch across, the yellow shore crab's carapace ranges from greenish yellow to pale brown, often mottled with darker spots. Their compact, rounded bodies and short, sturdy legs make them highly effective in Seattle's rocky tidal pools, where they squeeze into crevices and cling to rocks to avoid waves and predators. Their coloration also provides excellent camouflage, allowing them to blend with their surroundings and evade the watchful eyes of predators such as seabirds and larger fish.

One of the crab's most distinctive features is its claw behavior. Unlike some crabs, the yellow shore crab's claws are relatively small, allowing it to focus on scavenging rather than overpowering large prey. Using these claws, it nimbly picks through sand, algae, and small rocks in search of food. Yellow shore crabs are

omnivorous and highly opportunistic, feeding on algae, detritus, tiny crustaceans, and even carrion. This adaptable diet enables them to thrive in varied conditions and contributes to their reputation as "cleaners" of the tide pools, where they help break down organic matter and maintain a balanced ecosystem.

Yellow shore crabs are also highly social, often seen clustering together in cracks and crevices along the shoreline. During low tide, they may be found scurrying around in groups, exhibiting a surprising amount of activity for such a small creature. This social behavior, along with their hardiness, makes them an excellent indicator of tide-pool health. In fact, when yellow shore crab populations are strong, it often signifies that local tide pools are flourishing and capable of supporting a diverse array of species.

One of the quirkiest behaviors of the yellow shore crab is its ability to survive out of water for extended periods, provided it stays moist. When the tide goes out, these crabs can be seen "climbing" along rocks and even venturing onto damp sand. This unique adaptability has enabled them to take advantage of both marine and terrestrial resources, giving them a competitive edge in the ever-shifting intertidal zones of Puget Sound.

Where to See Them

Seattle's beaches are ideal for spotting these small but fascinating creatures, especially during low tide. Alki Beach, Carkeek Park, and Golden Gardens are popular locations where yellow shore crabs can be found hiding under rocks or nestled in tidal pools. Richmond Beach Saltwater Park and Discovery Park also provide excellent tide-pooling areas, where children and adults alike can observe these crabs darting around in search of food or hiding from larger animals.

Fish

Seattle's Salmon: Chinook, Coho, Sockeye, Pink, and Chum

In Seattle, few creatures hold as much cultural, ecological, and even culinary significance as salmon. Year in and year out, Chinook, coho, sockeye, pink, and chum salmon return to the rivers, lakes, and streams of the Lake Washington watershed, journeying through the Chittenden Locks in the Ballard neighborhood. These wild fish are more than just a marvel to observe; they are a testament to Seattle's unique connection to the natural world and an essential thread in the intricate tapestry of the Pacific Northwest's ecosystem.

The Chinook: King of Salmon

Also known as "king salmon" for its size and regal importance, Chinook salmon are the largest salmon species to pass through the Lake Washington watershed. Growing up to 40 pounds, they are famed for their rich, flavorful flesh and are highly prized both by humans and their natural predators. But more than their culinary appeal, Chinook are integral to the health of local ecosystems. They play a critical role as a food source for Seattle's beloved southern resident orcas, whose survival largely depends on the abundance of these hefty fish.

The life cycle of Chinook salmon is a remarkable feat of endurance and instinct. Hatched in the cold, gravel beds of rivers and streams, young Chinook spend their early lives in fresh water before migrating to the open ocean. Here, they spend up to five years maturing before beginning their journey home—a journey that takes them from the ocean, up Puget Sound, and finally through the Chittenden Locks into Lake Washington. From there, they move into the Cedar River, their primary spawning grounds within the watershed. Each fall, Seattle residents gather at viewing areas along the Locks to watch these magnificent fish leap and struggle against the current, a visible display of nature's resilience.

Coho Salmon:
The Resilient Acrobat

Coho, or "silver salmon," are known for their leaping ability and feisty behavior. While smaller than Chinook, coho are fierce fighters, darting through rivers and streams with remarkable speed and agility. Their acrobatic prowess makes them popular among sport fishers, but beyond their recreational appeal, coho are essential contributors to the ecosystem. As they decay after spawning, their nutrient-rich bodies help fertilize the riverbanks, nourishing trees, plants, and ultimately the entire watershed.

The life cycle of coho salmon begins in the smaller tributaries and streams connected to the Lake Washington watershed. These juveniles spend up to a year in fresh water, developing strength before heading to the Pacific. After one or two years in the ocean, they return to Seattle's waters, often arriving in late summer and early fall. Passing through the Chittenden Locks, they continue to Lake Washington and beyond, heading to their spawning sites in the Cedar River and Bear Creek. Coho salmon have shown resilience to changes in water flow and temperature, adapting to a more urbanized environment in ways other salmon struggle to. However, coho still face significant challenges due to habitat loss, pollution, and the warming waters of Puget Sound.

Sockeye Salmon:
The Colorful Nomad

Perhaps the most visually striking of Seattle's salmon species, sockeye salmon are famous for their vivid red coloration during spawning. Also called "red salmon," their unique appearance has earned them a special place in Seattle's salmon-watching spots. Sockeye differ from Chinook and coho in that they

require lakes for part of their life cycle, making the Lake Washington watershed one of the few urban areas where they can be observed in such numbers.

Sockeye begin life in lakes rather than streams. After hatching, young sockeye spend one to three years in freshwater lakes, such as Lake Washington, where they feed on plankton before heading to the ocean. Like other salmon, they eventually return to their birthplace to spawn. However, sockeye face the added challenge of passing through the Chittenden Locks, which connect Lake Washington to Puget Sound. Here, the narrow fish ladder at the Locks is crucial, allowing these lake-reliant salmon a safe passage through Seattle's urban landscape.

Each summer, Seattleites can witness sockeye gathering near the Locks, where their transformation from silvery ocean fish to brilliant red spawners is on full display. Their striking color change serves as an invitation to mates and a visible reminder of the mysterious transformations these fish undergo on their journey.

Pink Salmon: The People's Salmon

Pink salmon, also known as "humpies" for the pronounced hump that males develop during spawning, are the smallest and most abundant salmon species in Seattle's waters. Averaging 3 to 5 pounds, pinks may not have the size or rich flesh of Chinook, but they are highly valued for their accessibility and rapid life cycle. Their importance in the ecosystem lies in their sheer numbers; during odd-numbered years when pink salmon return to spawn, Puget Sound becomes a bustling habitat of fish and predators. This biennial return draws a wide range of wildlife, including seabirds, bears, and seals, all of which rely on the plentiful pink salmon for sustenance.

Pink salmon follow a straightforward, two-year life cycle, making them unique among salmon species in Seattle. Hatched in gravel beds along the lower sections of rivers, young pinks quickly migrate to the ocean, where they grow and mature over the next eighteen months. When they return to fresh water to spawn, they travel up Puget Sound and into Seattle's river systems, where they complete their life cycle. Their brief yet prolific presence makes each odd-year return a major ecological event. Seattle residents and visitors can view these determined fish at the Chittenden Locks or at places like the Duwamish River, where pink salmon gather in massive numbers, creating a vibrant scene of life and motion that underscores the resilience of Pacific Northwest salmon.

Chum Salmon: The Unsung Hero

Among Seattle's salmon species, the chum salmon, or *Oncorhynchus keta*, often flies under the radar compared to its more famous counterparts. Known for their ability to thrive in diverse habitats, chum salmon play a vital role in Seattle's freshwater and marine ecosystems. Unlike Chinook and coho, which prefer deep, fast-flowing waters for spawning, chum are less particular about spawning habitats, often choosing slower, shallow streams or gravel beds near river mouths. This flexibility allows chum to spawn in locations where other salmon species may not venture, contributing to genetic diversity and helping stabilize salmon populations overall.

Chum salmon are also notable for their role in nutrient cycling. As they complete their life cycle and die after spawning, their decaying bodies release nutrients like nitrogen and phosphorus back into the ecosystem. These nutrients feed the soil, benefiting plants, trees, and other organisms in the watershed. Chum, sometimes known as "dog salmon" due to their distinctive, canine-like teeth that develop during spawning, also differ from other salmon in their lower fat content, which makes them less of a target for sport fishing. However, they are highly valued by Native communities and commercial fisheries, contributing to

▲ Sockeye and Chinook salmon returning to spawn, as seen through the fish-ladder viewing window at Ballard's Chittenden Locks.

the cultural and economic landscape of the Pacific Northwest.

Chum salmon begin their lives in Seattle's rivers and streams, such as those feeding into Lake Washington and Puget Sound. Unlike species that spend significant time in fresh water, chum juveniles migrate to the ocean soon after hatching, spending minimal time in fresh water. This early migration strategy, known as "fry migration," reduces competition with other salmon species for freshwater resources and minimizes predation risks for young chum. In the ocean, chum spend between two and five years maturing before making their way back to their natal streams to spawn.

In late fall, chum salmon return to Seattle's freshwater bodies through the Ballard Locks and nearby tributaries. Their presence signals the end of the spawning season and is a popular attraction for Seattle residents, who often gather at viewing spots such as Piper's

Creek in Carkeek Park. As with other salmon, chum undergo significant physical changes as they prepare to spawn, with males developing large teeth and distinctive vertical bars along their bodies that range in color from green to purple. These transformations mark the end of their journey and serve as a visual testament to the power and endurance of Pacific Northwest salmon.

Chum salmon may not have the same status as Chinook or the visual impact of sockeye, but their presence in Seattle's waters is vital. Their adaptability, nutrient contributions, and role in stabilizing local salmon populations make them an unsung hero of Seattle's natural ecosystem.

Salmon's Connection to Seattle

The return of salmon is a cultural and environmental touchstone in Seattle. For generations, salmon have shaped the lives of the Coast Salish peoples, who have long understood the salmon's ecological and spiritual significance. The annual migrations of Chinook, coho, and sockeye are a reminder of Seattle's heritage and connection to the environment—a link that continues today as residents gather at places like the Chittenden Locks, also called the Ballard Locks, to witness these resilient fish return.

The Ballard Locks play a key role in supporting salmon migrations. Built in 1917 to link Lake Washington with Puget Sound, the Locks created a unique urban fish passage through which thousands of salmon pass each year. The fish ladder, a series of concrete steps and pools, allows salmon to navigate this engineered obstacle, and the viewing windows built into the ladder provide an educational platform for visitors. Watching these fish navigate the ladder is more than just a chance to see wildlife; it is an opportunity to connect with the cycles of nature that have continued in this region long before Seattle was a city.

Conservation Challenges and Efforts

The future of Seattle's salmon, however, is far from guaranteed. Urbanization, climate change, and pollution have created numerous challenges for these iconic fish. Increasing water temperatures in Puget Sound and local rivers can be deadly for salmon, as can toxins from road runoff, which impact coho particularly hard. Additionally, habitat degradation along the Lake Washington watershed has reduced the areas available for spawning, putting additional strain on already stressed populations.

In response, conservation efforts are underway to improve salmon habitat, reduce pollution, and restore riverbanks. Local organizations work alongside state agencies to plant native vegetation along waterways, which helps cool the water and provides safe habitats for young salmon. The Seattle community is also encouraged to use eco-friendly gardening practices and reduce chemical runoff, all of which contribute to creating a healthier habitat for salmon.

Seattle's Chinook, coho, sockeye, pink, and chum salmon are more than just fish; they are living symbols of resilience and an integral part of the region's identity. Each migration cycle from ocean to river echoes the wild pulse running beneath Seattle's urban landscape, a reminder to safeguard this natural heritage for generations to come.

Where to See Them

The Hiram M. Chittenden Locks features a fish ladder with viewing windows, allowing visitors to watch salmon navigate from Puget Sound to Lake Washington. Chinook are typically seen in August, coho in September, and sockeye from mid-June to mid-July.

Another great spot to see salmon spawning is Carkeek Park. Piper's Creek there is a prime destination to watch the fish jump obstacles in efforts to return to the patch of stream where they were born. Volunteer salmon stewards are often present during the peak of spawning season to provide information to the salmon-curious.

A little farther afield is the Cedar River, which starts high up in the Cascades and flows into the southern end of Lake Washington in Renton. In the late summer and fall, nature lovers can settle in at the Renton Library, built directly over the river, and watch the salmon spawn right below. Farther north, Bothell's North Creek is another lesser-known spot to catch some glimpses of the Pacific Northwest's favorite fish as they make their way to meet their maker.

Pacific Herring

Clupea pallasii

The Pacific herring is a small but essential fish in the ecosystems of Seattle and the broader Puget Sound region. Known for their silvery bodies and schooling behavior, these forage fish play a foundational role in the marine food web, connecting plankton to larger predators like salmon, seabirds, and marine mammals. Measuring 6 to 12 inches in length, Pacific herring are easily overlooked compared to the region's more iconic species, but their ecological importance cannot be overstated.

Pacific herring are a vital source of energy for countless marine species. Their diet primarily consists of plankton, which they filter from the water using their finely spaced gill rakers. By consuming vast amounts of plankton, herring convert microscopic organisms into a nutrient-rich food source for higher trophic levels. Chinook salmon, a critical species for southern resident orcas, depend heavily on herring as a food source, especially during key stages of their life cycle. Additionally, herring eggs and larvae provide sustenance for seabirds, crabs, and other fish, further underscoring their role as a cornerstone species in Seattle's marine ecosystems.

One of the most remarkable behaviors of Pacific herring is their mass spawning events,

which typically occur in late winter and early spring. Herring migrate to shallow, vegetated areas like eelgrass beds to spawn, depositing their adhesive eggs on submerged vegetation, rocks, and other surfaces. These spawning events attract a host of predators, creating a feeding frenzy that highlights herring's ecological significance. The eggs, known as roe, are prized not only by wildlife but also by humans, particularly in traditional Indigenous diets, where herring roe holds cultural and nutritional importance.

Pacific herring schools are an awe-inspiring sight, shimmering beneath the surface as their bodies reflect light in unison. This schooling behavior serves as a defense mechanism, as their numbers and synchronized movements confuse predators. Despite these natural defenses, herring populations face significant threats. Habitat degradation, climate change, pollution, and overfishing have all contributed to declines in herring abundance in some areas of Puget Sound. The loss of eelgrass beds, which serve as critical spawning habitats, has been particularly detrimental to herring populations near Seattle.

Efforts to restore and protect herring habitats are essential to maintaining healthy marine ecosystems in the region. Local conservation groups and government agencies are working to restore eelgrass beds, reduce water pollution, and implement sustainable fishing practices to support herring populations. Their recovery is not only crucial for the health of Puget Sound but also for the survival of iconic species like salmon and orcas that depend on herring for sustenance.

Where to See Them

Pacific herring are most often spotted in the shallow waters of Elliott Bay, especially near vegetated areas where eelgrass beds are present. During their spring spawning season, areas like Shilshole Bay and West Point in Discovery Park are excellent places to observe their shimmering schools and the bustling activity of predators drawn to their spawning events. Whether you're kayaking along Seattle's shoreline or watching from a ferry, Pacific herring reveal the intricate connections within the city's marine ecosystems, serving as a living reminder of the balance between predator and prey in the waters of Puget Sound.

Yellow Perch

Perca flavescens

Yellow perch, with their striking golden yellow bodies and bold black vertical stripes, are among the most recognizable fish in Seattle's freshwater ecosystems. Native to North America, these small, schooling fish are abundant in Lake Washington and other regional lakes, where their adaptability and resilience have made them a cornerstone of local aquatic ecosystems. Averaging 4 to 10 inches in length, yellow perch are prized by anglers for their tasty flesh and by predators for their abundance and accessibility.

Yellow perch are schooling fish, typically traveling in large groups that make them easy targets for anglers and predators alike. Their diet is diverse, ranging from zooplankton and aquatic insects to small fish, which they hunt with quick, darting movements. This varied diet allows yellow perch to thrive in a wide range of environments, from clear, deep waters to weedy shallows. Their opportunistic feeding behavior helps control insect and small-fish populations, playing an important role in maintaining the balance of the local ecosystem.

A unique characteristic of yellow perch is their rapid growth and reproduction. Females lay long, ribbon-like strings of eggs that are draped over submerged vegetation or structures in spring. These egg masses can contain tens of thousands of eggs, ensuring high reproductive potential. The young perch, or fry, grow quickly, forming dense schools that provide food for larger fish like bass, trout, and northern pikeminnow. This role as both predator and prey cements the yellow perch's importance in the food web, supporting a wide array of aquatic species in Seattle's lakes.

Despite their abundance, yellow perch face challenges in some parts of their range due to habitat changes and competition with invasive species. In Seattle's urbanized environment, water quality is a key factor influencing their success. Pollution, eutrophication, and the loss of aquatic vegetation can reduce suitable habitats for perch and the species they depend on for food. However, in healthy lake ecosystems like Lake Washington, yellow perch populations remain robust, highlighting the importance of conservation efforts to maintain water quality and aquatic habitats.

Yellow perch also provide significant recreational and cultural value. Their schooling behavior and predictable presence in shallow waters make them a favorite among local anglers, especially in summer when perch are most active. In addition to their role as a sport fish, perch are a key species in introducing new anglers, including children, to fishing, given their abundance and willingness to bite on baited hooks.

Where to See Them

Yellow perch are commonly found in the freshwater lakes of Seattle, with Lake Washington and Green Lake being prime spots for observation and fishing. They are most active during warmer months and can often be seen schooling near docks, piers, and the edges of aquatic vegetation. Whether viewed from a dock or caught on a fishing line, yellow perch offer a glimpse into the vibrant and interconnected aquatic ecosystems of Seattle's lakes, where they serve as both predators and prey in a thriving underwater world.

▲ A fisherman caught this yellow perch in Lake Washington, near Seattle in Kirkland's Juanita Bay.

Banana Slug

Ariolimax columbianus

Banana slugs are one of the Pacific Northwest's quirkiest and most captivating creatures. Known for their bright yellow coloring (though they can also be brown or greenish), these giant slugs can reach lengths of up to 10 inches, making them the second-largest terrestrial slug species in the world. While they may not inspire the same excitement as Seattle's marine or avian residents, banana slugs are essential to the local ecosystem, playing a vital role in forest health and nutrient cycling. In Seattle and surrounding areas, they are a unique find for curious hikers and nature enthusiasts.

The banana slug's signature bright yellow hue serves as both camouflage and a warning. Often found amid fallen leaves and damp forest-floor debris, they can blend with the environment due to their color, particularly under dappled sunlight. But it also warns predators that they produce a foul-tasting, numbing slime that deters most would-be diners. This mucus, or slime, is not just for defense. It helps them glide smoothly across rough surfaces, prevents dehydration, and even aids in reproduction, as slugs follow each other's slime trails to find mates.

One of the banana slug's defining traits is its diet. As a decomposer, it feeds on decaying plant material, fungi, and animal waste, breaking down organic matter into nutrients that enrich the soil. This makes them essential "forest recyclers," transforming waste into nutrient-rich soil that supports plant growth and sustains the forest ecosystem. Their activity enhances soil fertility and promotes

forest health, making banana slugs a keystone species in Pacific Northwest woodlands.

Banana slugs also have some unique biological traits. These slugs have both male and female reproductive organs and can reproduce alone if necessary, a trait known as *hermaphroditism* that ensures population resilience. Banana slugs prefer moist, cool environments, thriving in old-growth forests and damp woodlands. They are sensitive to habitat loss and climate changes that dry out forest floors, making conservation of their natural habitat essential to their survival.

Where to See Them

Seattle's surrounding parks and forests provide excellent opportunities to spot these fascinating creatures. Look for them along trails in damp woodlands, especially after rain, when they're most active. Discovery Park, Seward Park, and Carkeek Park are all excellent places within the city where banana slugs can be found in shaded forest areas.

Lewis' Moon Snail

Euspira lewisii

The moon snail, with its massive, spiraled shell and predatory instincts, is one of the Pacific Northwest's most fascinating beach dwellers. Known for their nearly hypnotic shells that can reach up to 6 inches across, moon snails are the giants of Seattle's sandy tidal zones. These carnivorous mollusks are more than just a striking sight on the beach; they play an essential role in the local marine ecosystem as active hunters and ecosystem engineers. For those who explore Seattle's shores, a moon snail encounter offers a glimpse into the hidden dynamics of life along the Puget Sound.

Moon snails have a smooth, round shell, usually in shades of pale brown or cream, which they carry on their muscular foot, an organ that can extend to more than twice the size of their shell. This foot helps the snail move along the sandy seabed and burrow deep into the substrate in search of prey. Moon snails are fierce predators of clams, a behavior that may surprise beachgoers familiar with the more herbivorous diets of smaller snails. Using a specialized mouthpart called a *radula*, moon snails bore perfectly round holes in clam shells to access the soft tissues inside, leaving empty shells scattered along the beach—a telltale sign of their presence.

The moon snail's diet makes it an important predator in the Puget Sound ecosystem, helping regulate clam populations. By preying on both abundant and invasive clam species, they maintain a balance in the intertidal zone, supporting biodiversity and preventing any one species from dominating. Although moon snails are themselves prey to some species of fish and seabirds, they are relatively well protected due to their large size and burrowing behavior.

One of the moon snail's most intriguing contributions to the ecosystem is its unique egg-laying process. During the breeding season, female moon snails produce large, rubbery egg collars that resemble sand rings. These collars are created by mixing sand with mucus and embedding thousands of tiny eggs within the structure. These sand collars are often found along Seattle's beaches, especially after low tide, and can sometimes be mistaken for a piece of discarded rubber tubing. These structures provide a temporary nursery where juvenile snails can develop within the safety of the sandy collar until they are ready to disperse, further supporting the moon snail population in the region.

Where to See Them

Seattle's tidal zones and sandy beaches offer prime locations for observing moon snails or their distinctive egg collars. Alki Beach, Golden Gardens, and Richmond Beach are ideal spots, especially during very low tides, when moon snails are more likely to be out hunting or resting on the sandy flats. Adventurous beachcombers may find empty shells with perfect round holes—the mark of a moon snail meal—or stumble upon the unusual egg collars scattered along the shore. The best time to visit is during summer's minus tides, when more of the intertidal zone is revealed, bringing moon snails and other sand-dwelling creatures into view.

Pacific Geoduck

Panopea generosa

Among Seattle's unique marine residents, the Pacific geoduck stands out as one of the most curious and storied. Known for its enormous, elongated siphon and deep burrowing habits, the geoduck (pronounced "gooey-duck") is the largest burrowing clam in the world and a fascinating member of the Puget Sound ecosystem. Although somewhat of a local celebrity due to its size and unusual appearance, this giant clam plays an essential role in maintaining the health and biodiversity of Seattle's coastal waters.

The Pacific geoduck can grow to weigh up to 3 pounds, with its siphon alone extending up to 3 feet beyond its shell. Unlike other clams, the geoduck's siphon cannot retract into its shell, giving it a unique, striking look. This siphon, which protrudes from the sand like an underwater periscope, is used to filter-feed, drawing in water to extract plankton and other microscopic organisms. The geoduck filters massive amounts of water daily, contributing to water quality by reducing suspended particles and excess nutrients, thus helping balance the ecosystem in the soft, sandy seafloor of Puget Sound.

Geoducks are incredibly long-lived, with some specimens believed to be over 100 years old, a lifespan that has earned them the title of one of the longest-living animals in the Pacific Northwest. Their longevity is partly due to their low predation risk: buried up to 3 feet deep, they are protected from many natural predators. However, moon snails, sea stars, and certain fish species have evolved to extract geoducks from the sediment, maintaining a delicate predator-prey balance within Seattle's underwater ecosystems.

One of the quirkiest aspects of geoduck behavior is their burrowing and feeding method. Using their muscular foot, juvenile geoducks burrow deep into the sediment, where they remain for life. The deeper they burrow, the more secure they are, making them challenging to extract by predators and, later, by human harvesters. This deep-seated

lifestyle and filter-feeding habit have led to geoducks being nicknamed "filtering giants of the Sound."

Geoducks have become a symbol of Pacific Northwest cuisine, highly valued for their sweet, briny meat in both local and international markets. In fact, geoduck farming is a growing industry in Washington state, where sustainable practices are used to cultivate these clams without depleting wild populations. This sustainable harvesting plays a role in Seattle's coastal economy and helps support awareness about the importance of maintaining balanced marine ecosystems.

Where to See Them

Because of their deep-burrowing nature, Pacific geoducks are rarely seen by casual beachgoers. However, their presence can sometimes be noted by observing "geoduck holes" in the sand, typically identifiable by small jets of water that spurt from the holes during low tide. For those eager to learn more, the Seattle Aquarium occasionally features exhibits and educational programs that showcase geoducks and other bivalves, shedding light on their ecology and impact on Puget Sound.

Adventurous locals and visitors can participate in licensed geoduck harvesting tours offered in nearby areas, like Hood Canal, where geoduck digging is a popular activity. With a guide, participants get a hands-on look at the effort required to extract these deep-burrowing clams and learn about the geoduck's significance to the Pacific Northwest.

Fly Agaric

Amanita muscaria

The fly agaric mushroom, with its iconic red cap speckled with white spots, is one of the most recognizable mushrooms in Seattle's forests. Often depicted in fairy tales and folklore, this striking mushroom adds an otherworldly charm to Seattle's woodlands, especially in autumn. While its bright colors are captivating, the fly agaric is known for its toxic and hallucinogenic properties, giving it a reputation as both a mystical and dangerous forest resident. Despite this, it plays an essential role in the local ecosystem, supporting trees and soil health in the Pacific Northwest.

Fly agarics are large, easily recognizable mushrooms with caps that can grow up to 12 inches across. The signature red or orange cap with white "warts" is both a warning to predators and a signal to foragers that this mushroom is not for eating. Containing psychoactive compounds like muscimol and ibotenic acid, the fly agaric can be toxic if consumed, causing hallucinations, nausea, and other effects. While traditionally used in shamanic rituals by some Indigenous cultures, it is generally considered unsafe to consume, especially without extensive preparation.

Despite its toxicity, the fly agaric is beneficial to Seattle's forest ecosystem. This mushroom forms a symbiotic relationship with trees, particularly conifers, by connecting to their roots through a network of fungal filaments known as mycorrhizae. Through this underground network, the fly agaric exchanges nutrients with its host tree, supplying water and minerals in exchange for sugars produced by the tree's photosynthesis. This partnership not only supports the tree's health but also contributes to the stability of the forest floor,

► The visually stunning fly agaric mushroom, named for its insecticidal properties, might trigger hallucinations if you consume it, but it might also kill you.

as mycorrhizal networks improve soil structure and nutrient cycling. The fly agaric's role as a mycorrhizal fungus makes it an essential part of the Pacific Northwest's forest ecology, helping maintain the health of wooded areas around Seattle.

The fly agaric also provides habitat and sustenance for various small forest creatures. Slugs and certain insects, immune to its toxins, feed on its flesh, while small mammals often use the mushroom as cover on the forest floor. Although not as directly involved in decomposition as some fungi, the fly agaric's presence supports a range of forest interactions, fostering biodiversity in Seattle's woodlands.

Fly agarics are not considered endangered, as they are widely distributed across the Northern Hemisphere, thriving in coniferous and mixed forests. Their resilience and adaptability to different climates and soil types make them a common sight in Seattle's woodlands, and they face no significant conservation threats. However, like many forest organisms, they benefit from the preservation of natural habitats and minimal disturbance of forest soils.

Where to See Them

In Seattle, fly agarics can be found in wooded parks and forests, particularly in areas dominated by conifers like fir and pine trees. Discovery Park, Seward Park, Magnuson Park, and the Washington Park Arboretum are excellent locations to spot these mushrooms during the fall months when they are most abundant. Their bright red caps stand out against the damp, earthy tones of the forest floor, making them relatively easy to find in shaded, moist areas.

Old Man's Beard Lichen

Usnea longissima

Old man's beard lichen, known for its delicate, hanging strands and pale green color, is one of the most intriguing and graceful organisms found in Seattle's forests. Resembling wisps of beard or Spanish moss, it drapes over tree branches and shrubs, creating an enchanting, almost mystical appearance in the Pacific Northwest's misty woodlands. Though it may look like a plant, old man's beard lichen is actually a combination of fungi and algae, working together to survive and thrive in one of the region's most unique partnerships.

It is easily recognized by its hair-like tufts that range from a few inches to nearly a foot in length, has a soft, springy texture, and is highly flexible, allowing it to sway with the wind and rain that Seattle's forests experience year-round. This lichen grows slowly but can live for decades, clinging to tree branches without harming its host. As an epiphyte, old man's beard relies on the air around it to absorb water and nutrients, which means it is highly sensitive to air quality. Because it requires clean, unpolluted air to thrive, the presence of beard lichen is often a sign of a healthy, low-pollution environment.

One of the unique roles of old man's beard in Seattle's ecosystem is its function as a bioindicator. Due to its sensitivity to air pollutants, beard lichen acts as a natural gauge for air quality; when air-pollution levels rise, it is often one of the first organisms to decline. This makes it an invaluable indicator for scientists studying environmental health and conservationists working to protect Seattle's natural spaces. The presence of lush, thriving beard lichen signals a clean, balanced ecosystem, while its absence can be an early warning of pollution-related issues.

It also plays a significant ecological role by providing shelter and nesting materials for birds, insects, and small mammals. Birds often use strands of it to line their nests, creating warm, insulated spaces for their

eggs and young. Certain insect species live exclusively within lichen tufts, finding refuge from predators and the elements. By offering food, shelter, and nesting material, beard lichen supports a micro-ecosystem of small organisms, reinforcing the complex web of life in Seattle's forests.

Old man's beard lichen has been used traditionally for its medicinal properties, particularly as an antimicrobial agent. Some Indigenous cultures have utilized *Usnea* as a remedy for infections and as a wound dressing, a practice based on its unique chemical compounds. While its medicinal uses have gained modern attention, it's important to remember that lichen grows slowly, and overharvesting can harm local populations, so conservation-minded practices are encouraged.

Where to See Them

Seattle's temperate rainforests provide ideal conditions for old man's beard lichen, which thrives in cool, damp, and shaded areas. Discovery Park, Seward Park, and the Washington Park Arboretum are excellent spots to observe it hanging from branches and shrubs. In these locations, it forms dense tufts on trees, especially in mossy, undisturbed areas.

Turkey-Tail Mushroom

Trametes versicolor

The turkey-tail mushroom, with its layered, fan-shaped caps and vivid bands of color, is one of Seattle's most distinctive fungi, bringing earthy charm to the city's woodlands and shaded parks. Known for its resemblance to a turkey's tail, this mushroom adds visual intrigue to Seattle's forests, growing on fallen logs, stumps, and decaying wood. Beyond its appearance, the turkey-tail mushroom is a crucial part of the local ecosystem, playing a vital role in nutrient recycling and forest health.

Turkey-tail mushrooms are named for their vibrant rings of color, which can include shades of brown, orange, blue, gray, and white. These colorful bands serve as camouflage, blending with the forest floor and fallen leaves. The mushroom's velvety texture and overlapping, shelf-like growth pattern add to its unique look, making it a favorite for foragers and nature photographers alike. Despite its appeal, turkey-tail is not considered edible due to its tough, leathery texture; however, it has a long history of medicinal use in teas and supplements, valued for its potential immune-boosting properties.

This mushroom is a decomposer, feeding on deadwood and breaking it down into nutrients that return to the soil. As they decompose, turkey-tail mushrooms release vital nutrients like nitrogen and phosphorus, enriching the forest floor and supporting new plant growth. Their role as decomposers makes turkey-tail mushrooms an essential part of Seattle's forest ecosystem, helping create

▼ Turkey-tail mushrooms are wood decomposers and contain medicinal compounds known to boost immunity.

rich, fertile soil that sustains the next generation of trees and plants. In this way, turkey-tail mushrooms act as nature's recyclers, turning decay into life and maintaining the health of Seattle's wooded areas.

Turkey-tail mushrooms also provide habitat for various small organisms. Insects, fungi-feeding beetles, and microscopic life-forms often inhabit these mushrooms, creating a mini-ecosystem within the mushroom itself. By providing shelter and a food source for these smaller species, turkey-tail mushrooms support biodiversity in Seattle's forests, reinforcing the intricate web of life that defines these habitats.

Though common in the Pacific Northwest, turkey-tail mushrooms face challenges from habitat loss and urban expansion. Preserving forested areas is essential for the survival of fungi like turkey-tail, which rely on decaying wood and undisturbed ecosystems to thrive. Fortunately, turkey-tail is resilient and widely distributed, with no immediate conservation concerns. In fact, its presence is often seen as an indicator of a healthy forest ecosystem.

Where to See Them

Turkey-tail mushrooms can be found in Seattle's moist, shaded woodlands, particularly where there is an abundance of fallen logs and decaying wood. Discovery Park, Seward Park, and the Washington Park Arboretum are excellent places to find these mushrooms throughout the year. Turkey-tail is especially noticeable in autumn, as the damp, cool weather encourages fungal growth and the forest floor becomes dotted with colorful turkey-tail clusters.

White Crustose Lichen

Lecanora, *Pertusaria*, and other genera

The white crustose lichen, often found in Seattle's urban and forested landscapes, is one of nature's most resilient yet understated organisms. Distinguished by its pale, crust-like appearance, white crustose lichen adheres tightly to rock surfaces, tree bark, and even concrete walls, adding a quiet, chalky layer to Seattle's natural scenery. This hardy lichen might go unnoticed due to its modest look, but it plays a crucial role in the ecosystem, supporting air quality and biodiversity in Seattle's temperate climate.

White crustose lichen, like all lichens, is a symbiotic partnership between fungi and algae (or sometimes cyanobacteria). The fungi provide a protective structure, while the algae photosynthesize, producing energy that sustains both organisms. This collaboration enables white crustose lichen to endure in exposed, nutrient-poor environments where other plants would struggle to survive. Unlike leafy or tufted lichens, crustose lichens grow flat against their substrate, forming a thin, rock-like crust. They often appear in shades of white, gray, or light blue, sometimes marked with fine cracks, resembling a layer of dry paint or chalk.

One of the most remarkable aspects of white crustose lichen is its extreme resilience. This lichen can withstand harsh conditions, including prolonged exposure to sunlight, rain, and wind. Due to its slow growth rate—often less than a millimeter per year—it can live for decades, and some species are even considered among the oldest living organisms on Earth. In Seattle, white crustose lichen is commonly found on tree bark, rock faces, and buildings, providing an essential ecological service by contributing to soil formation. As it grows, the lichen gradually breaks down the surface of the substrate, helping create soil particles over time.

White crustose lichen is also a bioindicator, meaning its health and presence indicate the quality of air in its environment. Sensitive to pollutants like sulfur dioxide, these lichens flourish in areas with clean air, while pollution causes them to decline. Observing healthy populations of white crustose lichen in Seattle's parks and urban spaces suggests relatively low levels of air pollution, providing a natural measure of environmental health.

Although white crustose lichen might not provide shelter like tufted lichens, it still contributes to the local ecosystem by supporting other small organisms. Tiny invertebrates, such as mites and springtails, feed on the organic material within lichen layers, helping support the base of the food web in Seattle's green spaces. These small, unassuming organisms play a part in nutrient cycling and contribute to the delicate balance of life on forest floors and urban surfaces alike.

Where to See Them

White crustose lichens are common throughout Seattle, found in nearly every green space where there are rocks, tree bark, or bare soil. Discovery Park, Seward Park, and the Washington Park Arboretum are excellent locations to observe this hardy lichen up close, particularly on older tree trunks and rocky outcrops. Its chalky crust is especially visible on granite or limestone rocks and can be seen along trails and on exposed tree trunks.

◄ White crustose lichen is a common sight on one of Seattle's most common trees, the red alder.

Trees and Shrubs

Bigleaf Maple

Acer macrophyllum

The bigleaf maple, named for its remarkably large leaves that can each span over a foot across, is one of Seattle's most captivating and ecologically vital trees. Found throughout the Pacific Northwest, this deciduous tree thrives in Seattle's mild, rainy climate and is often seen in parks, forests, and along city streets.

With its broad canopy, mossy bark, and golden fall color, the bigleaf maple provides shade, supports biodiversity, and plays a critical role in Seattle's natural ecosystems.

One of the most distinctive features of the bigleaf maple is its leaves—the largest of any native maple in North America. Each leaf has

▼ A bigleaf maple at Seward Park thrives against a backdrop of evergreen trees.

five deeply lobed segments and can grow up to 12 inches wide, creating a lush canopy that provides essential shade in Seattle's forests. In autumn, the tree transforms as its leaves turn shades of yellow and gold, carpeting the forest floor with a blanket of foliage that nourishes the soil as it decomposes. The tree's thick branches and broad leaves make it a favored choice for animals seeking shelter, from nesting birds to squirrels and insects.

Bigleaf maples are especially known for the diverse ecosystem they host on their bark. The moist Pacific Northwest climate encourages a rich growth of mosses, ferns, and lichens on the tree's trunk and branches. These epiphytes do not harm the tree but rather coexist with it, creating a micro-ecosystem that provides food, shelter, and nesting materials for insects, birds, and small mammals. This unique layer of mossy greenery not only adds visual character to Seattle's forests but also supports the city's urban wildlife in surprising ways.

In addition to its role in local habitats, the bigleaf maple is valued for its adaptability and soil-enhancing properties. Its leaves break down quickly, returning nutrients like calcium and potassium to the soil and supporting the growth of other plants. Bigleaf maples are also known for their resilience, growing in various soil types and recovering well after disturbances. This adaptability makes them a common sight in Seattle's green spaces, where they often populate riverbanks, slopes, and even reclaimed urban areas.

The bigleaf maple also holds cultural significance in the Pacific Northwest. Indigenous peoples have long used the wood and bark of the tree to make tools, utensils, and woven materials. Its wood, which has a unique, curly grain pattern, is still prized for furniture, musical instruments, and crafts today. Some even tap bigleaf maples to produce a mild, sweet syrup, adding to the tree's value as a resource.

While bigleaf maples are abundant, they face challenges from climate change and diseases such as "maple decline," a condition affecting the health and growth of trees in the region. Conservation efforts that maintain healthy soil, reduce pollution, and protect natural habitats are essential for supporting the long-term health of Seattle's bigleaf maples and their ecosystems.

Where to See Them

Bigleaf maples are easy to find throughout Seattle's parks and natural areas. Discovery Park, Seward Park, and the Washington Park Arboretum all feature these towering trees, especially along trails where their canopy offers cool shade in summer and vibrant color in fall. The trees' moss-laden trunks add to the charm of these parks, making them popular spots for nature walks and photography.

Bull Kelp

Nereocystis luetkeana

Bull kelp, with its towering stalks and floating bulbs, is a foundational species in the Pacific Northwest's coastal waters and plays a crucial role in Seattle's marine ecosystems. Known for its impressive size and unique appearance, bull kelp forms underwater forests that provide habitat, food, and protection for a variety of marine life. These kelp forests are essential to Seattle's coastal health, supporting biodiversity, stabilizing the shoreline, and contributing to the local environment in ways that are visible just below the surface of the Puget Sound.

Bull kelp is easily recognized by its long, flexible stipes (stalks) that can grow up to 100 feet, reaching from the seabed up to the water's surface. At the top of each stalk is a gas-filled bulb, or pneumatocyst, that keeps the kelp floating upright and allows the fronds to spread out and absorb sunlight near the surface. The kelp's fronds create a dense canopy that shades and shelters the underwater ecosystem, offering a protected environment where fish, crustaceans, and invertebrates can thrive.

In Seattle's coastal waters, bull kelp forests serve as essential habitat for countless species, from tiny plankton to larger fish like rockfish and salmon. The kelp's dense canopy and towering stalks create vertical structure and cover, attracting animals that use it for feeding, hiding, and breeding. Young fish find shelter in the kelp forests, safe from larger predators, while crabs, sea urchins, and sea stars live among the kelp's stipes and feed on the detritus that accumulates within these dense underwater groves. Seabirds, otters, and seals are also frequent visitors to kelp beds, hunting and foraging in this rich marine habitat.

Bull kelp is more than just a habitat provider; it also plays an essential role in maintaining coastal health. Through photosynthesis, bull kelp absorbs carbon dioxide and releases oxygen, improving water quality and reducing the effects of ocean acidification. Additionally, bull kelp's strong, anchoring holdfasts stabilize the seafloor, helping reduce erosion along shorelines and create a buffer that protects coastlines from the impact of waves. This stabilization is particularly valuable in regions like Seattle, where tides and currents can erode coastal areas.

While bull kelp is a naturally resilient species, it faces challenges from climate change, pollution, and warming ocean temperatures. Changes in water temperature and quality have contributed to a decline in kelp populations in some areas of the Pacific Northwest. Conservation efforts, including monitoring programs and the creation of marine protected areas, aim to preserve and restore these vital kelp forests. In Seattle, local conservation groups work to raise awareness about the importance of kelp ecosystems and to protect this essential resource.

▲ While kelp populations have seen significant declines over the last several decades, bull kelp seems to be thriving in Seattle's Elliott Bay, possibly due to the presence of artificial structures that provide suitable substrates for attachment. Ongoing research and conservation efforts aim to understand these patterns and support kelp recovery in Puget Sound.

Where to See Them

Bull kelp forests can be observed along Seattle's coastlines and are especially visible at low tide, when their floating bulbs and fronds can be seen on the water's surface. Alki Beach, Golden Gardens, and the shores of West Seattle offer some of the best spots for seeing kelp beds from shore, especially during calm days when the water is clear. Kayakers and divers exploring Puget Sound can experience kelp forests up close, gliding over or diving down to observe the rich, hidden life within.

Bull kelp's role in Seattle's coastal ecosystems as a habitat provider, carbon sink, and stabilizing force underscores its importance to the health of the Puget Sound. These underwater forests remind us of the interconnectedness of marine life and the ways in which even unseen habitats contribute to the vibrancy and resilience of Seattle's natural environment.

Devil's Club

Oplopanax horridus

Devil's club, with its sprawling spiny stems and broad, maple-like leaves, is one of Seattle's most formidable and fascinating plants. Known for its striking appearance and protective nature, this thorny shrub is a staple in the Pacific Northwest's moist forests and wetlands. Found in Seattle's natural areas and extending north through Alaskan rainforests, devil's club adds a distinct character to the region's landscapes, supporting wildlife and playing a unique role in Seattle's ecosystem.

Devil's club is instantly recognizable by its large, lobed leaves, which can grow up to a foot wide, and the intimidating spines that cover its stems and leaf veins. The plant's sharp, barbed thorns are a defense mechanism, deterring animals and people alike from getting too close. In late spring, devil's club produces clusters of small white flowers that resemble delicate umbrellas. These flowers give way to bright red berries in late summer, which are visually striking but inedible for humans, as they are toxic. The berries, however, are an important food source for birds and small mammals, which are unaffected by the plant's toxicity.

Devil's club thrives in Seattle's shaded, damp forests, particularly in low-lying areas

▶ Devil's club, although pesky to hikers, plays an important role in terms of ecosystem services, as it stabilizes soils and helps the forest recover from both natural disturbances, such as landslides or blowdowns, and human incursions like logging.

near streams, wetlands, and boggy soil. It grows well in these moist, nutrient-rich environments, where its extensive root system stabilizes soil along riverbanks and slopes, preventing erosion. By helping anchor the soil, devil's club supports the health of Seattle's riparian ecosystems and maintains water quality in the surrounding environment. Its presence is a good indicator of an intact, healthy wetland or forest understory, as the plant requires a stable, moist habitat to thrive.

The dense growth and thorns of devil's club provide excellent shelter for wildlife. Birds and small mammals use the plant's broad leaves and thorny branches as cover, creating a natural refuge within the forest understory. The berries, though toxic to humans, are a valuable food source for birds, which help disperse the seeds throughout the forest. In this way, devil's club contributes to both local biodiversity and the natural regeneration of Seattle's wild spaces.

In addition to its ecological importance, devil's club holds deep cultural significance for Indigenous peoples of the Pacific Northwest, who have long respected the plant for its medicinal and spiritual qualities. The roots and inner bark have been used in traditional medicine for a variety of ailments, including pain relief, arthritis, and infections. The plant is considered sacred in many Indigenous cultures, where it is used in spiritual practices and ceremonies. Though powerful, devil's club requires careful handling due to its sharp spines and potent properties.

While devil's club is not considered endangered, it faces some threats from habitat disturbance and urban development, which can disrupt the wetland and riparian zones it depends on. Conservation efforts aimed at protecting wetlands and streamside habitats help ensure that devil's club continues to thrive in Seattle's forests and beyond.

Where to See Them

In Seattle, devil's club can be found in several parks with moist, shaded forest environments. Seward Park, Discovery Park, and Carkeek Park all offer opportunities to observe this striking plant in its natural habitat, particularly along stream beds and wetland areas. Its large leaves and thorny stems make it easy to spot along shaded trails, but it's wise to admire devil's club from a distance to avoid its sharp spines.

Douglas Fir

Pseudotsuga menziesii

The Douglas fir is one of the most iconic trees in Seattle and throughout the Pacific Northwest, standing tall in the region's forests and city parks. Known for its towering height, rugged bark, and distinctive cones, the Douglas fir is not only a visual symbol of the Northwest but also an essential player in the local ecosystem. With some trees reaching heights of more than 250 feet and lifespans stretching beyond 500 years, Douglas firs are impressive giants that sustain and shelter a variety of life.

One of the most distinguishing characteristics of the Douglas fir is its thick, rough bark, which is highly resistant to fire. This resilience has allowed it to thrive in forests where fires periodically clear out smaller vegetation, giving the Douglas fir a competitive edge. The tree's cones are also unique, featuring bracts that resemble tiny "mouse tails" peeking out from between the cone scales—a quirky detail that makes Douglas fir cones easy to identify.

Douglas fir trees play a crucial role in Seattle's ecosystem by supporting diverse plant and animal communities. Their dense canopies offer shade and regulate temperature and humidity on the forest floor, creating a stable environment for shade-tolerant plants,

▲ Douglas firs are the dominant trees in a mature ancient- or second-growth forest, not to mention many backyards in and around Seattle.

mosses, and lichens to grow. The tree's thick foliage provides essential cover and nesting sites for birds, while mammals like squirrels and chipmunks rely on the seeds from the cones for food. As the tree ages, it may develop cavities that serve as nesting sites for birds, bats, and insects, creating a layered habitat that supports numerous species.

In addition to their ecological importance, Douglas fir trees have deep cultural and historical significance. Indigenous peoples of the Pacific Northwest have used Douglas fir for millennia, recognizing its strength and versatility. Its wood is durable and was traditionally used for building structures, canoes, and tools. Today, Douglas fir remains one of the most valuable timber species in North America, prized for its strength and resistance to decay, which makes it an important economic resource.

While Douglas firs are generally abundant in the Pacific Northwest, they face challenges due to logging, urban development, and climate change. The expansion of urban areas has reduced available habitat for these trees, while increasing drought conditions due to climate change have made young seedlings especially vulnerable. Nevertheless, conservation efforts to protect old-growth forests and promote sustainable forestry practices help maintain Douglas fir populations and preserve Seattle's natural landscape.

Where to See Them

Douglas firs can be found throughout Seattle's parks and green spaces, where they add grandeur to the landscape and provide a peaceful escape within the city. Discovery Park, Seward Park, and the Washington Park Arboretum are popular locations for spotting these towering trees. The forested areas within these parks offer an immersive experience, where visitors can walk among Douglas firs and observe the rich, biodiverse ecosystems they support.

English Ivy

Hedera helix

English ivy, with its lush green foliage and ability to climb nearly any surface, is one of Seattle's most widespread and controversial plants. Originally introduced as an ornamental ground cover from Europe, English ivy has spread aggressively throughout the Pacific Northwest, thriving in Seattle's mild climate and becoming an invasive species. While some people appreciate English ivy for the green coverage it provides on fences and in backyards, its impact on local ecosystems has led to ongoing efforts to control it and remove it from wild spaces around the city.

English ivy is easily recognizable by its glossy, dark green leaves, which are often lobed and arranged in dense, trailing vines. These vines can grow more than 90 feet long, allowing the ivy to quickly cover the ground, trees, fences, and even entire buildings. The plant's aerial roots secrete a sticky substance that enables it to cling to surfaces as it climbs, adding a picturesque, natural aesthetic to walls and structures. Because of its appealing look and its ability to create quick ground cover, English ivy has become a popular landscaping choice, creating a natural green backdrop in residential gardens across Seattle.

Despite its beauty, English ivy poses serious ecological risks. In Seattle's forests and parks, ivy grows rapidly, forming dense mats that choke out native plants by competing for sunlight, nutrients, and water. Ivy's thick ground cover prevents native plants from establishing, leading to a significant reduction in plant diversity. In wooded areas, ivy climbs tree trunks and can create heavy loads on branches, weakening trees and making them more susceptible to disease and wind damage. As it spreads, English ivy also disrupts the natural regeneration of forests, shading out young trees and shrubs that are crucial for maintaining forest health.

The dense growth of English ivy also affects wildlife. By displacing native plants, ivy reduces the available food and habitat for insects, birds, and small mammals that rely

English ivy is considered a noxious weed in and around Seattle, despite the fact that many homeowners love it for the natural screen it provides.

on native flora for survival. The ivy's dark mats provide limited resources and cover, which can result in a decrease in biodiversity in areas where it dominates. In particular, Seattle's native pollinators, such as bees and butterflies, are deprived of their usual nectar sources when ivy replaces flowering plants.

To combat these ecological impacts, many conservation groups and volunteers in Seattle work diligently to remove English ivy from public lands, often organizing ivy-pulling events in local parks like Discovery Park and Seward Park. The goal of these efforts is to restore native plants and create a more balanced and resilient ecosystem. Removing ivy is labor-intensive, as the vines are tenacious and can regrow from even small root fragments. However, regular maintenance has been effective in restoring some areas to their natural state, allowing native plants to thrive again.

While English ivy is viewed as a problem by many conservationists, some Seattle residents appreciate its visual appeal and use it to cover fences, walls, and garden beds. Its year-round greenery offers a natural aesthetic and privacy screening, making it popular in urban landscapes despite its invasive nature. However, many gardeners are now choosing native alternatives that provide similar coverage without harming local ecosystems.

Where to See Them

English ivy can be found throughout Seattle, both in urban and natural areas. In parks like Carkeek Park and along the Burke-Gilman Trail, ivy is often seen covering trees and forest floors, though restoration efforts are gradually reducing its spread. Ivy is also a common sight in residential neighborhoods, climbing fences and walls where it is deliberately cultivated.

English ivy's rapid spread and impact on Seattle's native ecosystems make it a contentious but prominent part of the city's landscape. While its greenery appeals to some, its role as an invasive species reminds us of the importance of choosing plants that support rather than harm the local environment.

Himalayan Blackberry

Rubus armeniacus

The Himalayan blackberry is one of Seattle's most contentious yet oddly beloved plants. This thorny, sprawling vine is an invasive species in the Pacific Northwest, but its juicy, flavorful berries make it hard to resist. Originally from Eurasia, Himalayan blackberry was introduced to North America in the late 19th century for its robust growth and delicious fruit. Today, it's found across Seattle's parks, green spaces, and even in backyards, where its dense thickets are as much a source of frustration as they are a hidden treasure for berry lovers.

Recognized by its thick, arching canes, sharp thorns, and clusters of five-lobed leaves, Himalayan blackberry can grow up to 15 feet tall, often forming impenetrable thickets. In spring, the plant produces clusters of small white or pale pink flowers, which give way to dark purple-black berries by mid- to late summer. The berries are sweet and juicy, making them popular with humans and animals alike. Come summer, many Seattleites brave the thorny vines to pick the ripe berries, which can be used in everything from jams and pies to syrups and snacks.

Despite its appeal, Himalayan blackberry is highly invasive, outcompeting native plants and spreading rapidly in Seattle's mild, wet climate. Its roots, known for their extensive network, can penetrate deep into the soil and re-sprout from even the smallest fragments, making it incredibly difficult to eradicate. Once established, Himalayan blackberry forms dense thickets that crowd out native vegetation, reducing biodiversity and altering local ecosystems. Its aggressive growth along riverbanks and wetlands can disrupt natural habitats, impacting water flow and displacing plants that wildlife rely on.

The blackberry's spread poses challenges for conservation efforts aimed at preserving Seattle's native flora. Efforts to control Himalayan blackberry often involve regular cutting, digging, and herbicide application, but the plant's resilience and tenacity make these tasks labor-intensive and ongoing. However, the plant's fruits provide a silver lining; they offer food for birds, mammals, and even people. Birds like robins and cedar waxwings feed on the berries, dispersing the seeds even farther in the process. For wildlife and residents alike, the summer berry season is one of the few redeeming qualities of this otherwise invasive plant.

Seattle residents have a love-hate relationship with Himalayan blackberry. On one hand, it provides free, tasty fruit in abundance, but on the other, it takes over landscapes with ease. Some local foragers, gardeners, and park enthusiasts make the best of its presence, taking advantage of the bounty it offers each year while participating in organized efforts to manage its spread. Community efforts to control Himalayan blackberry often emphasize removal where possible and replacement with native species that support biodiversity.

Where to See Them

Himalayan blackberry can be found in nearly every corner of Seattle, from overgrown roadsides to parks and backyards. Discovery Park, Carkeek Park, and along the Burke-Gilman Trail are popular places to find berry-laden brambles in summer, where residents and visitors alike can enjoy foraging—carefully navigating the thorny branches for the perfect berry.

For those interested in sustainable foraging, the summer months offer a chance to harvest this invasive species without guilt, as gathering the fruit doesn't harm local ecosystems and can even help limit the spread of its seeds. While Himalayan blackberry remains a challenge to Seattle's native landscapes, its delicious berries provide a seasonal reward, making it a plant that locals can't help but hate to love.

Kinnikinnick

Arctostaphylos uva-ursi

Kinnikinnick, also known as bearberry, is a low-growing evergreen shrub that weaves through Seattle's forests, parks, and coastal areas. Recognized for its dense, mat-like growth and tiny, bright red berries, kinnikinnick adds a pop of color to Seattle's green spaces and plays a unique role in the Pacific Northwest's ecosystem. Known for its resilience and adaptability, kinnikinnick is an important ground cover that stabilizes soil, provides food and shelter for wildlife, and enhances biodiversity in and around Seattle.

One of kinnikinnick's most distinctive features is its small, leathery leaves, which remain green year-round and form a dense, spreading carpet on the forest floor. The leaves are rounded, dark green on top, and lighter beneath, offering a subtle contrast that makes kinnikinnick easily recognizable. In spring, the plant produces clusters of small, pinkish white, bell-shaped flowers that attract bees and other pollinators. These flowers are followed by bright red berries in late summer and fall, which remain on the plant well into winter, providing a welcome burst of color during Seattle's gray, rainy months.

Kinnikinnick's sprawling growth habit makes it an effective ground cover, particularly on slopes and in disturbed soils. Its extensive root system helps stabilize soil, preventing erosion on Seattle's hillsides, riverbanks, and coastal bluffs. This soil-stabilizing quality is invaluable in urban green spaces and natural areas where erosion can threaten the integrity of trails and habitats. By covering the ground with its dense foliage, kinnikinnick also helps retain moisture, reduces the spread of invasive species, and provides a nurturing environment for native plants to thrive.

For wildlife, kinnikinnick is an important source of food and shelter. The berries, while tart and mealy for human tastes, are a favorite of birds, including grouse and waxwings, as well as small mammals like squirrels and chipmunks. In winter, when other food sources are scarce, these berries provide critical sustenance for wildlife. The plant's low, dense structure also provides ground cover and hiding places for small animals, offering a haven in open areas and along forest edges.

Kinnikinnick has a long history of traditional use by Indigenous peoples, who valued the plant for its medicinal and ceremonial properties. The leaves were used in teas for treating various ailments, while the berries were sometimes eaten fresh or dried. Its common name, kinnikinnick, comes from an Algonquian word meaning "smoking mixture,"

as the leaves were often mixed with tobacco and other herbs for ceremonial smoking.

While kinnikinnick is not considered endangered, it can sometimes struggle in urban settings where habitat fragmentation, soil disturbance, and competition from invasive species create challenges. However, its adaptability to various soil types and light conditions makes it a resilient presence in Seattle's natural areas, where it thrives in sunny to partially shaded environments.

Where to See Them

Kinnikinnick can be found in many of Seattle's parks and along trails where ground cover and erosion control are priorities. Discovery Park, Carkeek Park, and Magnuson Park all offer excellent opportunities to observe kinnikinnick's lush green mats covering forest floors and slopes. The plant is especially prominent in areas with well-drained soil and plenty of sunlight, such as open forest edges, bluffs, and rocky outcrops.

Nootka Rose

Rosa nutkana

The Nootka rose, with its fragrant pink blossoms and abundant hips, is one of Seattle's most beautiful and ecologically important native plants. This hardy wild rose thrives in the Pacific Northwest's varied landscapes, from coastal bluffs to forest edges, bringing vibrant color and supporting biodiversity across Seattle. Named after the Nootka Sound on Vancouver Island, the Nootka rose has a special place in the region's natural and cultural heritage, serving as a valuable source of food and shelter for wildlife and a symbol of resilience in the wild Seattle landscape.

The Nootka rose is easily recognized by its lovely, single-petaled flowers, which bloom in shades of pink and are often about 2 inches wide. In early summer, these flowers bring bright, cheerful color to Seattle's forests and meadows, filling the air with a light, sweet fragrance that attracts pollinators. The Nootka rose's leaves are made up of five to seven serrated leaflets, giving the plant a soft, bushy appearance. By late summer, the flowers give way to large, round, reddish orange rose hips, which persist into fall and winter, providing a valuable food source for birds and mammals.

One of the Nootka rose's primary roles in the ecosystem is as a food source. Its flowers attract bees, butterflies, and other pollinators, while its rose hips are consumed by a variety of birds, including robins, waxwings, and grouse. Small mammals, such as squirrels and deer, also browse on the rose hips, finding nourishment in their vitamin-rich flesh. These rose hips, which are high in vitamin C and antioxidants, were traditionally eaten by Indigenous peoples, who valued them for their nutritional and medicinal properties.

Beyond providing food, the Nootka rose offers crucial shelter for wildlife. Its dense, thorny thickets create safe nesting sites and protection from predators, making it a favorite shelter for small birds and mammals. In open fields and along forest edges, where there may be little other cover, the Nootka rose's thick

growth offers a haven for wildlife, contributing to the biodiversity and stability of Seattle's natural areas.

Culturally, the Nootka rose holds special significance for Indigenous peoples of the Pacific Northwest, who have used its flowers, hips, and bark for centuries. The plant's rose hips were traditionally dried and made into teas or used as food during the winter months, while the bark was sometimes used in basketry and rope-making. Today, Nootka rose is also popular among foragers and gardeners alike, valued for both its beauty and its beneficial properties.

The Nootka rose is well adapted to Seattle's climate, thriving in both full sun and partial shade and tolerating a wide range of soil types. While it is a hardy plant, Nootka rose benefits from conservation efforts that protect native plant habitats, as invasive species and habitat loss can threaten its populations in some areas.

Where to See Them

Nootka rose can be found throughout Seattle's parks, along trails, and in open meadows where its flowers and berries stand out among the greenery. Discovery Park, Seward Park, and Magnuson Park are all excellent locations to see Nootka rose in its natural habitat. Along trails and forest edges, these roses add a splash of pink in the early summer and are often clustered in dense thickets that provide cover for small animals.

Pacific Madrone

Arbutus menziesii

The Pacific madrone, with its smooth, peeling bark and dramatic red-orange hue, is one of Seattle's most distinctive and captivating trees. Known for its striking appearance and resilience, the madrone stands out in Seattle's forests, adding vibrant color and unique texture to the landscape. Found along the Pacific Coast from California to British Columbia, the Pacific madrone is especially at home in the Pacific Northwest's mild, coastal climate. This evergreen broadleaf plays an important ecological role, supporting biodiversity and enriching Seattle's wild spaces.

The madrone's most recognizable feature is its bark, which peels away in thin layers, revealing a smooth, orange or reddish surface beneath. Over time, the bark matures to a greenish gray, creating a mosaic of colors that change throughout the tree's lifespan. The tree's glossy, dark green leaves are leathery and thick, contrasting beautifully with the vivid bark and adding to the madrone's visual appeal. In spring, clusters of small, white, bell-shaped flowers bloom, attracting pollinators like bees and hummingbirds. By autumn, these flowers give way to bright red-orange berries that are a favorite food for local birds and mammals.

The Pacific madrone thrives in dry, well-drained soils and is often found on rocky outcrops, coastal bluffs, and sunny slopes. Unlike many trees in the region, madrones prefer sunny exposures and are highly drought-tolerant, relying on deep root systems to access moisture during dry spells. This adaptability allows them to withstand the rain-soaked winters and dry summers typical of Seattle's climate. Madrones are often seen growing alongside Douglas firs, Garry oaks, and shore pines, where their striking bark and foliage add diversity to the Pacific Northwest's forested slopes.

Ecologically, the Pacific madrone plays a vital role in Seattle's forest ecosystems. The tree's berries are a rich food source for many bird species, including robins, thrushes, and woodpeckers, while its dense foliage provides shelter for birds, insects, and small mammals.

Because it is a slow-decomposing hardwood, fallen madrone branches and logs contribute to forest structure, providing habitat for invertebrates and fungi that break down the wood and enrich the soil. This decay process is essential for nutrient cycling, supporting the long-term health and productivity of forest ecosystems.

The Pacific madrone also holds cultural significance in the Pacific Northwest. Indigenous peoples have long valued the tree for its medicinal and practical uses, utilizing its bark and leaves in teas, as well as for treating skin ailments and digestive issues. The dense, hard wood of the madrone has traditionally been used for carving tools and making firewood due to its excellent burning qualities.

While the Pacific madrone is well suited to its environment, it faces threats from urbanization, disease, and changing climate conditions. Fungal infections like "madrone canker" can weaken trees, especially in areas where habitat fragmentation and human development have increased stress on madrone populations. Conservation efforts focused on protecting native habitats and reducing pollution are crucial for supporting the health and longevity of Seattle's Pacific madrone populations.

Where to See Them

Pacific madrones are commonly found on Seattle's coastal bluffs and on the ledges and hilltops of its forested parks. (In fact, Seattle's Magnolia neighborhood was misnamed back in 1857 when a naval geographer mistook all the madrone trees there for magnolias.) These days, Discovery Park, Carkeek Park, and Lincoln Park all provide excellent opportunities to see these beautiful trees up close, often on exposed slopes and rocky areas with plenty of sunlight. Their eye-catching bark and foliage make madrones a highlight along many of the city's hiking trails.

Pacific Rhododendron

Rhododendron macrophyllum

The Pacific rhododendron, with its vibrant pink blooms and broad evergreen leaves, is a standout in Seattle's wild landscapes and the official flower of Washington State. Found throughout the Pacific Northwest, this stunning shrub is a beloved resident of Seattle's forests and a symbol of the region's natural beauty. Known for its showy blossoms and adaptability, the Pacific rhododendron adds color to forested areas, supports local wildlife, and plays a unique role in Seattle's diverse ecosystem.

Pacific rhododendrons are easily recognized by their large, leathery leaves and spectacular clusters of pink to purple flowers, which bloom in late spring to early summer. Each flower cluster can contain up to twenty individual blossoms, making a mature rhododendron a vibrant splash of color against the darker greens of the forest. The plant's evergreen leaves are thick and glossy, helping it retain moisture during dry summers and withstand the rain-soaked winters typical of Seattle. This evergreen foliage also makes it a year-round feature in local forests, providing visual interest even in the depths of winter.

In the wild, Pacific rhododendrons thrive in the understory of mixed forests, often growing alongside Douglas fir, western hemlock, and other Pacific Northwest giants. They prefer acidic, well-drained soils and are commonly found on slopes, in forest clearings, and along the edges of woodlands. While they can tolerate partial shade, Pacific rhododendrons are often found in areas with filtered sunlight, where they can receive a balance of light and shade. This adaptability allows them to flourish in Seattle's varied topography, from forested hillsides to coastal bluffs.

Ecologically, Pacific rhododendrons provide food and habitat for a variety of wildlife. Their flowers attract pollinators such as bees, butterflies, and hummingbirds, which feed on the nectar and assist in the plant's reproduction. The dense foliage offers shelter for small

animals, including birds and insects, making the rhododendron a small but valuable haven in the forest understory. Additionally, as evergreen plants, they contribute to soil stability and help prevent erosion on slopes, which is essential in maintaining the health of Seattle's forested areas.

Pacific rhododendrons have a long cultural history in the Pacific Northwest. Indigenous peoples of the region traditionally used parts of the rhododendron for medicinal purposes, as well as for making dyes. The plant's resilience and beauty have made it a popular ornamental shrub as well, leading to its adoption in gardens and parks throughout the city. Its designation as Washington's state flower in 1959 reflects its cultural significance and its deep-rooted connection to the region's identity.

While Pacific rhododendrons are not currently endangered, their natural habitats face threats from urban expansion and habitat fragmentation. Conservation efforts that protect forests and maintain the integrity of natural habitats are crucial to ensuring that these beautiful shrubs continue to thrive in Seattle's green spaces.

Where to See Them

Seattle offers many places to see Pacific rhododendrons in the wild, particularly in parks and natural areas with native forests. Discovery Park, Seward Park, and the Washington Park Arboretum all feature Pacific rhododendrons, especially along trails where filtered sunlight and the forest edge provide ideal growing conditions. During the bloom season, these parks transform into a tapestry of pink and purple blossoms that are a treat for nature lovers and photographers alike.

For a more immersive experience, the Rhododendron Species Botanical Garden in nearby Federal Way is a treasure trove of rhododendron varieties, including the native Pacific rhododendron. This garden showcases the diversity of the genus and provides an educational look at the species' role in Pacific Northwest ecosystems.

Red Alder

Alnus rubra

The red alder, with its smooth, silvery bark and distinctive serrated leaves, is one of Seattle's most adaptable and ecologically important trees. Found throughout the Pacific Northwest, red alders thrive in disturbed and moist soils, making them common along riverbanks, wetlands, and roadsides. Known as a "pioneer species," the red alder is often one of the first trees to colonize cleared or disturbed areas, setting the stage for a thriving forest ecosystem. In Seattle's woodlands and green spaces, red alders contribute to soil health, support wildlife, and play a significant role in the region's natural regeneration.

Red alders are recognizable by their pale, grayish bark that often becomes mottled with patches of white lichen, giving the trunks a speckled appearance. In spring, their broad, toothed leaves emerge with a vibrant green color before fading to a more muted shade. One of the tree's unique characteristics is that its leaves remain green until late autumn, often turning brown without falling off entirely. This contributes organic material to the forest floor gradually, nourishing the soil with a steady supply of nutrients as the leaves decompose.

The red alder is a nitrogen-fixing tree, which is a key reason for its importance in Seattle's ecosystems. Its roots host bacteria called *Frankia* that absorb nitrogen from the air and convert it into a form usable by plants. This process enriches the soil, making it more fertile for other trees and plants. As a result, red alders play a vital role in forest succession, improving the soil quality in disturbed areas and creating a fertile environment for other species, including Douglas fir, western hemlock, and various understory plants.

Wildlife also benefits from the presence of red alders. The trees produce small, cone-like catkins that are a food source for birds such as siskins, chickadees, and finches. Insects, too, are drawn to the alder's foliage and wood, in turn attracting larger animals like woodpeckers and other insectivorous birds. Red alder's bark and branches provide nesting and sheltering sites, while fallen logs and branches create valuable habitat for amphibians, fungi, and small mammals, contributing to the biodiversity of Seattle's forests.

Red alders have been historically used by Indigenous peoples for various purposes. The tree's bark contains tannins and produces a red dye, which has been used to color baskets, clothing, and other materials. Alderwood, known for its smooth, even grain, was also used in carving and crafting, and today it remains a popular choice for cabinetry and furniture.

While red alder is a common tree in the Pacific Northwest, climate change and urban development pose challenges to its habitat. Although it is resilient, the tree relies on access to moisture and open spaces, making conservation of riparian zones and disturbed habitats important for maintaining red alder populations in urban settings like Seattle.

Where to See Them

Red alders can be found throughout Seattle's green spaces, particularly in areas near water. Discovery Park, Carkeek Park, and the Washington Park Arboretum offer excellent locations to see these trees up close, especially along streams and wetlands. Red alders are also common along the Burke-Gilman Trail and in many neighborhood parks, where their role in soil improvement and wildlife support is on full display.

▲ Red alders may colonize disturbed landscapes, laying the groundwork for bigger trees to come later.

▲ A red alder in Ravenna Park stares back at you.

Salal

Gaultheria shallon

Salal, with its glossy leaves and dark purple berries, is one of the Pacific Northwest's most versatile and ecologically important plants. Found abundantly in Seattle's forests, parks, and coastal areas, this evergreen shrub plays a vital role in supporting local ecosystems. Its dense, leafy thickets provide shelter for wildlife, its berries offer a nutritious food source, and its hardy nature makes it an important ground cover that stabilizes soil in Seattle's woodlands.

One of the most distinctive features of salal is its tough, leathery leaves, which remain green year-round and help the plant retain moisture during dry summer months. The shrub's leaves are oval-shaped and often glossy, making salal easy to spot in the understory of Seattle's forests. In late spring and early summer, salal produces clusters of small, bell-shaped, pink or white flowers that attract a variety of pollinators, including bees and hummingbirds. By late summer, the flowers give way to dark blue or purple berries, which are a favorite among both wildlife and foragers.

Salal is a foundational species in Pacific Northwest ecosystems, providing year-round habitat and food for animals. Birds, such as towhees, juncos, and thrushes, feed on the berries, while small mammals, including squirrels and raccoons, also rely on salal as a food source. In the thick foliage, these animals find protection from predators and harsh weather, making salal a crucial refuge in Seattle's forested areas. The plant's dense growth also provides ideal cover for nesting birds and insects, supporting a biodiverse community within its leafy confines.

In addition to its role as a food source and shelter, salal is essential for soil health and erosion control. Its deep, spreading root system stabilizes soil on slopes and helps prevent erosion, especially in Seattle's coastal and hilly regions. Salal is well adapted to the

region's wet winters and dry summers, allowing it to thrive in areas where other plants might struggle. By creating a lush, ground-level canopy, salal protects young trees and other understory plants, providing a shaded, moist environment that helps them establish and grow. In this way, salal acts as a "nurse plant," supporting the health and regeneration of Pacific Northwest forests.

Salal has also been important to Indigenous peoples of the Pacific Northwest, who have long used its berries for food and its leaves for medicinal purposes. The berries were traditionally eaten fresh, dried, or mixed with other foods, while the leaves were used in poultices to treat minor wounds. Today, salal continues to be valued for its edible berries, and its branches are harvested sustainably for floral arrangements, adding to its cultural and economic significance.

Where to See Them

Salal can be found in nearly every forested area around Seattle. Discovery Park, Seward

Park, and Washington Park Arboretum all offer excellent opportunities to see salal thriving in its natural habitat. The shrub is often found along trails, where its dense foliage lines the paths and creates a verdant undergrowth. In the late summer, these parks also offer a chance to see salal in full berry, as its purple fruits dot the landscape.

Salmonberry

Rubus spectabilis

Salmonberry, with its vibrant pink flowers and bright orange-to-red berries, is a staple of Seattle's natural landscapes and an essential part of the Pacific Northwest ecosystem. Growing abundantly along trails, riverbanks, and in forested areas, this hardy deciduous shrub is one of the first plants to bloom in spring, signaling the end of winter and providing an early food source for pollinators, wildlife, and foraging enthusiasts. Salmonberry's cheerful blooms, tasty fruit, and ecological importance make it a beloved plant in and around Seattle.

One of the first signs of spring in Seattle is the sight of salmonberry's magenta flowers dotting the understory of the city's woodlands. The plant's distinctive flowers, with their five-petal structure, bloom as early as March, offering one of the earliest food sources for pollinators such as bees and hummingbirds. The shrub itself can grow between 3 to 12 feet tall, with thorny stems and trifoliate leaves resembling those of its close relatives, the raspberry and blackberry. In late spring and early summer, the flowers give way to juicy, edible berries that range in color from bright orange to deep red, with a flavor that varies from tart to sweet, depending on ripeness.

Salmonberry plays a significant role in Seattle's ecosystem, supporting a wide range of wildlife. Birds, including robins, thrushes, and wrens, feed on its berries, while mammals like bears, raccoons, and small rodents also benefit from this seasonal food source. The dense thickets of salmonberry provide essential cover and nesting habitat for birds and small animals, creating a safe space within Seattle's forests and along riverbanks. In particular, the early bloom of salmonberry supports hummingbirds and bees at a time when few other plants are flowering, giving it a unique place in the region's seasonal cycle.

Salmonberry is also an important part of the cultural heritage of the Pacific Northwest. Indigenous peoples have long harvested the berries as a food source, eating them fresh or combining them with fish roe, a pairing that led to the plant's common name, "salmonberry." The berries are still popular with local foragers, who prize them for their mildly sweet taste and high water content, which make them refreshing snacks during spring and summer hikes. While the berries aren't widely cultivated, their availability in the wild makes them an accessible treat for those who explore Seattle's natural areas.

Though salmonberry is native to the Pacific Northwest, it sometimes competes with other invasive shrubs for space. Fortunately, salmonberry is a resilient species that thrives in a variety of habitats, from moist, shaded forests to the edges of sunny trails, making it well suited to Seattle's varied terrain. Its ability to stabilize soil along slopes and riverbanks helps prevent erosion, supporting the health of nearby streams and rivers, which in turn benefits local fish populations, including the salmon with which it shares its name.

Where to See Them

Salmonberry is a common sight in Seattle's parks and green spaces, especially during spring, when its bright pink flowers are in bloom. Discovery Park, Seward Park, and Ravenna Park are ideal places to see salmonberry in its natural habitat, often growing along trails and near water sources. By early summer, these same parks offer opportunities to forage for the colorful berries, which hang in clusters and are easily accessible to those who recognize them.

Sitka Spruce

Picea sitchensis

The Sitka spruce, with its towering height and striking blue-green needles, is a defining tree of Seattle's coastal forests and the Pacific Northwest's misty landscapes. Known for its rapid growth, impressive size, and adaptability to moist environments, the Sitka spruce is the largest of the spruce species, reaching heights of over 300 feet in some cases. In Seattle's cool, damp climate, this majestic tree thrives, playing a crucial role in local ecosystems and offering a fascinating look into the region's natural history.

One of the distinctive features of Sitka spruce is its stiff, sharp needles that have a subtle bluish tint, giving the tree a unique, silvery appearance. The needles are short and prickly, arranged radially around each twig, which distinguishes the Sitka from its

▼ Ready for the Pacific Northwest's signature rain, hikers pass a huge Sitka spruce tree.

evergreen neighbors. Its bark is thin and scaly when young but thickens and develops deep grooves as it ages, providing extra resilience in Seattle's cool, wet environment.

Sitka spruces are often found near streams and coastal areas, where the high humidity and rich, well-drained soils provide ideal growing conditions. Unlike many trees, Sitka spruces are particularly tolerant of salty air, making them well suited to the Pacific coastline. Their branches and roots help stabilize soil along stream banks, reducing erosion and supporting the delicate balance of riparian habitats. As they grow, they create a canopy that regulates light, moisture, and temperature on the forest floor, allowing an abundance of ferns, mosses, and other shade-loving plants to flourish.

In the Pacific Northwest ecosystem, Sitka spruces play a vital role in supporting wildlife. Their tall trunks and spreading branches offer nesting sites for birds such as bald eagles, warblers, and owls. The dense canopy provides shelter from the elements, while fallen branches and logs become habitat for a range of creatures, from insects to amphibians and small mammals. When a Sitka spruce falls and begins to decompose, it enriches the soil with nutrients that benefit the next generation of forest life, becoming what is known as a "nurse log." These nurse logs are characteristic of Seattle's coastal forests, as they nurture saplings, moss, fungi, and even small animals, creating a micro-ecosystem on the forest floor.

Historically, Sitka spruce has been valued for its light, flexible wood, which has been used by Indigenous communities for boat-building, tools, and musical instruments. During World War I, the wood was prized for its use in aircraft construction, due to its strength-to-weight ratio. Today, Sitka spruce remains important for timber and conservation, as sustainable practices ensure that the tree continues to thrive while supporting local economies.

Where to See Them

Sitka spruce trees can be seen in several parks and green spaces around Seattle. Discovery Park and Seward Park are excellent locations to observe Sitka spruces up close, where they mingle with Douglas fir and western hemlock, creating diverse and layered forest habitats. Their presence in these parks helps maintain the rich biodiversity of Seattle's green spaces.

◄ Sitka spruce is monoecious, meaning it has both male and female cones on the same tree.

Thimbleberry

Rubus parviflorus

Thimbleberry, with its broad, velvety leaves and delicate white flowers, is a beloved and ecologically significant shrub in Seattle's wild spaces. Found in forests, meadows, and along trails, thimbleberry is a key part of the Pacific Northwest's plant community, providing shelter, food, and seasonal beauty to the Seattle area. With its soft, raspberry-like fruits and vibrant foliage, thimbleberry adds both visual appeal and practical value to Seattle's ecosystems.

Thimbleberry is recognizable by its large, maple-like leaves, which can grow up to 8 inches across. The leaves are soft and fuzzy, giving them a texture that sets thimbleberry apart from other shrubs. In spring, clusters of large white flowers bloom, each with five petals, attracting pollinators such as bees, butterflies, and flies. By early summer, the flowers give way to the bright red, slightly flattened berries that give the plant its name. The berries, which look like tiny thimbles, are delicate and easily crushable, making them somewhat difficult to transport but a delightful treat to enjoy fresh from the plant.

Thimbleberry's role in the ecosystem is multifaceted, supporting a range of wildlife. The flowers provide an early nectar source for pollinators, and the leaves offer shelter for insects and small creatures. The berries are an important food source for many species, including birds like robins, thrushes, and jays and mammals like squirrels, raccoons, and bears. The shrub's dense, sprawling growth pattern creates a natural undergrowth that provides protective cover for birds and small animals, making thimbleberry thickets valuable nesting sites within Seattle's green spaces.

Unlike some of its prickly relatives in the *Rubus* genus, such as blackberry and raspberry, thimbleberry is thornless, making it more accessible to both wildlife and humans. Its thorn-free stems and soft leaves make thimbleberry easy to approach, adding to its popularity among foragers and nature lovers. The berries are mildly sweet with a hint of tartness, and while they're not as juicy as blackberries, their delicate flavor has made them a traditional treat. Indigenous peoples of the Pacific Northwest have long enjoyed thimbleberries as a seasonal food, often eating them fresh or drying them for later use. The leaves and bark were also used in traditional medicine for their soothing properties.

Thimbleberry is well suited to Seattle's climate and thrives in both full sun and partial shade, especially in moist, well-drained soil. Its adaptability allows it to grow along forest edges, stream banks, and open trails, making it a common sight in Seattle's natural areas. The plant's extensive root system helps stabilize soil, preventing erosion in forested areas and along riverbanks, which supports the health of Seattle's watersheds and contributes to the stability of local ecosystems.

Where to See Them

Thimbleberry is widespread in Seattle's parks and trails, where it thrives in both forested areas and open spaces. Discovery Park, Seward Park, and Carkeek Park are excellent places to spot thimbleberry, especially along trails, where the shrub often grows in sunny patches and along paths. During summer, the bright red berries can be seen hanging from the plants, providing a tempting snack for foragers who recognize them.

Western Hemlock

Tsuga heterophylla

The western hemlock, with its feathery needles and gracefully drooping branches, is a quintessential part of Seattle's lush forest landscape. Often found in the dense, moist woodlands of the Pacific Northwest, this evergreen tree embodies the serene, misty beauty that defines the region. Known for its adaptability and distinct appearance, the western hemlock plays a crucial role in Seattle's ecosystems, supporting both plant and animal life and contributing to the resilience of Pacific Northwest forests.

One of the defining characteristics of the western hemlock is its elegant, lacy foliage. The needles are short, soft, and vary in length, giving each branch a textured, delicate appearance. Unlike many conifers, western hemlocks have slightly drooping tops and branches that

sweep gracefully downward, giving the tree a refined silhouette. This drooping shape helps the tree shed excess moisture in Seattle's rainy climate, protecting its foliage from fungal growth and damage.

Western hemlock trees can reach impressive heights, with mature trees growing over 200 feet tall and some specimens living for several centuries. Despite this grandeur, western hemlocks are surprisingly shade-tolerant, thriving in the understory of old-growth forests where sunlight is sparse. This adaptability allows them to grow alongside towering Douglas firs and red cedars, filling in the spaces below the canopy and contributing to the forest's layered structure.

In Seattle's ecosystems, western hemlocks serve as foundational species. Their branches provide nesting sites for birds such as chickadees and owls, while their bark and wood are home to various insects and fungi, which support a diverse range of animal life. Fallen hemlock logs are a crucial part of the forest floor, decomposing slowly and releasing nutrients that enrich the soil for new plant growth. Mosses, ferns, and lichens often cling to these decomposing logs, creating microhabitats that support smaller creatures like salamanders, beetles, and even small mammals.

Western hemlock trees are also culturally significant to the Indigenous peoples of the Pacific Northwest, who have long recognized the tree's medicinal and practical uses. Its bark, which contains tannins, has traditionally been used for tanning hides and creating natural dyes, while its foliage has been used in teas and remedies. Today, western hemlock remains valuable for timber, but sustainable forestry practices help ensure that it continues to thrive in Seattle's forests.

While western hemlocks are generally widespread and abundant, they face challenges from climate change and invasive species. Increased temperatures and changes in precipitation patterns can stress these moisture-loving trees, making them more susceptible to pests like the hemlock looper caterpillar. Conservation efforts in Seattle and surrounding areas focus on protecting old-growth stands, promoting forest health, and managing threats to ensure the long-term survival of western hemlock populations.

Where to See Them

Western hemlocks are easy to find in Seattle's natural areas and parks, where they contribute to the city's distinctive green landscape. Discovery Park, Seward Park, and the Washington Park Arboretum offer excellent opportunities to observe these trees up close. The cool, shaded paths through these parks are lined with western hemlocks, creating a lush, peaceful environment where visitors can appreciate their beauty and significance.

Western Red Cedar

Thuja plicata

The western red cedar, known as the "tree of life" in Pacific Northwest Indigenous cultures, is one of Seattle's most cherished and ecologically important trees. Revered for its towering height, fragrant wood, and rich cultural history, this graceful evergreen plays a vital role in the Pacific Northwest's forest ecosystems. The western red cedar is instantly recognizable by its reddish brown bark that peels in long, thin strips, and its delicate, scale-like foliage that gives off a distinct, sweet aroma. A key player in the temperate rainforests of Seattle and across the Pacific Northwest, the western red cedar stands as a symbol of resilience, history, and natural beauty.

Growing up to 200 feet tall and living for over a thousand years, western red cedars are often among the oldest trees in the forest.

▲ A pair of western red cedar trees join a western swordfern just off the ravine trail in Ravenna Park.

◄ You can always tell a western red cedar by the fibrous, stringy texture of its thin, reddish bark.

173

The bark's layered, fibrous texture and natural resistance to decay make it an exceptionally hardy tree, well suited to Seattle's wet climate. Its roots extend deep into the ground, stabilizing soil and supporting the health of riparian zones by reducing erosion along streams and rivers. This root system also helps the tree absorb nutrients from moist soil, allowing it to thrive in Seattle's damp woodlands.

In addition to their impressive stature, western red cedars create a shade canopy that helps regulate the temperature and humidity of the forest floor. Their dense foliage allows for a wide variety of mosses, ferns, and shade-loving plants to thrive beneath them, fostering a rich understory that supports diverse animal life. The tree's foliage also provides essential cover for birds, including chickadees and owls, while its branches are ideal nesting sites for larger birds such as bald eagles. Fallen cedar branches and trunks provide critical habitat for insects, amphibians, and small mammals, making western red cedars key contributors to Seattle's ecosystem.

Culturally, western red cedars have deep roots in the lives of the Indigenous peoples of the Pacific Northwest. For thousands of years, they have used cedarwood and bark for practical and ceremonial purposes, crafting canoes, totem poles, baskets, clothing, and even housing. The tree's rot-resistant wood was valued for its durability and warmth, while the bark was woven into mats, baskets, and clothing. To this day, western red cedar remains a powerful symbol of cultural heritage and environmental stewardship in the region.

In recent years, climate change has posed challenges to the western red cedar. Increasingly dry summers and warmer temperatures have stressed some populations, particularly young trees, as they rely on a steady supply of moisture. Conservation efforts to preserve Seattle's mature red cedar stands are essential to maintain the health and resilience of local forests, as these trees play a foundational role in the Pacific Northwest's ecosystems. Tree Action Seattle, a nonprofit with the mission of protecting and celebrating Seattle's cooling and carbon-sequestering urban trees for the sake of climate justice and resilience, stages awareness-raising events to help save landmark western red cedars and other big, old trees on private property that is being redeveloped.

Where to See Them

Western red cedars are common throughout Seattle's parks and green spaces. Discovery Park, Seward Park, Ravenna Park, and Washington Park Arboretum offer excellent opportunities to observe these magnificent trees up close, where they tower above trails and create lots of peaceful shade. Walking through these parks, one can often spot younger cedars growing alongside older specimens, highlighting the tree's continuity and regenerative power.

Western Swordfern

Polystichum munitum

The western swordfern, with its lush, feathery fronds and year-round greenery, is one of Seattle's most iconic and resilient plants. Known for its adaptability and vibrant presence, this evergreen fern plays a crucial role in the Pacific Northwest's forest ecosystems, providing essential ground cover, stabilizing soil, and supporting local wildlife. In Seattle's forests, parks, and shaded landscapes, the western swordfern brings texture and color, contributing to the health and beauty of wild Seattle.

The swordfern is easily recognized by its long, pointed fronds that can reach up to 5 feet in length. Each frond is lined with serrated, blade-like leaflets, giving the plant a sword-like appearance that inspired its common name. Its dense, fountain-like growth pattern creates a sweeping green ground cover that fills forest understories and shaded trails, making it a familiar sight in Seattle's green spaces. The plant's deep green color persists throughout the year, adding vibrancy to Seattle's often cloudy and rainy landscape, even in winter when other plants may be dormant.

One of the key ecological roles of the western swordfern is its ability to stabilize soil and prevent erosion. The fern's fibrous roots extend widely through the soil, helping hold it in place on slopes and along stream banks, particularly in Seattle's hilly and coastal areas. By anchoring the soil, the fern helps prevent landslides and erosion, creating a stable foundation for other plants and young trees to grow. This role is especially important in Pacific Northwest forests, where heavy rainfall can quickly erode unprotected soils.

Western swordferns also create microhabitats that support a variety of species. The dense fronds provide shelter and cover for small animals, including birds, insects, and amphibians, offering protection from predators and harsh weather. The shade and moisture retained under the fern's canopy create a cool, humid environment that nurtures mosses, fungi, and other moisture-loving plants, enriching the forest floor's biodiversity. Many species of beetles, spiders, and small mammals use the bases of swordferns as places of refuge, helping form a miniature ecosystem within Seattle's woodlands.

This fern has deep cultural significance as well. Indigenous peoples of the Pacific Northwest have used the western swordfern for centuries for practical and medicinal purposes. The fronds were used to line baskets, wrap food, and provide bedding, while the roots were sometimes used in teas or medicinal poultices. Today, the fern is still appreciated for its ornamental beauty and its value in landscaping and ecological restoration.

Western swordferns are hardy and adaptable, able to thrive in Seattle's wet winters and dry summers. They grow well in shaded, forested areas and are highly tolerant of a variety of soil types, making them resilient in both natural and urban settings. However, they can be affected by habitat disturbance, soil compaction, and invasive species, which can threaten their populations in some areas.

Where to See Them

Seattle's parks and forests are filled with western swordferns, which thrive in shaded, moist environments. Discovery Park, Seward Park, and Ravenna Park are excellent locations to see swordferns flourishing along trails and under tree canopies. These ferns are often found in clusters, carpeting the forest floor and creating a lush, green understory that is perfect for exploring and photographing.

► Swordferns are constant companions in Pacific Northwest forests.

FIELD TRIPS

Volunteer Park

Escape the concrete jungle at this historic oasis in the heart of Seattle, where leafy landscapes, cultural landmarks, and serene spaces offer a peaceful retreat.

Nestled in the Capitol Hill neighborhood, Volunteer Park offers a lush, green escape for anyone looking to reconnect with nature without leaving the city. This 48-acre park is one of Seattle's oldest and most iconic green spaces, with a rich history and diverse array of plants, wildlife, and peaceful spots for reflection.

Originally designed by the famed Olmsted Brothers, Volunteer Park offers something for everyone, whether you're a plant enthusiast, birdwatcher, or just someone seeking tranquility amid natural beauty.

Exploring Volunteer Park's Botanical Gems

As you enter Volunteer Park, the first thing you'll notice is the sprawling, manicured lawns punctuated by towering trees. These include native species like Douglas fir, western hemlock, and bigleaf maple, alongside non-native but equally impressive trees such as ginkgo, horse chestnut, giant sequoias, and coast redwoods. For plant lovers, these trees are just the beginning.

A centerpiece of the park is the Volunteer Park Conservatory, a Victorian-style glasshouse filled with an impressive variety of tropical and subtropical plants. Inside, you'll discover a world of ferns, orchids, bromeliads, and even cacti, meticulously arranged in themed rooms. This century-old conservatory is a peaceful haven, providing a year-round escape into greenery and warmth, especially on chilly Seattle days.

Just outside the conservatory is a beautiful seasonal garden, where you can stroll through flower beds filled with roses, tulips, and other blooming plants depending on the time of year. The park's commitment to horticulture makes it a perfect spot to enjoy both native and exotic flora in a curated setting.

► Volunteer Park is one of only a few locations around Seattle where you can see coast redwood trees. These giants, which can live longer than 1500 years and grow to 300 feet or taller, are native to Northern California—so the specimens growing around here were planted or transplanted by enterprising gardeners and park planners during the city's early years after white settlement.

FIELD TRIP 1

Wildlife and Birdwatching in Volunteer Park

Despite its location in the city, Volunteer Park teems with wildlife, especially birds. If you're an avid birdwatcher, bring your binoculars and be prepared for sightings of species like the great blue heron, red-winged blackbird, American crow, and northern flicker. In the early morning or late afternoon, you might even spot a bald eagle soaring overhead.

The park's pond, though small, attracts ducks, Canada geese, and other waterfowl. As you walk through the park's wooded areas, keep your ears open for the songs of chestnut-backed chickadees, and if you're lucky, you might catch a glimpse of a belted kingfisher darting by.

For those who enjoy spotting less-common species, the tree-lined paths and open fields make it easy to find a variety of migratory birds during the spring and fall seasons. Warblers, thrushes, and flycatchers can often be seen passing through, taking advantage of the park's ample food sources and shelter.

Volunteer Park's Tranquil Spaces

One of the defining features of Volunteer Park is its serene atmosphere, even when busy with visitors. Many find solace near the park's reflecting pool, a calm, quiet spot framed by manicured shrubs and towering evergreens. The stillness of the water provides a mirror-like reflection of the sky and surrounding trees, offering a perfect moment of calm in the middle of the city.

The Seattle Asian Art Museum, housed within the park, adds a cultural element to the experience, but even outside, the surrounding lawns and gardens invite you to sit, relax, and enjoy the natural beauty. It's not uncommon to find visitors practicing yoga, meditating, or simply enjoying a book on the expansive grass lawns.

▼ Blushing bromeliad, native to the tropical rainforests of the Amazon but also found inside the hot and humid Volunteer Park Conservatory, changes the color of its central leaves to a vibrant red or pink just before blooming, giving the appearance of blushing—and signaling to pollinators that it's ready to reproduce.

▲ A northern flicker rests on a dead tree snag, scouting for its next snack.

The park is also home to the historic Volunteer Park water tower, which is open to visitors who want a panoramic view of the city. Climbing to the top offers sweeping vistas of the Seattle skyline, framed by trees and greenery.

A Brief History of Volunteer Park

Originally used as a cemetery in the late 1800s, the land was transformed into a park in the early 20th century. The Olmsted Brothers were hired to design the space, and they crafted it with both aesthetics and conservation in mind, ensuring that it would serve as a green haven for future generations. The park's name, Volunteer Park, was chosen in honor of those who volunteered to fight in the Spanish-American War, adding a touch of local history to its rich tapestry.

Since its creation, Volunteer Park has been a beloved space for Seattleites to connect with nature and each other. It is a living reminder of the city's commitment to preserving natural spaces within its urban landscape.

Conservation and Sustainability

Volunteer Park isn't just a place to enjoy the beauty of nature—it's also a site where conservation efforts are constantly in play. The city works hard to preserve the park's natural ecosystems, removing invasive plant species and encouraging the growth of native plants that sustain local wildlife.

Interpretive signs throughout the park educate visitors about the importance of native plants and the role they play in supporting local birds, insects, and mammals. The park also hosts community gardening programs, workshops, and volunteer opportunities, fostering a deeper connection between residents and their environment.

▲ Even though Volunteer Park is smack-dab in the middle of urban Seattle, coyotes frequently make their rounds there.

Hidden Gems: Secret Gardens and Art

Volunteer Park is full of little surprises. Tucked behind the conservatory, you'll find a small, secluded fern garden, where you can escape the main pathways and take in the lush greenery in peace. This spot is particularly refreshing on a warm summer day, as the thick canopy overhead provides welcome shade.

The park also boasts a number of public art installations, including the iconic "Black Sun" sculpture by artist Isamu Noguchi. This sculpture, which resembles an abstract eclipse, is perfectly placed to align with the Space Needle in the distance, creating a stunning visual effect when viewed from just the right angle.

For art lovers, the Seattle Asian Art Museum is an additional draw, but even those who don't venture inside will appreciate the park's thoughtful integration of art and nature, which encourages visitors to see the landscape through a creative lens.

A Perfect Day at Volunteer Park

Whether you're wandering the meandering paths, relaxing by the reflecting pool, or exploring the flora inside the conservatory, a visit to Volunteer Park offers a peaceful respite from the hustle of city life. It's a space where art, history, and nature intertwine, creating a harmonious blend of urban parkland and natural beauty.

A day spent here is more than just a park visit; it's an opportunity to reconnect with the simple, grounding pleasure of being surrounded by trees, flowers, birds, and the soft sounds of the natural world. As you leave, you'll likely feel rejuvenated, having taken a step back from the everyday chaos and into the serene embrace of Volunteer Park.

Wild on the Inside at The Spheres

In the heart of Seattle's bustling South Lake Union neighborhood, The Spheres stand as a futuristic oasis, seamlessly blending urban innovation with nature. These glass-domed structures, part of online retailer Amazon's headquarters, house a breathtaking indoor rainforest filled with more than 40,000 plants from across the globe. Designed to provide employees with a workspace infused with biophilic elements, The Spheres also offer limited public access, allowing visitors to experience a thriving ecosystem unlike any other in the city.

Inside, towering trees stretch toward the curved ceilings, while waterfalls and lush greenery create an environment that feels worlds away from the surrounding skyscrapers. The temperature and humidity are carefully controlled to mimic a tropical cloud forest, making it an ideal habitat for a diverse collection of plant life, including rare orchids, bromeliads, and massive ficus trees. Winding pathways lead visitors through multilevel gardens, where they can observe how plants from different continents coexist in a meticulously curated environment.

Beyond their botanical wonders, The Spheres demonstrate how nature can be integrated into modern urban life. The structure itself is a marvel, designed to maximize light penetration and create a microclimate where plants and people can thrive together. For the public, this space offers a rare opportunity to engage with nature in a setting that prioritizes both sustainability and well-being.

Seattle is known for its proximity to the outdoors, but the Amazon Spheres bring a slice of that experience into the heart of the city, proving that even in a technology-driven world, nature remains essential. Whether for plant enthusiasts, architecture lovers, or those simply seeking a moment of tranquility, The Spheres provide a unique and immersive way to reconnect with the natural world without leaving downtown.

Washington Park Arboretum

Leave the city behind and take a walk around the world at this 230-acre lakeside arboretum harboring hundreds of beautiful and expertly maintained native and exotic plants.

▼ Red maples are among the deciduous trees that put on a foliage display at the Arboretum in fall.

The Washington Park Arboretum, nestled on the shores of Lake Washington in Seattle, is a sprawling botanical haven, offering visitors a peaceful escape from the urban bustle while showcasing a vast array of plant species from around the world. Managed by the University of Washington and the City of Seattle, the Arboretum is a living museum where horticulture meets conservation, education, and nature immersion.

As you step into the Arboretum, you are immediately enveloped by the towering canopy of Douglas fir, western hemlock, and western red cedar trees. These native giants create a lush backdrop for the various themed gardens within the park. The Arboretum is home to both native plants and exotics from similar climates around the globe, providing a diverse and visually stunning landscape.

A meander through the Arboretum's winding paths introduces you to various plant collections, each carefully curated to tell a story about the interconnectedness of ecosystems. The Pacific Connections Garden is a highlight, where you can explore flora from regions sharing the Pacific Ocean's rim, such as New Zealand, Chile, and China. The New Zealand forest in particular showcases unique species like the southern rata, with its striking red flowers, and the silver fern, a symbol of New Zealand's wild landscapes.

The Woodland Garden is another gem, featuring a serene pond and pathways lined with native ferns, trillium, and vine maple. In spring, this area bursts into bloom with azaleas, rhododendrons, and magnolias, offering a colorful display that delights the senses.

▼ Weeping willows and a wide variety of other trees line the scenic and serene shoreline of Duck Bay, an inlet of Lake Washington bordering the Arboretum.

Throughout the year, the Arboretum transforms with the changing seasons. Spring is a time of rebirth, when cherry blossoms and magnolias paint the landscape with delicate pinks and whites. Summer brings lush greenery and fragrant gardens filled with lilies and roses. As autumn arrives, the Arboretum's Japanese maples put on a stunning show of fiery reds, oranges, and yellows, creating a breathtaking contrast against the evergreen backdrop. Even in winter, the Arboretum remains a serene destination, with conifer collections providing rich greens and the bare branches of deciduous trees adding a sculptural element to the landscape.

The Arboretum is not only a plant lover's paradise but also a sanctuary for wildlife. Over 200 bird species have been spotted here, making it a birdwatcher's dream. The varied habitats—ranging from woodlands to wetlands—attract an array of avian visitors. Great blue herons wade in the marshy shores of Lake Washington, while bald eagles soar overhead, scanning for fish. The Arboretum's ponds and streams provide ideal nesting grounds for mallards and wood ducks, while songbirds such as warblers, chickadees, and sparrows flit through the trees.

If you listen closely as you wander through the Arboretum's wooded areas, you may hear the tapping of pileated woodpeckers echoing through the forest, or the soft trill of a Pacific wren hidden among the underbrush. The dense plant life provides excellent cover for smaller creatures like chipmunks, squirrels, and occasionally a shy raccoon.

A visit to the Arboretum wouldn't be complete without a stroll along the boardwalks of Foster Island, a unique section of the park that extends out into Union Bay. This wetland habitat is teeming with life, offering visitors a chance to see great blue herons, red-winged blackbirds, and turtles basking on logs in the sun. The boardwalk leads you over water, through cattails and willow groves, making you feel as though you've left the city far behind.

During the warmer months, dragonflies and damselflies dart over the water, adding a magical quality to the wetland scenery. The island is also a prime location for spotting beavers and otters, who frequent the area's waterways, leaving behind evidence of their nighttime forays in the form of gnawed branches and dammed streams.

The Arboretum places a strong emphasis on education and sustainability. The Graham Visitors Center, located near the park's entrance, serves as a hub for information on the Arboretum's plant collections and wildlife. Visitors can learn about ongoing conservation efforts, sustainable gardening practices, and the importance of preserving biodiversity through interpretive displays, guided tours, and seasonal workshops.

Throughout the year, the Arboretum hosts a variety of events and educational programs for all ages. In spring and fall, the Arboretum hosts plant sales, where visitors can purchase rare and native plants for their own gardens. There are also guided birdwatching walks, horticultural tours, and workshops on topics ranging from pruning techniques to climate-resilient gardening.

Sustainability is at the heart of the Arboretum's mission. Many of the plantings are chosen not only for their beauty, but for their ability to thrive

▲ Giant horsetails bunch up at the waterline.

◀ The otherworldly bark of a Japanese flowering cherry adds a pinch of scarlet-orange to the Arboretum's diverse colorway.

▶ A red-eared slider patrols the shoreline of Duck Bay.

in Seattle's temperate climate with minimal water and maintenance. The Arboretum also serves as a testing ground for new conservation strategies, including the cultivation of climate-resilient species that may better adapt to the challenges posed by climate change.

The Arboretum's commitment to sustainability is also evident in its maintenance practices. Fallen leaves are left to decompose naturally, enriching the soil, and the park's wetlands act as natural water filters, improving the quality of water that flows into Lake Washington.

The Washington Park Arboretum is open year-round, offering visitors a peaceful retreat in the heart of the city. Whether you're a plant enthusiast, a birdwatcher, or someone simply seeking a quiet place to reconnect with nature, the Arboretum has something to offer in every season. The combination of lush plant collections, diverse wildlife, and tranquil landscapes makes it one of Seattle's most cherished natural spaces.

A visit to the Arboretum is a reminder of the beauty and complexity of the natural world, right in the middle of a bustling metropolis. From towering trees to delicate flowers, from bird song to the gentle rustling of leaves, the Arboretum invites you to slow down, breathe deeply, and appreciate the wonders of nature.

Enjoy the Zen at Seattle's Japanese Garden

Nestled within Washington Park Arboretum, the Japanese Garden offers a serene, meticulously designed space that transports visitors to a tranquil corner of Japan. Inspired by traditional Japanese garden principles, this 3.5-acre oasis features carefully curated plantings, including vibrant azaleas, irises, and Japanese maples, which provide stunning color displays year-round. In spring, the cherry blossoms create a delicate pink cloud, while in autumn, the fiery red maples steal the show.

The garden's design emphasizes harmony between nature and human craftsmanship. Meandering paths,

serene ponds, and rustic wooden bridges invite quiet reflection and exploration. Evergreen shrubs like Japanese holly and bamboo lend a sense of timelessness, while intricate stone lanterns and koi-filled ponds highlight Japanese aesthetics.

What sets the Japanese Garden apart is its dedication to seasonal change, where each visit offers a different experience, from the lush greens of summer to the crisp beauty of winter's bare branches. This peaceful retreat within the Arboretum captures the spirit of Japanese gardening—combining beauty, simplicity, and natural harmony in an urban oasis. The Japanese Garden (admission fee required) is open Tuesday through Sunday year-round, with hours changing seasonally.

◄ The views at the Japanese Garden change dramatically depending on the season.

▲ Koi fish subsist on small insects, crustaceans, and plant materials in the water, but in summer, staff at the Japanese Garden augment the fish's natural diet with commercial pelletized "koi chow."

Union Bay Natural Area

Join abundant wildlife passing through this former sawmill and dump site transformed into a natural oasis along the shores of Lake Washington.

On the northeastern shore of Lake Washington, tucked between the University of Washington campus and the waters of Union Bay, lies the Union Bay Natural Area (UBNA), a unique ecosystem that blends restoration, research, and recreation. Covering nearly 74 acres, UBNA is one of Seattle's most dynamic nature spaces, hosting a blend of wetlands, meadows, and riparian habitats that teem with wildlife. It's a place where both seasoned birdwatchers and casual walkers can immerse themselves in Seattle's natural diversity.

The Evolution of Union Bay

The story of Union Bay Natural Area is one of dramatic transformation. Before it became a landfill in the mid-20th century, the area was part of Union Bay, a natural inlet of Lake Washington. The lowering of Lake Washington's water level in 1916, due to the construction of the Lake Washington Ship Canal, drained much of the wetland, significantly altering the landscape. For decades, the site served as a city dump until it was capped in the 1960s.

In the 1970s, the University of Washington initiated efforts to rehabilitate the area, removing invasive species and planting native vegetation. Today, UBNA stands as an ecological success story, where natural processes have largely reclaimed a human-altered environment. It is now part of the Union Bay Natural Area and Montlake Fill, offering a unique combination of natural beauty and a living laboratory for ecological research.

A visit to UBNA provides a firsthand look at how reclaimed land can become a vital natural habitat, supporting not only flora and fauna but also the local community's love for outdoor exploration and nature-based learning.

▲ The permanent ponds at Union Bay Natural Area provide lots of habitat and forage for waterfowl and amphibians, among others.

Plants of the Wetlands and Meadows

UBNA's landscape is defined by its diverse vegetation, supporting plant species that thrive in its combination of wetland and meadow ecosystems. Tall, native grasses sway across the meadows, including varieties like tufted hairgrass and red fescue, which add texture and movement to the landscape. These grasses provide essential cover for small animals and ground-nesting birds, while also stabilizing the soil and preventing erosion.

In the wetter parts of the natural area, a rich array of sedges, rushes, and cattails line the edges of the marshlands. Common tule, a tall, spiky

191

grass-like plant, grows in thick clusters, offering crucial habitat for birds and amphibians. Look closely, and you might notice arrowhead plants, with their distinctive triangular leaves, and water smartweed, which blooms with tiny pink flowers during the warmer months.

Willows and red alders are some of the hardier trees thriving around the wetlands, with willows in particular providing habitat for insects, which in turn attract the many bird species that frequent the area. The striking red osier dogwood, with its red stems visible in winter, adds color to the landscape, and its white berries are an important food source for birds as autumn transitions to winter. Along the drier, upland areas, shrubs like Nootka rose and snowberry contribute to the area's floral diversity, their blooms attracting pollinators like bees and butterflies throughout spring and summer.

Birds of Union Bay Natural Area

With its varied habitats, UBNA is a premier birdwatching destination in Seattle. The area hosts more than 200 bird species, making it a paradise for both casual and serious birders.

Waterfowl are some of the main attractions. In spring and fall, migratory species like northern pintails, green-winged teal, and lesser scaup can be spotted dabbling in the shallow waters of Union Bay. Resident species, such as mallards and gadwalls, are frequently seen feeding in the marshes year-round. In winter, UBNA becomes a hub for spotting buffleheads, American wigeons, and even the occasional trumpeter swan, which find sanctuary here during the colder months.

Shorebirds are also drawn to UBNA's mudflats, especially during migration seasons. Greater and lesser yellowlegs can be seen foraging along the water's edge, along with killdeer and the occasional sandpiper. In late summer, spotted sandpipers make their appearance, easily identified by their distinctive "teetering" as they move along the shoreline in search of food.

Raptors frequent the skies above UBNA as well, scanning the landscape for small mammals and birds. Red-tailed hawks are the most common sight, often seen circling high above the meadows. In spring, the call of the osprey becomes a familiar sound, as these fish-hunting birds nest near Union Bay and dive dramatically into the water to catch fish. Bald eagles, too, are common visitors, drawn by the bay's abundant food sources. They can often be seen perched on the tallest trees along the shoreline or gliding over the water in search of fish.

Songbirds and smaller birds thrive among UBNA's shrubs and trees. Common yellowthroats, with their bright yellow chests and black masks, flit through the willow thickets, while American goldfinches add their vibrant colors to the landscape. In spring, listen for the bubbly song of marsh wrens and the chattering of black-capped chickadees. Warblers, including yellow-rumped and Wilson's warblers, pass through during migration, their vivid colors providing a delightful burst of life amid the greenery.

▲ A painted lady butterfly alights on a western red cedar's scale-like needles.

Insects, Amphibians, and Other Wildlife

The wetland habitat of UBNA makes it an ideal environment for amphibians, including Pacific tree frogs and long-toed salamanders. On warm, rainy evenings in spring, Pacific tree frogs sing their distinctive "ribbit" calls, marking the start of breeding season. In the shallow ponds, you might spot rough-skinned newts swimming gracefully or resting among the submerged vegetation.

Butterflies and bees thrive in UBNA's meadows, where flowering plants like yarrow, goldenrod, and aster bloom throughout summer. During sunny days, painted lady and western tiger swallowtail butterflies flit through the open meadows, stopping occasionally to feed on nectar-rich flowers. Dragonflies and damselflies are plentiful near the water, with species like the common green darner and the blue dasher darting over the marshes in pursuit of smaller insects.

The wetland and meadow habitats also support a variety of mammals, from muskrats, which build their lodges in the marshy areas, to coyotes, which occasionally roam the natural area, though they're rarely seen during daylight hours. Small mammals such as rabbits and voles can sometimes be spotted along the trails, especially near dusk when they emerge from cover to forage.

Seasonal Changes and Scenic Views

Each season brings new highlights to UBNA, making it a fascinating place to explore year-round. Spring is marked by the arrival of migratory birds, blooming wildflowers, and the return of amphibian activity as frogs and newts emerge to breed. Summer sees an explosion of greenery, with grasses, shrubs, and flowers in full bloom, attracting pollinators and offering food for young wildlife.

In autumn, the landscape takes on a golden hue as willows, alders, and dogwoods turn color, and the area becomes quieter as migratory birds head south. Winter brings a stark beauty, as frost covers the grasses, and the bare branches of trees reveal the silhouettes of birds perched high above.

Connecting with Nature and Community

Union Bay Natural Area is a place of community engagement, with regular restoration projects led by the UW Botanic Gardens and local volunteers. These efforts include removing invasive species like Himalayan blackberry and encouraging the growth of native plants, ensuring the health of UBNA's diverse ecosystem. Interpretive signs along the trails offer information about the area's flora, fauna, and ecological importance, making it a learning experience as well as a natural escape.

For those who love nature photography, UBNA provides ample opportunities, from sunrise reflections on Lake Washington to close-ups of waterfowl in the marshes. The site's trails are gentle and well-maintained, making them accessible for all ages, whether you're an avid birder, a family looking for a weekend outing, or a solo walker seeking tranquility in nature.

Union Bay Natural Area stands as a living testament to Seattle's commitment to urban ecology and habitat restoration. Whether you're marveling at a hawk soaring above, listening to the frogs' evening chorus, or watching the wildflowers sway in the summer breeze, UBNA offers a slice of wilderness in the city—a reminder of the resilience and beauty of nature right in Seattle's backyard.

Yesler Swamp—A Hidden Jewel

At the eastern edge of UBNA lies Yesler Swamp, a smaller but equally fascinating natural area that adds another layer of ecological and historical significance. Yesler Swamp is named for Henry Yesler, an early Seattle settler who operated a sawmill near the site in the 19th century. The swamp once served as a log-storage pond, and remnants of this history can still be seen today.

Yesler Swamp is one of the last remaining swamps in Seattle, offering a glimpse into the region's presettlement landscapes. Unlike UBNA's open grasslands and wetlands, the swamp features a dense canopy of native trees such as willows, red alders, and cottonwoods.

Beneath this leafy cover, a rich understory of skunk cabbage, sedges, and ferns thrives, creating a lush environment that feels worlds away from the bustling city nearby.

A well-maintained boardwalk winds through the swamp, providing visitors with an intimate view of its unique ecology. This area is particularly important for its role as a breeding ground for amphibians and a habitat for wood ducks, kingfishers, and other water-loving birds. In winter, the swamp takes on an almost mystical quality, with bare branches reflected in still waters, making it a favorite spot for photographers and nature lovers alike.

▼ Following the boardwalk into Yesler Swamp gets you deep into nature, even though the hustle and bustle of the University of Washington's urban campus is just a stone's throw away.

Ravenna Park

Duck into this 50-acre forested ravine and follow the course of the trickling creek as it cuts through the forest primeval and gives a glimpse of how Seattle used to look.

Nestled in Seattle's northeast, Ravenna Park offers a retreat into an enchanting slice of the Pacific Northwest, showcasing towering old-growth trees, dense ferns, trickling streams, and plentiful wildlife. Covering more than 50 acres, this park is known for its deep ravine, where a rich variety of plant and animal life flourishes year-round. For nature lovers, Ravenna Park is a mini-wilderness hidden right in the heart of the city, where every season brings its own highlights and discoveries.

The Ancient Trees of Ravenna

One of the park's most remarkable features is its forest of towering trees, which once included ancient giants believed to be over 1000 years old. Although most of these original old-growth trees were removed in the early 20th century, remnants of this natural legacy live on in the towering Douglas firs, western hemlocks, and bigleaf maples that line the ravine today.

Douglas firs dominate the park, their straight trunks stretching skyward, some reaching heights of more than 100 feet. These trees, with their deeply furrowed bark and whorls of needled branches, provide a habitat for all kinds of creatures, from squirrels and owls to insects that thrive in the thick, textured bark. Western hemlocks, known for their soft needles and elegant, drooping tops, thrive in the shady parts of the park. Beneath these towering evergreens, bigleaf maples spread their broad, lobed leaves, offering an impressive autumn display as they turn bright yellow and orange each fall.

In addition to these native giants, you'll find pockets of red alders and vine maples, whose brilliant red and yellow hues create a fiery contrast against the deep green evergreens in autumn. The forest canopy is diverse, capturing the essence of Pacific Northwest woodlands while providing shelter to animals and shade for the park's undergrowth.

◄ The varied foliage of Ravenna Park is evident in this bird's-eye autumn view of the ravine.

A Carpet of Ferns and Forest Flora

One of the things that sets Ravenna Park apart is the lush, layered understory blanketing the forest floor. Walking along the trails, you're likely to notice the dense carpets of swordferns, hardy native plants that thrive in the damp, shaded areas. Their long, toothed fronds unfurl in all directions, creating a green carpet beneath the towering trees. In addition to swordferns, bracken and lady ferns add to the diversity, their delicate fronds filling gaps in the forest undergrowth.

The understory is also rich with the waxy, holly-like leaves of Oregon grape, a common sight in Pacific Northwest forests. In spring, bright yellow flowers appear, later producing purple berries that feed local wildlife. Salal, another key component of the understory, grows in dense thickets with glossy leaves and clusters of dark purple berries that sustain birds through the colder months. Spring brings a burst of color to the understory with wildflowers like trilliums, bleeding hearts, and woodland violets, each dotting the forest floor with bright whites, pinks, and purples.

Ravenna Creek: A Quiet, Vital Waterway

The heart of Ravenna Park is its ravine, where Ravenna Creek flows through the dense forest. While most of the creek was redirected underground years ago, a section still winds through the park, creating a natural water source for plants and animals alike. Walking along the ravine trail, you might catch

▼ Raccoons might be the most frequently seen mammals in Ravenna Park, besides humans and their dogs.

▲ A dark-eyed junco alights on a young red alder branch.

the soft sound of water trickling over rocks, a reminder of the creek's presence even when it's hidden by dense vegetation.

Near the creek, moisture-loving plants such as skunk cabbage and lady ferns thrive. Skunk cabbage, with its broad leaves and distinctive yellow flowers, appears each spring, filling the air with its earthy scent. This plant is an early bloomer, offering food and shelter to small animals emerging from winter dormancy. The creek banks also provide a perfect habitat for red osier dogwood, identifiable by its bright red stems, which add a splash of color against the greenery. In winter, these vibrant red stems stand out, adding a burst of color to the park's landscape.

Wildlife Wonders: Birds, Mammals, and More

Ravenna Park is alive with wildlife, from birds and insects to small mammals. Birdwatchers flock to the park year-round, binoculars in hand, as the park's mixture of habitats supports a rich diversity of bird species. You might hear the distinct call of the Pacific wren, a small brown bird that loves to hide among fallen logs and brush. Golden-crowned kinglets, with their distinctive yellow head stripes, flit through the upper branches, and in winter, these tiny birds often form mixed flocks with black-capped chickadees, red-breasted nuthatches, and dark-eyed juncos.

Larger birds are also common. Look up, and you might spot a red-tailed hawk circling above, scanning for small mammals below, or even a barred owl perched silently among the trees, waiting for dusk to hunt. The creek attracts water-loving birds, such as mallards and great blue herons, which can occasionally be seen wading through the shallow pools in search of small fish or insects.

Mammals are frequent visitors to the park's quieter areas. Raccoons are known to explore the creek banks, especially at night, while eastern gray squirrels make their homes in the park's trees, busily foraging for acorns, seeds, and berries. Occasionally, visitors spot a coyote, especially in the early morning or evening hours. Coyotes help control the population of smaller mammals, and while they're shy around humans, they play an important role in maintaining the park's ecological balance.

Seasonal Splendor

Every season in Ravenna Park brings something new to discover. Spring transforms the park into a burst of green, as ferns unfurl and wildflowers blossom. Trilliums, with their striking white petals, are one of the first signs of spring, often popping up along the trails and providing an early source of nectar for pollinators.

In summer, the shady canopy keeps the park refreshingly cool, attracting walkers and picnickers alike. The creek remains a haven for dragonflies

and damselflies, which flit over the water's surface. Fall is perhaps the most stunning season, as bigleaf maples and vine maples light up the park with hues of red, yellow, and orange. The forest floor is carpeted with fallen leaves, creating a picturesque autumn scene. In winter, the park becomes a tranquil, misty escape; bare branches create a stark beauty, and evergreens stand out even more vividly, while the understory's bright red osier dogwood adds warmth to the cold landscape.

Community Engagement with Nature

Ravenna Park is more than just a green space; it's a beloved community spot that brings people together through nature. Local groups often host volunteer days for trail maintenance and native plant restoration, helping control invasive species like English ivy and Himalayan blackberry. These efforts ensure that the park remains a healthy, vibrant ecosystem for both plants and wildlife. Interpretive signs along the trails provide educational information about the park's ecology, making it a great spot for families and nature enthusiasts to learn about Seattle's native flora and fauna.

Whether you're there to spot birds, hike the trails, or simply enjoy the serenity of the forest, Ravenna Park offers an escape from the bustle of the city. It's a place where you can reconnect with nature, witness the seasons in their full splendor, and immerse yourself in the rich tapestry of Seattle's natural environment. With its towering trees, diverse plant life, and bustling wildlife, Ravenna Park is a reminder of the wild beauty that lies within reach for Seattle's urban dwellers.

▲ Oregon grape is a native, holly-like evergreen shrub used extensively by Coast Salish peoples as a medicine with antimicrobial and anti-inflammatory properties.

► Sitka spruce trees, unmistakable for their jigsaw-puzzle bark, thrive at the bottom of Ravenna Park's dark and moist ravine.

FIELD TRIP 4

Green Lake Park

Flock like the birds to Green Lake in the center of north Seattle to immerse yourself in the sights and sounds of elemental nature for just a little while.

Nestled in the heart of Seattle, Green Lake is a vibrant urban park that offers much more than a picturesque spot for jogging, kayaking, or picnicking. This beloved destination is also a haven for local wildlife and a living showcase of the Pacific Northwest's natural diversity. Encircled by a 2.8-mile trail and surrounded by neighborhoods bustling with activity, Green Lake's tranquil waters and abundance of greenery provide an essential refuge for plants, animals, and people alike.

For nature enthusiasts, Green Lake offers an opportunity to experience the dynamic interplay between urban life and the wild world. From bird-watching to observing seasonal plant cycles, this park is a microcosm of the larger ecosystems that define the Seattle region.

A Diverse Ecosystem at the Heart of Seattle

At the center of Green Lake Park lies the lake itself, a shallow, 259-acre body of water that supports a variety of aquatic and terrestrial life. The surrounding parklands include grassy fields, forested patches, and areas of restored wetlands that together form a thriving ecosystem.

The lake's waters are teeming with fish species such as rainbow trout, largemouth bass, and yellow perch, making it a popular spot for anglers. Aquatic plants like duckweed and fragrant water lilies float on the surface, while submerged vegetation provides habitat for invertebrates and small fish.

Encircling the lake, native trees like bigleaf maple, Douglas fir, and western red cedar form a natural canopy that shelters wildlife and shades visitors

▲ Duck Island just off Prospect Point along the northwest shoreline of Green Lake looks like it has always been there, but was actually built by FDR's Works Progress Administration in 1936.

on sunny days. Beneath these giants, shrubs like red-flowering currant and snowberry create a dense understory, bursting into bloom in spring and offering food and shelter for birds and insects.

A Birdwatcher's Delight

Green Lake is a magnet for bird lovers, with over 200 bird species recorded in the park throughout the year. Whether you're a seasoned birder or just starting out, you're likely to spot some of the region's most charismatic avian residents.

The lake's surface often glimmers with the movement of waterfowl. Mallards are the most common, their iridescent green heads brightening the scene, but sharp-eyed observers can also spot American wigeons, ring-necked ducks, and the occasional hooded merganser. During the winter months, migratory species like buffleheads and gadwalls make Green Lake their temporary home, offering a seasonal treat for birdwatchers.

203

In the trees and along the shoreline, songbirds such as black-capped chickadees, golden-crowned kinglets, and red-winged blackbirds fill the air with their calls. The lake is also a favored hunting ground for great blue herons, which can often be seen stalking the shallows with their deliberate, graceful movements.

Above it all, bald eagles and red-tailed hawks circle the skies, keeping a watchful eye on the park's abundant prey. These majestic raptors serve as a reminder of Green Lake's role in supporting not just its immediate inhabitants but the wider web of life in the city.

▲ American coots gather en masse in spring and summer on Green Lake.

Small Mammals and Hidden Creatures

While the birds may steal the show, Green Lake is also home to an array of mammals and smaller wildlife. Gray squirrels are ubiquitous, darting through trees and scavenging for acorns. At dusk, look for rabbits grazing quietly on the grassy lawns or the occasional raccoon foraging near the water.

If you venture to the quieter, wilder edges of the park, you might spot muskrats swimming near the shoreline or signs of beaver activity, such as gnawed branches and small dams. These industrious animals play a crucial role in maintaining the wetland habitats around the lake.

Seasonal Blooms and Native Plants

Green Lake Park also showcases the natural beauty of the Pacific Northwest's plant life, particularly during the spring and summer months. The park's native landscaping efforts have introduced a variety of species, including Pacific ninebark, vine maple, and Oregon grape, which contribute to the area's ecological health and visual appeal.

Taiga Wetlands

In 2022, the nonprofit Friends of Green Lake anchored two 650-square-foot islands that provide native plant habitat for birds and other wildlife in the middle of Green Lake, not far from Duck Island. Besides welcoming birds up top, these "Taiga Wetlands"—named after Taiga Hinckley, a valued employee of the Green Lake Boathouse who died tragically during an evening paddle—also sequester nutrients from the lake for uptake by the plants above and to augment the thick microbial biofilm on the roots underneath, which support fish habitat and a diverse community of aquatic macroinvertebrates (for example, mayflies, midges, and mites).

▼ Green Lake's Taiga Wetlands

In early spring, the iconic cherry blossoms near the lake's eastern edge draw crowds, their delicate pink and white flowers heralding the changing season. Later in the year, wildflowers like lupines, yarrow, and fireweed provide bursts of color along trails and open meadows, attracting pollinators like bees and butterflies.

The park's wetlands, located near the northern and southern ends of the lake, are especially vibrant. Cattails and sedges dominate these areas, providing shelter for amphibians like Pacific tree frogs and creating feeding grounds for waterfowl.

Exploring Green Lake's Natural Side

Green Lake's accessibility makes it easy for visitors to immerse themselves in its natural wonders. The loop trail is the park's most popular feature, offering a scenic walk or bike ride that brings you up close to the lake's plants and wildlife. Along the trail, interpretive signs highlight key features of the park's ecology, helping visitors learn about the importance of urban green spaces.

For a more leisurely experience, rent a kayak or paddleboard to explore the lake's waters and catch glimpses of fish, turtles, and birds up close. Birdwatchers may want to bring binoculars to spot some of the rarer species that frequent the park, especially during migration seasons.

Green Lake is also a fantastic destination for families, with areas like the Woodland Lawn offering plenty of space for children to explore and learn about nature.

Conservation in Action

Green Lake Park is not only a recreational gem but also a site of ongoing conservation efforts. Invasive species like Himalayan blackberry and English ivy are regularly removed by volunteers, and native plants are reintroduced to restore the park's natural balance. These efforts ensure that Green Lake continues to support the wide variety of species that call it home.

Community involvement plays a big role in preserving the park's ecosystem. Events like habitat-restoration days and guided nature walks invite locals and visitors to become active stewards of this cherished green space.

▼ Green Lake is a 259-acre true oasis in the middle of north Seattle.

A Green Escape in the Emerald City

Green Lake is a testament to the resilience of nature within an urban setting. Its thriving ecosystems and rich biodiversity offer a glimpse into the natural beauty that defines the Pacific Northwest, all within easy reach of downtown Seattle. Whether you're birdwatching, enjoying a peaceful walk, or simply soaking up the scenery, Green Lake provides a space to reconnect with the wild world amid the city's hustle and bustle.

For anyone seeking a deeper connection with nature in Seattle, Green Lake stands as a reminder of the importance of preserving green spaces and the many ways they enrich our lives. It's more than a park—it's a living sanctuary for plants, animals, and people alike.

Pioneering Local and Global Conservation at Woodland Park Zoo

Not far from Green Lake, Woodland Park Zoo offers a variety of immersive exhibits, such as the African Savanna and the Tropical Rain Forest, where visitors can observe a diverse range of animals in habitats that mimic their natural environments. The zoo also features seasonal events and hands-on experiences, including behind-the-scenes tours and animal encounters designed to engage the public in wildlife preservation and environmental sustainability.

Woodland Park Zoo is also a leader when it comes to both local and global conservation. Locally, the zoo is committed to protecting species native to the Pacific Northwest. One of its key initiatives focuses on the northern spotted owl, an endangered species that faces grave threats from habitat destruction and competition with the invasive barred owl. The zoo collaborates with local wildlife agencies to support breeding programs and recovery strategies aimed at preserving these iconic birds. It also contributes to the restoration of salmon populations in the region. Chinook and coho salmon, which are vital to the ecosystem of the Pacific Northwest, are struggling due to habitat loss, pollution, and climate change. Woodland Park Zoo partners with organizations that work to remove barriers to salmon migration, restore riparian habitats, and address the environmental pressures that endanger these fish. Alongside these efforts, the zoo is helping protect local pollinators, including native bees and butterflies, which are essential for maintaining the health of local ecosystems and agricultural systems.

The zoo's conservation efforts extend beyond Washington state, focusing on species and habitats around the world. Woodland Park Zoo supports a variety of projects aimed at protecting endangered species in their natural environments; one notable example is its work to conserve gorillas in Central Africa. The zoo collaborates with other institutions to prevent poaching, address human-wildlife conflict, and protect the rainforests that these great apes call home. The zoo's commitment to tigers is another example of its global conservation reach. By working with partners in India, Southeast Asia, and Russia, the zoo helps ensure the protection of tiger habitats, while also supporting anti-poaching efforts and programs to reduce the illegal wildlife trade. Similarly, the zoo is deeply involved in penguin conservation, especially for the endangered Humboldt penguins of South America. Through collaborative efforts, the zoo helps protect the coastal habitats these birds rely on, which are threatened by overfishing and climate change.

In addition to habitat protection, Woodland Park Zoo participates in breeding and reintroduction programs to help bolster endangered species populations. The zoo is involved in Species Survival Plans (SSPs) that coordinate breeding efforts for a variety of endangered animals. For instance, it has helped breed red wolves, an endangered species from the southeastern United States, and Przewalski's horses, a wild horse that had nearly gone extinct. By contributing to global breeding efforts, Woodland Park Zoo helps ensure genetic diversity within these species and supports their eventual reintroduction into the wild. Through these efforts, the zoo is not only preserving species in captivity but also playing a role in their resurgence in their native habitats.

At the core of the zoo's mission is education, and it has a strong focus on engaging the public in conservation efforts. Through immersive exhibits and interactive experiences, visitors gain insights into the challenges faced by endangered species and the environmental issues threatening ecosystems worldwide. Its educational programs are designed to inspire people of all ages to take action in their own lives to support conservation.

The zoo's commitment to sustainability is also evident in its own operations. Woodland Park Zoo is dedicated to reducing its environmental impact through practices such as energy conservation, waste reduction, and using sustainable materials in its exhibits. For instance, it runs a comprehensive composting program and has invested in water-saving technologies to reduce its ecological footprint. These efforts align with its broader conservation goals by modeling environmentally responsible behavior for the community. Additionally, the zoo is actively involved in local habitat-restoration projects, working with environmental organizations to help restore wetlands and forests in the Pacific Northwest, ensuring that these vital ecosystems remain healthy and resilient.

Woodland Park Zoo's collaborative approach to conservation extends to its partnerships with more than thirty conservation organizations around the world. It works closely with groups like the World Wildlife Fund (WWF), the Wildlife Conservation Society (WCS), and the International Union for Conservation of Nature (IUCN). By sharing research, resources, and expertise, these

▲ Peacocks stroll the grounds freely at the Woodland Park Zoo.

collaborations amplify the impact of the zoo's work and enable it to reach more areas of the globe in need of conservation intervention.

Technology also plays a key role in the zoo's conservation efforts. The zoo uses cutting-edge tools, such as satellite tracking and camera traps, to monitor wildlife populations in their natural habitats. These technologies allow researchers to gather data on species behavior, migration patterns, and population health, which informs conservation strategies. The zoo also supports scientific research in areas such as reproductive technologies, helping increase the genetic diversity of endangered species through artificial insemination and other techniques.

Through these diverse and interconnected efforts, Woodland Park Zoo plays a crucial role in the preservation of wildlife and ecosystems. Its commitment to both local and global conservation, combined with its educational outreach and sustainable practices, ensures that it continues to be a leader in the effort to protect our planet's natural heritage.

Magnuson Park Wetlands

Poke around the web of trails that cuts through these teeming wetlands in the middle of Magnuson Park for an immersion in nature you wouldn't expect at the site of a former naval airbase.

Tucked along Lake Washington's western shore, Magnuson Park's wetlands are a remarkable restored habitat set within the sprawling 350-acre Warren G. Magnuson Park. Once home to a naval air station, the wetlands today are a flourishing ecosystem of ponds, marshes, and native plant life, providing a sanctuary for wildlife and an immersive experience for nature lovers. As one of Seattle's largest urban restoration projects, the Magnuson Park wetlands showcase the beauty and diversity of wetland habitats, all against the backdrop of one of Seattle's best-loved parks.

From Military Airfield to Nature Haven

The Magnuson Park wetlands are the result of a restoration project that began in the early 2000s, transforming paved areas and degraded landscapes into thriving natural habitats. Designed to improve local water quality, enhance biodiversity, and create sustainable green space, the project incorporated wetlands, meadows, and upland forest areas. By adding natural water filtration and flood protection, these wetlands offer benefits to the local environment while creating vital habitat for plants and wildlife. Today, Magnuson Park wetlands stand as a testament to the resilience of nature, where flora and fauna thrive once more.

A Tapestry of Native Plants

The Magnuson Park wetlands are home to an impressive variety of native plants that have taken root and now define the landscape. Near the marshy

◄ A boardwalk leads into the Magnuson Park wetlands, a 154-acre network of native wildlife habitat that looks like it has always been there, but was in fact installed by Seattle Parks and its partners over six years, beginning in 2006.

► The shallow ponds of the Magnuson Park wetlands are a haven for Pacific chorus frogs and other native amphibians.

ponds, look for swathes of cattails, whose tall, spiked stalks provide crucial cover for birds and small animals. Their fluffy seed heads release in fall, spreading with the wind and adding a soft, natural texture to the water's edge.

The wetlands are dotted with Pacific willows, red alders, and Sitka spruce, all native trees well suited to this area. Pacific willows, with their slender branches and narrow leaves, provide shade and shelter for animals along the water's edge. Red osier dogwood, recognizable by its vibrant red stems in winter, stands alongside native shrubs like snowberry and Nootka rose. Snowberry's small white berries are not only visually striking but provide sustenance for birds in colder months, while Nootka rose flowers bring delicate, pink blooms in spring, attracting pollinators like bees and butterflies.

The open, meadow-like areas surrounding the wetlands are rich with grasses and wildflowers, including native sedges, rushes, and goldenrod. In summer, these meadows burst into a profusion of color as lupines, daisies, and asters come into bloom, attracting pollinators and creating a vibrant backdrop to the wetlands. In fall, goldenrods and asters go to seed, providing additional food sources for birds and small mammals as winter approaches.

Birds: Stars of the Wetlands

Magnuson Park wetlands are a prime birdwatching location, drawing a wide variety of species that rely on these wetlands for food, shelter, and nesting sites. The ponds and waterways attract waterfowl like mallards, gadwalls, and northern shovelers, while American coots and pied-billed grebes can often be seen diving for food beneath the water's surface. In spring and fall, migratory birds including green-winged teal, buffleheads, and even the occasional hooded merganser make brief appearances, adding seasonal diversity to the park's bird population.

Shorebirds, including greater yellowlegs and spotted sandpipers, are frequently found along the muddy shores of the ponds, where they forage for invertebrates in the shallow water. Their long legs and quick, darting movements make them easy to spot as they search for small creatures among the vegetation.

Songbirds also abound here, flitting through the shrubs and trees along the trail. Listen for the melodic songs of yellow warblers, black-capped chickadees, and white-crowned sparrows, all of which are common visitors to the park. The bright yellow plumage of the yellow warbler is a delightful sight against the greenery of the shrubs and trees. In the understory, Pacific wrens and song sparrows forage on the ground, while tree swallows swoop through the air in pursuit of insects.

Raptors, too, are drawn to the rich ecosystem of the wetlands. Red-tailed hawks are common here, often seen perched on snags or soaring overhead as they scan for prey. Bald eagles, frequently spotted around Magnuson Park, occasionally glide over the wetlands, adding a majestic presence to the area. During migration season, sharp-shinned hawks may also make an appearance, further diversifying the avian inhabitants of these wetlands.

Amphibians, Reptiles, and Insects

The wetlands provide an ideal habitat for amphibians, whose populations benefit from the abundance of clean water and natural vegetation. Pacific chorus frogs are among the park's most common amphibians, their distinctive "ribbit" calls ringing out in spring and early summer as they breed. Rough-skinned newts, with their dark, warty skin and bright orange bellies, also thrive in these habitats, swimming through the ponds and hiding in the undergrowth. Both species play an essential role in the ecosystem, acting as both predator and prey in the wetland food web.

Dragonflies and damselflies are plentiful around the wetland ponds, where they flit over the water in a colorful display. Species like the blue dasher and common green darner dart above the surface, feeding on smaller insects and providing an important food source for birds and amphibians. Monarch butterflies, though rare, can sometimes be spotted fluttering around the meadows, where milkweed and other flowering plants offer nectar.

During summer, bees and other pollinators swarm around the wildflowers, particularly attracted to goldenrod, lupine, and asters. These insects are crucial to the health of the wetlands' plant life, supporting the growth and reproduction of the native flora that, in turn, sustains the entire ecosystem.

The Dynamic Seasonal Changes

Each season brings its own unique beauty to the Magnuson Park wetlands. In spring, the wetlands awaken with an explosion of fresh growth. Tree buds open, wildflowers bloom, and migratory birds arrive, adding splashes of color and activity. Frogs begin their mating calls, and young ducks and goslings can be seen paddling through the ponds.

By summer, the wetlands are lush and full, with thick foliage and wildflowers at their peak. Dragonflies hover above the ponds, while bees and butterflies feast on the blooming plants. This is also a great time for birdwatchers, as fledgling birds begin to venture out on their own.

► The striking red stems of the red osier dogwood stand out vividly during winter, adding a splash of color when most other plants are bare and brown.

In autumn, the wetlands take on a quieter, golden tone. Willows, dogwoods, and alders display their fall colors, and as leaves drop, the wetland's skeleton emerges, revealing the shapes and structures of the trees and shrubs. Birds feed heavily on berries, seeds, and insects as they prepare for winter or migration.

Winter brings a sense of tranquility, with frost-tipped grasses and bare branches casting reflections in the ponds. The wetland remains active even in the coldest months, with hardy waterfowl, raptors, and resident songbirds making it their winter home. A quiet walk through the park on a chilly morning reveals subtle signs of life, from animal tracks in the mud to the calls of wintering birds.

Connecting with Magnuson's Wild Heart

The Magnuson Park wetlands are more than a natural escape; they're a model of ecological restoration and a reminder of nature's resilience. Local organizations and volunteers continue to play a crucial role in maintaining and enhancing the park's biodiversity, hosting community work parties and educational programs to engage the public in conservation efforts.

Whether you're an experienced birdwatcher, a family looking to explore Seattle's wildlife, or a solo walker seeking serenity, the Magnuson Park wetlands offer a profound connection to the natural world. With every season revealing new layers of life, this vibrant habitat is a reminder of the incredible beauty and diversity that can thrive within an urban landscape.

▲ Red alder trees bordering wetland waterways are biding their time until industrious American beavers need their wood to improve a nearby lodge or redirect the water flow just so. Indeed, beavers have played an increasingly larger role in maintaining and improving the watery landscapes of the Magnuson Park wetlands in recent years.

Meadowbrook Pond

Explore the heart of the Thornton Creek watershed that is the ecological lifeblood of Northeast Seattle past, present, and future.

▼ Meadowbrook Pond is a naturalistic but nevertheless man-made catchment system that drains stormwater overflows from the two forks of Thornton Creek that merge just to the north.

Nestled in the heart of northeast Seattle's Meadowbrook neighborhood, Meadowbrook Pond offers a surprising slice of tranquility and rich biodiversity. This urban wetland, part of the larger Thornton Creek watershed, is an impressive example of natural engineering within the city, designed to help manage stormwater while creating habitat for plants and wildlife. Tucked behind quiet residential streets, the pond feels like a hidden gem where visitors can stroll along boardwalks, pause at observation points, and immerse themselves in a vibrant natural setting just minutes from bustling streets.

From Flood Control to Wildlife Refuge

Meadowbrook Pond was created as part of a flood-control and habitat-restoration project in the late 1990s. Originally a simple floodplain, it was reimagined into an engineered pond system that filters stormwater and protects downstream areas from flooding. Today, this well-managed ecosystem channels excess water from the nearby Thornton Creek while providing a sanctuary for local plants, animals, and migratory birds. In addition to its practical purpose, Meadowbrook Pond serves as a haven for wildlife in the middle of an urban landscape, benefiting both the environment and those who come to enjoy its natural beauty.

Diverse Flora Along the Pond

The vegetation around Meadowbrook Pond reflects the region's diverse native flora. Wetland species dominate the landscape, creating a complex habitat where each plant contributes to the ecosystem's health. At the pond's edges, common cattails sway in the breeze, their fluffy seed heads visible in fall, while clusters of hardstem bulrush, with their slender, tubular stalks, provide essential shelter for aquatic creatures.

In the wetter areas, Pacific willows and red alders grow in abundance, their roots stabilizing the soil and helping filter the water. Pacific willows, with their soft, downy leaves, add a delicate green hue in spring, while alders enrich the soil with nitrogen, supporting other plants around the pond. Near the shore, look for western red cedar and Sitka spruce with big roots that help stabilize the shoreline. These evergreens also provide year-round cover for wildlife.

In drier sections of the park, native shrubs like snowberry, with its white berries, and Nootka rose, a native wild rose that blooms in early summer, draw in pollinators and small animals. The shrubs and trees also support a variety of mosses and lichens, which add layers of texture and greenery. In spring and summer, watch for lupines and goldenrod dotting the meadows with bursts of purple and yellow, attracting bees and butterflies.

Birdwatching Highlights

Meadowbrook Pond is a birder's paradise, especially during migration seasons. A variety of species find shelter, food, and nesting sites here, making it an ideal spot for birdwatching year-round. Mallards, Canada geese, and gadwalls are among the common waterfowl that frequent the pond, their chicks visible in spring as they paddle behind their parents. Look closely, and you may spot the smaller green-winged teal, a dabbling duck with a distinct iridescent patch on its wings.

The trees and shrubs around the pond are home to numerous songbirds, such as the black-capped chickadee, spotted towhee, and white-crowned sparrow. American robins are also plentiful, foraging on the ground for insects and worms. In spring and summer, colorful yellow warblers and American goldfinches can be seen flitting through the foliage, adding bright yellow flashes against the green backdrop.

Raptors often visit the area, particularly red-tailed hawks and Cooper's hawks, which are drawn by the smaller birds and mammals around the pond. Ospreys, known for their fishing skills, occasionally make an appearance, diving into the water to catch fish.

Amphibians, Reptiles, and Insects

The still waters and dense vegetation around Meadowbrook Pond provide ideal conditions for a variety of amphibians and insects. One of the most notable residents is the Pacific chorus frog, whose characteristic "ribbit" call is a familiar sound during spring and early summer. These small green and brown frogs are commonly seen along the water's edge, where they find ample shelter and food.

Dragonflies and damselflies are frequent visitors in the warmer months, with species like the blue dasher and common green darner skimming the pond's surface, hunting smaller insects. They play an essential role in controlling mosquito populations, adding another layer of ecological balance to the pond. Native butterflies, including the western tiger swallowtail and cabbage white, are also common sights, fluttering around the wildflowers and shrubs on sunny days.

Occasionally, visitors may spot garter snakes basking on rocks or the banks, especially during spring and summer. These nonvenomous reptiles thrive in the wetland's cool, damp environment, where they hunt for frogs, fish, and insects, helping keep the pond's ecosystem in balance.

Seasonal Changes and Habitat Highlights

Each season at Meadowbrook Pond brings unique sights and sounds, making it a place worth visiting throughout the year. In spring, the pond comes alive with fresh growth, as trees leaf out, wildflowers bloom, and birds return to nest and raise their young. The air is filled with birdsong, and the pond's

▼ Mallards are among the waterfowl that feel right at home here at Meadowbrook Pond.

◄ Pacific aster is one of many wildflower species popping up around Meadowbrook Pond in spring and summer.

perimeter is vibrant with blossoming flowers and budding trees. Pacific chorus frogs add their calls to the seasonal chorus, creating a symphony of nature that is unmistakable.

During summer, the pond is at its fullest, with dense green vegetation and tall cattails lining the shore. Dragonflies zip above the water, while pollinators visit the wildflowers in the meadow areas. The tall trees provide shade and refuge for songbirds, and the pond's resident waterfowl, including ducks and geese, are frequently seen paddling across its surface.

Autumn at Meadowbrook Pond is a quieter, contemplative time. Trees like bigleaf maple and red alder shift to shades of gold and rust, and berries become a food source for migrating birds as they prepare for their journeys. The pond's water levels may drop, but the park's peaceful ambiance is heightened, with colorful leaves casting reflections in the still waters.

In winter, the wetlands take on a stark beauty. Bare branches reveal the structure of the trees, and the evergreens stand out even more against the winter landscape. Waterfowl like mallards and Canada geese remain, joined by wintering species such as northern pintails and American wigeons. Winter also brings opportunities to spot raptors, as leafless trees make it easier to see hawks perched overhead.

A Community Effort in Conservation

Meadowbrook Pond's success as a wetland habitat is due in large part to the work of local volunteers and conservation groups who continue to maintain and enhance the space. Regular community cleanups, invasive-species removal efforts, and habitat-restoration projects keep the area vibrant and healthy. Interpretive signs around the pond help educate visitors on the importance of wetland ecosystems and encourage respectful engagement with the natural surroundings.

Whether you're an avid birder, a photographer, or simply looking for a peaceful stroll through nature, Meadowbrook Pond provides a serene and biodiverse retreat. It's a testament to Seattle's dedication to preserving green spaces and offers a perfect example of how urban areas can harmoniously support both people and wildlife.

◄ Nootka roses bloom in the late summer and early fall at Meadowbrook Pond.

Daylighting Thornton Creek

It's hard to believe that unassuming little Thornton Creek, as it trickles through portions of northeast Seattle before emptying into Lake Washington at Matthews Beach, could be a major ecological feature of the metro area. But indeed it is, dominating a 7400 acre watershed that encompasses some 7 percent of the city's 84-square-mile footprint. The creek consists of two branches that come together at Meadowbrook Pond. The north fork flows out of Ronald Bog to Twin Ponds Park in Shoreline, then under Interstate 5 and through the Jackson Park golf course before cutting southeast toward Meadowbrook Pond. Meanwhile, the south fork starts near North Seattle College and flows south below Northgate—which used to be a big bog—before zigzagging east through three small parks and under several large roads and meeting the north fork at its Meadowbrook Pond confluence.

These bodies of water once flowed freely, supporting a rich ecosystem, including abundant runs of salmon and other native species. However, with Seattle's rapid urbanization in the early to mid-20th century, much of the creek was buried in culverts, and many of its tributary streams were diverted or encroached upon, leading to severe habitat degradation.

Efforts to restore Thornton Creek have been ongoing for decades, with one of the most ambitious goals being to "daylight" portions of the creek—reopening sections that were previously confined to pipes and culverts. This restoration work has been championed by community activists, environmental groups, and the City of Seattle. While some sections have been successfully uncovered, such as portions near Thornton Creek's headwaters in the Meadowbrook neighborhood, challenges remain in fully daylighting the creek through its urbanized sections.

The revitalization efforts also include the creation of Meadowbrook Pond in the 1990s, designed to mitigate flooding and improve water quality. The pond filters stormwater before it flows into Thornton Creek, enhancing both water quality and wildlife habitat. Restoration projects have focused on removing invasive plant species, replanting native vegetation, and improving fish passage, while community involvement continues to be a key part of the work.

Today, Thornton Creek is a crucial part of the watershed, providing habitat for salmon and other wildlife. Despite its challenges, ongoing conservation efforts aim to restore and protect the creek's health, with a vision of revitalizing this vital waterway as an ecological and community asset for generations to come.

Carkeek Park

Explore ocean beaches, coastal wetlands, forested trails, and salmon-bearing creeks in this 220-acre natural gem in northwest Seattle.

Nestled in northwest Seattle along Puget Sound, Carkeek Park is a hidden gem, blending beaches, forested trails, wetlands, and creeks into a captivating natural haven. Carkeek Park's 220 acres invite exploration for those drawn to the Pacific Northwest's coastal forests and marine ecosystems. Known for its varied terrain and thriving habitats, the park offers visitors a serene escape filled with opportunities to observe diverse plant life, wildlife, and sweeping views of the Olympic Mountains across Puget Sound.

Coastal Beach and Intertidal Zones

Carkeek Park's beach along Puget Sound is a primary draw, providing a window into the marine life and natural beauty of Seattle's waterfront. At low tide, the intertidal zone reveals a landscape teeming with life, from barnacles and mussels clinging to rocks to colorful sea stars and anemones nestled among tidal pools. For those interested in marine biology, the park's beach offers a glimpse of the interconnectedness of these coastal ecosystems.

Shellfish like clams and mussels filter the seawater, playing a critical role in the ecosystem's health, while small crabs scuttle between rocks, seeking food and shelter. Seabirds, including sandpipers and black oystercatchers, forage along the shoreline, their beaks probing the sand for marine invertebrates. You might even catch a glimpse of harbor seals bobbing in the water, their curious faces briefly surfacing before they vanish beneath the waves.

Golden sunsets at the beach highlight the park's western-facing views, where Puget Sound's waters meet the dramatic silhouette of the Olympic Mountains, creating an unforgettable sight. Evenings are an ideal time to watch bald eagles and osprey soaring overhead, scanning the water for fish.

► A classic driftwood-festooned Pacific Northwest ocean beach is just one of the natural charms on display at Carkeek Park in northwest Seattle.

FIELD TRIP 8

Piper's Creek and Salmon Spawning

Running through the heart of Carkeek Park is Piper's Creek, a salmon-bearing stream that adds a dynamic ecosystem to the park. Every fall, Piper's Creek becomes the stage for an incredible wildlife spectacle: the return of chum and coho salmon. This salmon run has been carefully supported by restoration efforts, which have improved water quality and habitat conditions along the creek.

During spawning season in November and December, visitors can witness the salmon battling upstream to lay their eggs, a journey filled with obstacles as they navigate rocks, fallen branches, and swift currents. The life cycle of salmon plays a vital role in the ecosystem, providing nutrients to the surrounding forest and feeding wildlife, including raccoons, birds, and other creatures. This restoration success story is a powerful reminder of nature's resilience and the importance of conservation.

Walking along the creek trail, you'll notice an array of riparian plants like red alder, willow, and salmonberry that thrive along the water's edge. These native plants create shade, regulate water temperature, and provide cover for young fish, creating a nurturing environment for salmon during

▲ A chum salmon negotiates yet another obstacle on its way upstream to spawn in Piper's Creek.

critical life stages. Interpretive signs along the creek share information about the salmon's journey, helping visitors understand the importance of this natural process.

Temperate Rainforest and Native Flora

For those who enjoy a hike through classic Pacific Northwest landscapes, Carkeek Park's forested trails offer a perfect mix of tranquility and immersion in nature. The park's trails wind through a canopy of towering trees, including Douglas fir, western red cedar, and bigleaf maple, creating shaded pathways with soft, mulchy earth underfoot. The trails provide an immersive experience in a rich temperate rainforest, especially during spring and summer, when the understory comes alive with ferns, trilliums, and wildflowers.

In the understory, swordferns and lady ferns form dense patches, while salal and Oregon grape add pops of green throughout the year. Spring brings forth blooms of red-flowering currant and thimbleberry, which attract a variety of pollinators, including bees and butterflies. Along the trails, the earthy aroma of damp moss and cedar creates a grounding sensory experience, allowing hikers to fully appreciate the park's thriving ecosystem.

For bird enthusiasts, Carkeek's forested area is a haven for local and migratory birds. Songbirds like Pacific wrens, black-capped chickadees, and varied thrushes flit through the foliage, while woodpeckers can often be heard tapping on tree trunks as they forage for insects. Higher up in the canopy, red-tailed hawks and Cooper's hawks keep a watchful eye, occasionally swooping down in pursuit of small mammals.

Wetlands and Native Wildlife

In addition to the beach, creek, and forest, Carkeek Park boasts wetlands that are crucial for supporting biodiversity. These moist, low-lying areas create unique habitats for species that thrive in wetland conditions. The wetland areas are home to skunk cabbage, a striking plant with large green leaves and a bright yellow bloom that appears in early spring. While its scent may not be appealing, skunk cabbage is an important source of food for insects and an early bloomer in the Pacific Northwest.

Wetlands are important stopover points for amphibians like Pacific tree frogs and rough-skinned newts, especially during the rainy season. Tree frogs are more commonly heard than seen, their evening chorus filling the air during spring and early summer. The wetland areas also attract a variety of waterfowl, including mallards and wood ducks, which add color and movement to the landscape.

This habitat diversity in Carkeek Park supports mammals as well. Visitors may catch a glimpse of raccoons foraging near the creek, squirrels scurrying along branches, and occasionally even a shy coyote slipping through the trees at dusk. These animals are a reminder of the park's wild heart and its place as a sanctuary for Seattle's urban wildlife.

Nature and History in Harmony

Carkeek Park's coastal ecosystems coexist with Seattle's rich history. The land was originally a gathering place for the Coast Salish people, and their connection to this area adds depth to the experience of walking its trails. In the 1920s, the park was developed into a public green space, and since then, efforts to restore its natural ecosystems have led to it becoming one of the city's most cherished parks. Today, community involvement through volunteer programs and educational initiatives helps maintain the park's natural beauty.

Interpretive signs along the trails offer insight into the park's plants, animals, and cultural heritage, helping visitors appreciate the interconnectedness of these ecosystems. Restoration projects, such as invasive plant removal and creek restoration, highlight ongoing efforts to preserve Carkeek's natural integrity, ensuring it remains a refuge for future generations of people and wildlife alike.

A Coastal Escape into Nature's Abundance

Whether exploring the beach, walking the forested trails, or watching salmon return to Piper's Creek, a visit to Carkeek Park provides a multifaceted experience of Seattle's diverse natural world. The park's combination of coastal, forest, and wetland habitats makes it an invaluable green space that reveals the richness of Pacific Northwest ecosystems. As you leave the park, you're likely to feel a sense of renewal and connection, having spent time in a space where the rhythms of nature flow uninterrupted.

In a city known for its bustling energy, Carkeek Park offers a quiet escape into nature, where you can enjoy the subtle beauty of native plants, observe wildlife, and feel the coastal breeze. It's a reminder that even within an urban environment, nature is always close by, waiting to be discovered and celebrated.

◄ In Piper's Creek, chum salmon return from the ocean to their natal stream, where females dig gravel nests called *redds*, deposit their eggs, and males fertilize them, ensuring the next generation before both adults die shortly after spawning.

Commodore Park

Check out nesting herons, hungry sea lions, and spawning salmon at this small but wildlife-rich park along the south side of Seattle's Chittenden Locks where the lake meets the ocean.

Tucked away in Seattle's Magnolia neighborhood, Commodore Park is a serene green space that offers a window into the natural rhythms of the Pacific Northwest. While small, this unassuming park is a hub of ecological activity, uniquely situated at the confluence of the Lake Washington Ship Canal and Salmon Bay. With its rich blend of forested trails, waterways, and abundant wildlife, Commodore Park is an urban gem for nature enthusiasts, birdwatchers, and anyone curious about the interplay of city and wilderness.

A Gateway to the Wild: The Ship Canal and Beyond

Commodore Park's location near the Ballard Locks (officially the Hiram M. Chittenden Locks) places it at the crossroads of a bustling natural corridor. This is where fresh water from Lake Washington flows into Puget Sound, creating a passage that salmon and other fish navigate during their annual migrations. This vital link draws a wide range of wildlife, making the park a hotspot for observing the interconnectedness of marine and terrestrial ecosystems.

The park's proximity to the Locks also means it offers a front-row seat to one of Seattle's most dramatic natural spectacles: salmon returning to their spawning grounds. From late summer to early fall, you can watch coho, sockeye, and chinook salmon as they make their way up the fish ladder. This annual event attracts not only curious human spectators but also an array of predators, including sea lions and harbor seals eager to feast on the abundance of fish.

A Heron Rookery: The Majestic Great Blue Heron

One of Commodore Park's most enchanting features is the nearby heron rookery, nestled in the forested canopy just across the canal in Kiwanis Ravine. Great blue herons, Seattle's largest wading birds, have made this area their home for decades. The rookery is one of the largest in the city, with dozens of nests high in the red alder trees, and serves as a critical breeding site for these iconic birds.

From February to June, visitors can witness the herons engaged in their nesting rituals. Males gather sticks and other materials to construct intricate nests, while females lay eggs and tend to their young. The sight of these stately birds, with their long legs and sinuous necks, flying over the canal or perched on the trees, is a highlight for nature lovers. On quiet mornings, their guttural croaks echo across the park, a sound that feels both prehistoric and deeply tied to the local environment.

During the breeding season, heron activity is especially lively, with adults bringing fish and amphibians to feed their growing chicks. Observing this rookery is a reminder of the delicate balance required to maintain urban wildlife habitats and the importance of preserving these spaces for future generations.

Sea Lions and Salmon: A Dynamic Food Chain

As salmon make their way through the Ballard Locks into Lake Washington and its tributaries, they bring with them a ripple effect that impacts the entire food web. Commodore Park is one of the best spots to see this drama unfold, especially during the salmon run.

▲ Commodore Park's famous heron rookery is in the red alder trees on the south (left) side of the Chittenden Locks pictured here.

▼ The viewing windows at Chittenden Locks allow visitors to check out salmon navigating the "fish ladder" separating freshwater Lake Union with saltwater Puget Sound.

► Seattle City Council designated the great blue heron as the city's official bird in 2003.

Sea lions, drawn by the promise of an easy meal, congregate in the waters near the Locks. These agile marine mammals can often be seen surfacing with salmon clamped firmly in their jaws. While their presence can be controversial—particularly among fishermen—they are a natural part of this ecosystem, playing their role as opportunistic predators.

Harbor seals are also frequent visitors, often bobbing near the canal's edges or lounging on nearby rocks. For those with a keen eye, the occasional river otter may even make an appearance, darting through the water in search of smaller fish or crustaceans.

Birdlife Beyond the Herons

While the heron rookery is a star attraction, Commodore Park is also home to a variety of other bird species that thrive in its mixed habitats. Ospreys and bald eagles are regular visitors, drawn to the canal's fish-rich waters. These raptors can be seen swooping low over the water or perched high in trees, scanning for their next meal.

Smaller birds, like kingfishers, black-capped chickadees, and song sparrows, add to the park's avian diversity. During migration seasons, birdwatchers may spot warblers, swallows, and other transient species passing through. The park's location along the waterway makes it an important stopover for many birds, providing both food and shelter during long journeys.

A Green Oasis for All Seasons

The natural beauty of Commodore Park isn't limited to its wildlife. The park's trails wind through a lush landscape of native plants and trees, offering a peaceful retreat from the city. Bigleaf maples, red alders, and western red cedars provide shade and structure, while shrubs like snowberry and Indian plum add seasonal interest with their flowers and berries.

In spring, the park bursts into life with blooming wildflowers and fresh green growth. Summer brings long days and the opportunity to watch dragonflies darting over the water. In fall, the changing leaves paint the park in shades of gold and red, creating a picturesque backdrop for walks along the canal. Even in winter, Commodore Park has its charms, with moss-covered trees and the soothing sound of water flowing through the canal.

Conservation and Community Engagement

Commodore Park's vibrant ecosystems owe much to ongoing conservation efforts. Volunteer groups regularly work to remove invasive species like English ivy and Himalayan blackberry, replacing them with native plants that provide food and shelter for wildlife. The preservation of the heron rookery

▲ A sailboat makes its way from saltwater Puget Sound into freshwater Lake Union via the Chittenden Locks in the Ballard neighborhood of Seattle.

and nearby wetlands is a testament to the dedication of local conservationists who recognize the importance of protecting urban green spaces.

Educational programs and guided walks further enrich visitors' experiences, offering insights into the park's history, ecology, and wildlife. These initiatives foster a sense of stewardship, encouraging the community to actively participate in maintaining this natural treasure.

A Quiet Escape in the Heart of the City

Despite its proximity to bustling Ballard and Magnolia, Commodore Park feels like a world apart. Its tranquil trails, vibrant wildlife, and unique location along the Ship Canal make it a must-visit destination for anyone looking to connect with nature in Seattle. Whether you're watching herons tend to their nests, marveling at sea lions chasing salmon, or simply enjoying the peaceful sounds of the water, the park offers a rare glimpse into the wild side of urban life.

For residents and visitors alike, Commodore Park serves as a reminder of the importance of preserving these green spaces—not just for the wildlife that depends on them, but for the inspiration and solace they provide to all who come to explore their wonders.

Discovery Park

Perched on a bluff overlooking Puget Sound, Discovery Park is a breathtaking 534-acre escape into the Pacific Northwest's natural beauty. Nestled in Seattle's Magnolia neighborhood, this expansive green space is the city's largest park, offering a stunning diversity of landscapes—from dense forests and open meadows to sandy beaches and windswept bluffs. For hikers, birdwatchers, and nature lovers, it is a treasure trove of ecosystems that reveal the region's incredible biodiversity.

Discovery Park's extensive trail network invites exploration, whether you're taking a leisurely walk or embarking on the iconic Discovery Park Loop Trail. Each step through the park immerses visitors in a dynamic blend of wilderness and tranquility, providing an unmatched urban sanctuary.

A Tapestry of Ecosystems

Discovery Park is a mosaic of habitats, each teeming with unique plants and wildlife. The park's transformation from its former life as Fort Lawton into a natural haven has resulted in an extraordinary variety of ecosystems, reflecting the Pacific Northwest's ecological richness.

The forests, with their towering Douglas firs, western red cedars, and bigleaf maples, create shaded pathways filled with the earthy scent of damp moss and cedar. Beneath the trees, swordferns and salmonberry bushes provide shelter for small mammals and nesting birds. The meadows, dotted with wildflowers like lupines and yarrow, offer open spaces with sweeping views of Puget Sound. These rolling prairies attract pollinators and serve as hunting grounds for raptors like red-tailed hawks.

► The loop hike at Discovery Park takes you down to the Puget Sound shoreline, where (on the way to West Point Lighthouse) this curlycup gumweed steals the show with its yellow flowers.

FIELD TRIP 10

On the park's western edge, the dramatic Magnolia Bluff provides panoramic vistas of the Olympic Mountains and Mount Rainier. Coastal shrubs like Nootka rose and snowberry cling to the bluffs, their roots stabilizing the slopes while providing food and habitat for wildlife. Below, the park's beaches are a hub of marine activity. Tide pools reveal crabs, sea stars, and anemones at low tide, while gulls and cormorants patrol the shoreline. Scattered wetlands throughout the park support amphibians like Pacific chorus frogs and salamanders, while also attracting waterfowl such as mallards and wood ducks.

The Discovery Park Loop Trail: A Journey through Nature

The 2.8-mile Discovery Park Loop Trail is the park's centerpiece, guiding visitors through its varied ecosystems. Relatively flat and accessible, the trail is a microcosm of the park's diverse landscapes.

It begins in the forest, where hikers are enveloped by the cool shade of towering evergreens. Black-capped chickadees and golden-crowned kinglets flit through the trees, while delicate woodland wildflowers like trilliums bloom in spring. Emerging from the forest, the trail opens into meadows alive with wildflowers and pollinators in the summer months. These open spaces also offer clear views of the Cascade Mountains on sunny days.

The path then ascends to the iconic Magnolia Bluff, where breathtaking vistas of Puget Sound stretch to the horizon. Bald eagles often soar overhead, and harbor seals can sometimes be spotted in the waters below. A side trail leads to the beach, where tide pools invite exploration and the rhythmic sound of waves adds a meditative quality. The loop finishes by winding through a mix of forest and meadow, offering new perspectives and the chance to encounter even more wildlife.

Wildlife-Watching Opportunities

With more than 270 bird species recorded, Discovery Park is a haven for birdwatchers. Bald eagles, osprey, and peregrine falcons hunt along the bluffs, while songbirds like Pacific wrens and red-breasted nuthatches thrive in the forest. During the winter months, waterfowl such as buffleheads and goldeneyes gather in the waters off West Point, adding seasonal variety to the park's avian life.

The park also supports a variety of mammals, from squirrels and rabbits to the occasional black-tailed deer. Marine mammals like harbor seals and California sea lions are frequently seen near the beaches, while the intertidal zones teem with life, including anemones, barnacles, and sea stars. The surrounding waters attract salmon, which draw larger predators and highlight the interconnectedness of the park's ecosystems.

▲ The well-marked trail system through Discovery Park makes it easy to get lots of steps in—not to mention great views and fresh air—without getting lost.

► Freakishly large trees like this bigleaf maple make you realize what the forests of Seattle must have looked like when the Denny Party first landed here in 1851.

FIELD TRIP 10

Conservation and Community Involvement

Discovery Park is not just a recreational gem—it's a vital part of Seattle's natural heritage. Conservation efforts focus on restoring native habitats, removing invasive species, and protecting sensitive areas from overuse. Volunteers play an integral role in these efforts, participating in habitat-restoration projects and educational programs.

One of the park's most significant restoration projects is the transformation of West Point. Once an industrial site, it has been reimagined as a thriving coastal habitat, complete with native vegetation and restored beaches. These initiatives ensure that Discovery Park remains a sanctuary for wildlife and a place of inspiration for visitors.

A Sanctuary in the City

Discovery Park is more than a green space; it's a refuge for both people and wildlife. Its forests, meadows, bluffs, and beaches offer something for everyone, whether you're exploring tide pools, watching bald eagles soar, or simply enjoying a peaceful walk through the woods.

This remarkable park invites visitors to slow down and reconnect with the natural world. It's a reminder of the rich heritage of the Pacific Northwest and the importance of preserving urban wild spaces for future generations. For anyone seeking a moment of serenity or an adventure into nature, Discovery Park is an essential destination, showcasing the wonders of Seattle's wild heart.

▲ Catching the sun setting over Puget Sound and the Olympic Mountains is a key attraction of an evening visit to Discovery Park.

Bringing Marine Nature to the City at the Seattle Aquarium

Perched on Pier 59 with panoramic views of Elliott Bay, the Seattle Aquarium serves as both a gateway to the wonders of marine life and a cornerstone of local conservation efforts. With its mission to "Inspire Conservation of Our Marine Environment," the aquarium offers visitors of all ages an opportunity to connect with the unique ecosystems of the Pacific Northwest and beyond, right in the heart of downtown Seattle.

A NEW ERA: THE OCEAN PAVILION

The newest feature of the Seattle Aquarium is the Ocean Pavilion, opened in August 2024. This new wing represents a transformative addition to the facility, furthering its commitment to education, conservation, and immersive experiences. This state-of-the-art exhibit space bridges the gap between the aquarium and the city's iconic waterfront, offering a seamless blend of urban life and marine wonder.

The Ocean Pavilion highlights the interconnectedness of global marine ecosystems, with a particular focus on the Coral Triangle, a biodiversity hotspot in the Pacific Ocean. Visitors will marvel at the vibrant reef habitats and encounter species like zebra sharks, coral catsharks, and colorful reef fish. The pavilion's design incorporates advanced sustainability features, including water-saving systems and energy-efficient lighting, aligning with the aquarium's eco-conscious ethos.

Beyond its exhibits, the Ocean Pavilion aims to deepen public understanding of how local actions impact global oceans. Interactive elements and storytelling platforms emphasize issues like ocean acidification, coral bleaching, and plastic pollution, empowering visitors to become active participants in marine conservation.

IMMERSIVE EXPERIENCES FOR ALL

The Seattle Aquarium invites guests to explore the marine world through interactive exhibits that highlight the diversity and complexity of aquatic life. From the mesmerizing 120,000-gallon Window on Washington Waters habitat, which replicates a coastal reef and features species like wolf eels, rockfish, and sea anemones, to the playful antics of sea otters and harbor seals, the aquarium provides a front-row seat to marine ecosystems.

One of its most beloved exhibits, the Underwater Dome, immerses visitors in a 360-degree view of a 1-million-gallon tank teeming with sharks, rays, and schools of local fish. The touch pools in the Life on the Edge habitat encourage hands-on exploration, allowing visitors to gently interact with tide-pool creatures like sea stars, urchins, and hermit crabs.

For families, the aquarium offers a range of programs, including storytelling sessions, feeding demonstrations, and themed events like Octopus Weekend, where the awe-inspiring giant Pacific octopus takes center stage.

LOCAL CONSERVATION IN ACTION

Beyond its exhibits, the Seattle Aquarium is a leader in marine conservation in the Pacific Northwest. Its dedicated team of scientists and volunteers works to protect species and habitats essential to the health of Puget Sound.

One notable initiative is the aquarium's involvement in efforts to restore kelp forests, a critical habitat for marine species that is rapidly disappearing due to climate change and human activity. By partnering with local organizations and using innovative methods like underwater drones to monitor kelp beds, the aquarium contributes valuable data to guide restoration projects.

The Seattle Aquarium is also committed to protecting iconic species like salmon and orcas. Through collaboration with regional agencies, the aquarium supports projects to improve salmon spawning habitats and reduce pollution in local waterways, ensuring a sustainable food supply for the southern resident killer whale population.

Another focus is on sea otter conservation, as these charismatic animals play a vital role in maintaining the health of kelp forest ecosystems. The aquarium participates in monitoring wild sea otter populations along the Washington coast and supports research to understand the challenges they face from oil spills and disease.

INSPIRING GLOBAL CHANGE

The aquarium's reach extends beyond the Puget Sound region, as it plays a key role in global conservation efforts. As a member of the Association of Zoos and Aquariums (AZA), it participates in Species Survival Plans (SSPs) to ensure the genetic diversity of vulnerable marine species. The institution also hosts international workshops on sustainable fisheries, helping address the overfishing crisis that threatens marine biodiversity worldwide.

EDUCATION AND ENGAGEMENT

At the heart of the Seattle Aquarium's mission is its dedication to education. Its Marine Science Club and Beach Naturalist programs inspire young conservationists, while its partnerships with local schools bring marine science into the classroom.

The aquarium also offers unique opportunities for the public to engage with its work. Visitors can join seasonal beach walks led by naturalists, where they learn about the intertidal zones of Puget Sound, or attend lectures from marine biologists on topics ranging from ocean acidification to whale behavior.

With the addition of the Ocean Pavilion and a strong conservation ethic, the Seattle Aquarium not only brings the magic of the marine world to the city but also empowers visitors to become stewards of the ocean.

▼ Sea otters are among the big attractions at the Seattle Aquarium.

TRIP 11

Alki Beach

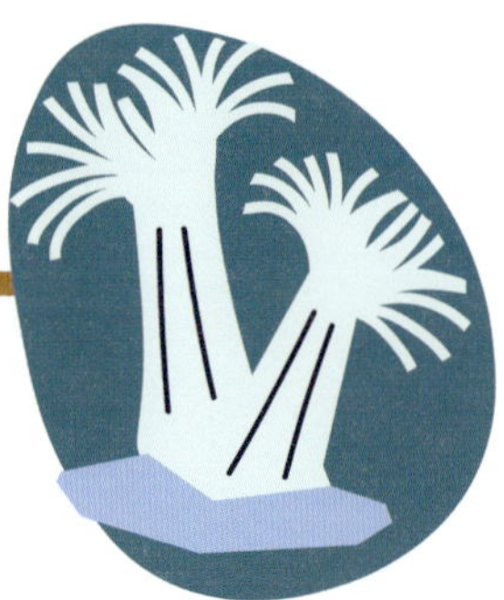

Investigate tide pools, spot marine mammals, and walk scenic trails at this vibrant coastal ecosystem along Puget Sound.

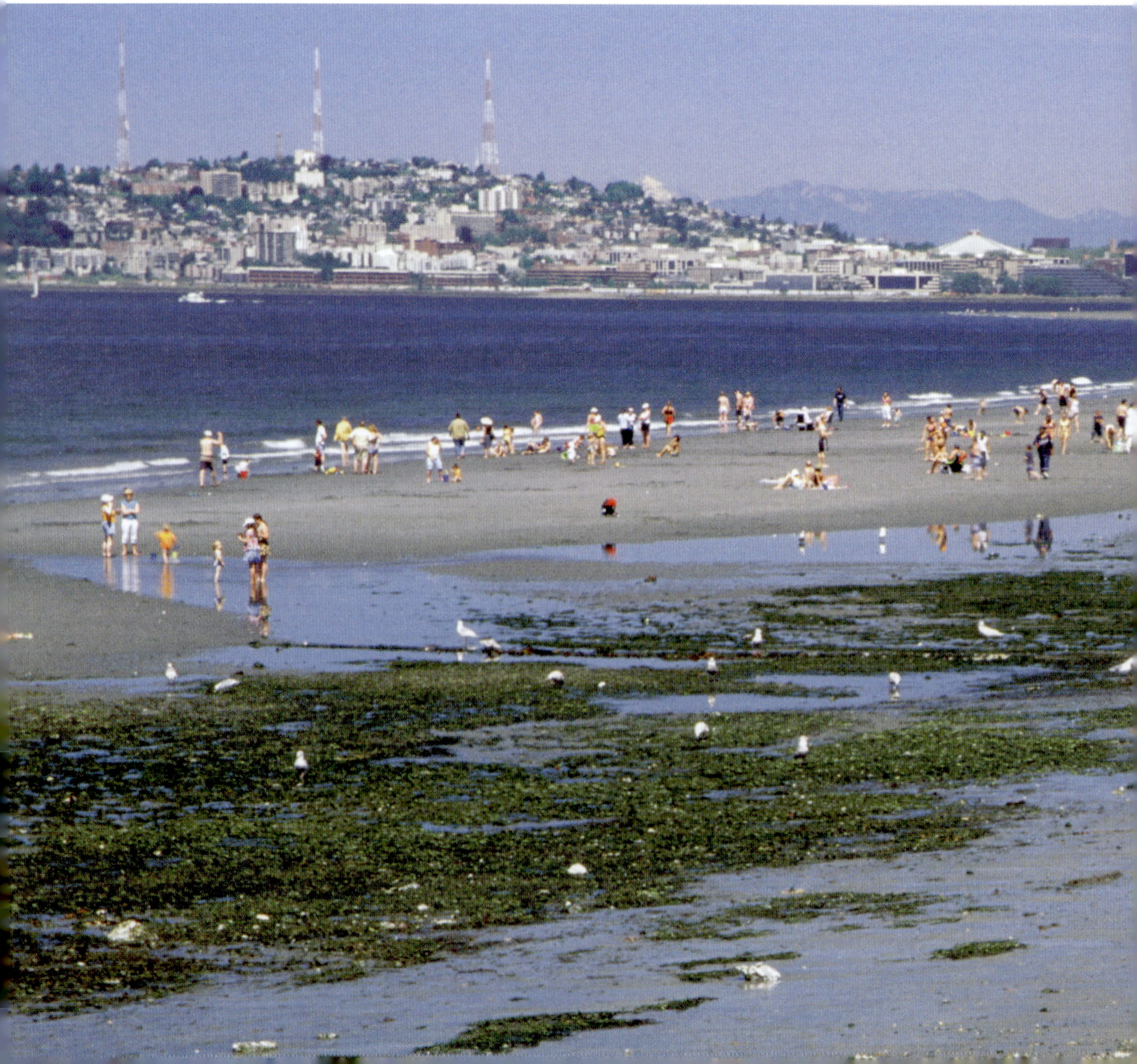

Seattle's Alki Beach, stretching over 2 miles along the city's western shore, offers a breathtaking blend of oceanfront views and a thriving ecosystem. Known for its sandy beaches, striking skyline views, and vibrant marine life, Alki Beach provides an enchanting escape for nature lovers and city dwellers alike. Its coastal setting makes it a rare gem in Seattle, a place where tidal pools teem with marine life, beach grasses sway in the breeze, and shorebirds and marine mammals thrive just a stone's throw from the city.

Coastal Habitats and Marine Life

One of the most captivating aspects of Alki Beach is its diverse coastal ecosystem. At low tide, the sandy shoreline reveals a series of tidal pools that attract local families, nature enthusiasts, and marine biology students. These pools brim with marine creatures like sea anemones, small crabs, sea

▼ "When the tide is out, the table is set." Before the arrival of the Denny Party, low tide at Alki Beach provided a twice-daily source of food for Coast Salish peoples, when edible shellfish and other marine life were exposed and ready for the taking.

▲ It's not unusual to see groupings of one to two dozen brants offshore of Alki Beach, feeding on eelgrass during winter when the pickings are otherwise slim.

◄ Giant kelp populations off the coast of Seattle have experienced significant declines over the past century due to rising water temperatures, pollution, and habitat loss.

stars, and barnacles. Each pool is a delicate microcosm where unique adaptations come to life, allowing these animals to survive the tidal ebb and flow. Bright orange and purple sea stars cling to rocks, while sea anemones sway gently in the shallow water, their tentacles waiting to ensnare small prey. Alki's tide pools provide a window into the hidden life beneath the ocean's surface and are truly a treat for anyone interested in marine biology.

In the intertidal zone, kelp and seaweed line the beach, providing vital food and shelter for an array of fish and invertebrates. The kelp forests that lie just beyond the beach's shallows support small fish and draw in larger predators like seals and river otters, often seen splashing near the shore. For those lucky enough to visit early in the morning or late in the evening, it's not uncommon to spot harbor seals swimming close to the beach, occasionally hauling out to rest on rocks along the shore.

A Birdwatcher's Paradise

Alki Beach is a haven for birdwatchers, offering an opportunity to spot both shorebirds and more elusive coastal species. Seagulls are a constant presence, of course, but they share the beach with many other birds, particularly in spring and fall, when Alki becomes a popular stop for migrating species. Western sandpipers, dunlins, and sanderlings can often be seen darting along the water's edge, poking their slender beaks into the sand in search of small invertebrates.

Winter months bring brants, small dark geese that feed on eelgrass along the shore. The presence of these brants is a sign of a healthy ecosystem, as they rely on nutrient-rich waters to sustain their long migration. Great blue herons are also a common sight, their slow, patient stalking and sudden strikes a testament to their efficiency as hunters. Occasionally, bald eagles soar overhead, scanning the beach for fish or small mammals, while cormorants dive underwater in search of their next meal. For birdwatchers, a visit to Alki offers endless opportunities to see some of the Northwest's iconic avian residents up close.

Native Plants and Coastal Flora

Alki Beach is more than just sand and sea; its surrounding areas host a variety of native plants that have adapted to the coastal environment. Beach grasses like dunegrass and saltgrass line the shore, stabilizing the sand and providing shelter for small animals. The hardy foliage is a testament to the resilience of coastal plants, which must survive the harsh conditions of salt spray, shifting sands, and strong winds. Wild roses, known for their fragrant pink blossoms, bloom along the edge of the beach in spring and summer. These hardy plants add a splash of color and attract bees and butterflies, creating a brief, beautiful reminder of the beach's seasonal changes.

Farther back from the shore, you'll find coastal shrubs like salal and snowberry. Salal's thick, waxy leaves and small, edible berries are a favorite of both birds and small mammals. Snowberries, meanwhile, produce delicate white berries that often persist into winter, offering a vital food source when other plants have gone dormant. These native plants help form a protective buffer between the beach and inland areas, promoting soil stability and creating habitats for smaller creatures.

Marine Mammals and Occasional Visitors

The waters off Alki Beach are rich with marine life, and on lucky days, visitors might spot one of the ocean's larger residents. Harbor seals are commonly seen in the waters around Alki, sometimes hauling out on nearby rocks to sun themselves. Kayakers and paddleboarders often encounter these curious animals, who may poke their heads above water to observe the passing visitors. In spring and early summer, sea lions can sometimes be heard barking from a distance, adding a unique coastal soundtrack to the Alki experience.

In recent years, Alki Beach has become known as a good place to observe the occasional orca pod passing through Puget Sound. These magnificent creatures are often seen from November through January as they follow migrating salmon. Onlookers gather along the shoreline, hoping for a glimpse of dorsal fins cutting through the water or a tail slap signaling the orcas' presence. Humpback whales have also been spotted from Alki's shores, offering residents and visitors a rare chance to see these majestic animals up close without leaving land.

Connecting with Nature along the Trails

Adjacent to the beach, the Alki Trail extends along the waterfront, providing a scenic path for walkers, joggers, and cyclists. The trail winds along the shoreline, with views of the Olympic Mountains to the west and the Seattle skyline to the east, creating a panoramic experience of Seattle's natural beauty. Small green spaces along the trail, such as Constellation Park, offer interpretive signs that introduce visitors to the marine life and ecosystems visible from the shore. Benches positioned at scenic spots along the trail offer quiet places to pause, observe the scenery, and enjoy the breeze.

Conservation and Community Involvement

Alki Beach is not only a place to appreciate nature but also a community-focused space where conservation efforts are strong. Local organizations work to protect the delicate intertidal habitats from overuse and pollution, with a focus on educating visitors about respectful interaction with tide

▲ Alki Beach is one of the best places on land to see orca whales when they venture into Elliott Bay.

pools and marine life. Programs that remove invasive plants and protect native flora help maintain the beach's unique ecosystem. Beach cleanup events, hosted by volunteer groups, play a vital role in keeping Alki's shoreline clean and safe for wildlife.

Interpretive signs educate visitors about the importance of local ecosystems, highlighting how every plant and animal contributes to the overall health of Puget Sound. These efforts underscore Alki's value not only as a recreational space but also as a place of natural preservation and ecological awareness.

A Day at Alki Beach

Whether you're exploring the sandy shoreline, observing marine life in the tidal pools, birdwatching, or simply strolling along the Alki Trail, a day at Alki Beach is a reminder of the natural beauty that can be found just outside Seattle's urban core. Alki offers a unique blend of ocean views, wildlife sightings, and peaceful green spaces, making it a beloved destination for locals and tourists alike. For those seeking a deeper connection with Seattle's coastal ecosystems, Alki Beach provides an immersive experience—one where the rhythms of nature, from the tide's rise and fall to the calls of shorebirds, invite visitors to pause, observe, and appreciate the natural world just steps away from the city.

Schmitz Preserve Park

Look for owls, chipmunks, and other local animal celebrities among the ancient trees of this old-growth forest sanctuary right in West Seattle.

Tucked away in the heart of West Seattle, Schmitz Preserve Park offers a rare, immersive natural experience that feels worlds away from the bustling city. This 53-acre park is one of Seattle's last remaining old-growth forests, with towering trees, winding trails, and a peaceful atmosphere that transports you deep into nature. Despite being surrounded by urban development, Schmitz Preserve Park retains a wild, untouched quality that makes it a must-visit for nature lovers, hikers, and anyone seeking solace in the forest.

A Walk through Ancient Forests

One of the most striking features of Schmitz Preserve Park is its towering canopy of ancient trees. Unlike most urban parks, Schmitz Preserve retains a significant portion of its original old-growth forest, with some trees estimated to be over 400 years old. As you step into the park, you are greeted by the sight of towering Douglas firs, western red cedars, and bigleaf maples, their branches forming a dense canopy overhead. The cool, shaded trails are soft underfoot, cushioned by layers of fallen needles and leaves, while the air is filled with the scent of damp earth and wood.

◄ A walk through Schmitz Preserve Park yields views of some of the biggest trees within Seattle's city limits, such as this imposing western red cedar tree that could be more than 1000 years old.

These trees aren't just impressive because of their size—they also offer a glimpse into what Seattle's landscape looked like before the city's development. Walking among them feels like stepping back in time, offering a rare opportunity to experience an ecosystem that has remained largely undisturbed for centuries. The park's dense understory, filled with ferns, mosses, and huckleberries, adds to the sense of being in a true wilderness, even though you're just minutes from the city streets.

Wildlife-Watching in the Preserve

Schmitz Preserve is a haven for wildlife, making it a fantastic destination for birdwatchers and nature enthusiasts alike. The thick forest provides shelter and food for a wide range of species, from common birds to less frequently seen animals. If you're quiet and patient, you may spot a pileated woodpecker hammering away at a tree, hear the soft calls of Pacific wrens in the under-brush, or catch sight of an occasional coyote darting through the woods.

For birdwatchers, the park offers a unique blend of forest species that can be hard to find elsewhere in the city. Keep an eye out for chestnut-backed chickadees, golden-crowned kinglets, and spotted towhees flitting between the branches. During the spring and fall migrations, you might also be lucky enough to spot warblers, thrushes, and other migratory birds using the park as a stopover.

The small creek that winds through the park also attracts wildlife. If you visit after a rainfall, you'll likely hear the creek's gentle babbling as it flows through the ravine, providing water for the forest's inhabitants. Amphibians like Pacific chorus frogs are known to frequent the area, and in the quieter moments, their calls add a layer of natural sound to the forest's symphony.

The Trails of Schmitz Preserve Park

Schmitz Preserve Park offers several miles of rustic trails that meander through the forest, perfect for hiking, walking, or simply taking in the natural beauty. Unlike more developed parks, the trails here are intentionally left in a more rugged state, with minimal signage and little in the way of mani-cured pathways. This adds to the sense of adventure, as each turn in the trail reveals new sights, whether it's a fallen log covered in bright green moss or a sunlit clearing surrounded by towering trees.

The main trail runs through the heart of the park, taking you along the edges of the ravine carved by Schmitz Creek. Side trails branch off into quieter, more secluded areas, offering opportunities for exploration. You might find yourself crossing small wooden bridges, ducking under low-hanging branches, or pausing to admire the play of light filtering through the trees.

What makes Schmitz Preserve's trails especially unique is the way they immerse you fully in the forest. There are no paved roads cutting through, no buildings interrupting the landscape. It's just you and the woods, with the sounds of rustling leaves, bird calls, and the occasional creak of a branch in the wind.

A Legacy of Preservation

Schmitz Preserve Park owes its existence to the foresight of Ferdinand and Emma Schmitz, who donated the land to the city in 1908. Their goal was to protect the area's natural beauty from the rapid development that was sweeping across Seattle at the time. Thanks to their generosity, the park

◄ Leaves of the piggyback plant, a native ground cover in coastal areas up and down the west coast, jockey for space on the forest floor among fallen branches.

► Schmitz Creek cuts a narrow but well-defined course through the middle of Schmitz Park.

remains one of the few places in the city where visitors can experience an old-growth forest in its natural state.

Over the years, the park has been carefully preserved, with minimal development to ensure the protection of its fragile ecosystem. It stands as a testament to Seattle's early commitment to conservation and the preservation of green spaces for future generations. Today, Schmitz Preserve is managed with a focus on maintaining the natural environment, which means invasive species are regularly removed, and efforts are made to support the health of the native plants and animals.

Hidden Corners and Quiet Moments

While Schmitz Preserve Park is not a large park by acreage, it feels expansive thanks to its dense forest and winding trails. It's easy to find a secluded spot where you can sit quietly and take in the sounds of the forest. Unlike more crowded parks, Schmitz Preserve tends to attract visitors looking for a quiet, reflective experience, making it a perfect spot for meditative walks or peaceful escapes from the noise of daily life.

In the early morning, the park is particularly serene, with the sun casting dappled light through the trees and the trails often empty. Whether you're looking to connect with nature, take a quiet walk, or enjoy a moment of solitude, Schmitz Preserve Park offers a rare opportunity to do so in a truly wild setting.

A Seattle Treasure

Schmitz Preserve Park may not have the manicured lawns or art installations of other Seattle parks, but what it does offer is a raw, untouched glimpse of the region's natural beauty. It's a place where you can experience the Pacific Northwest's forests in their full glory, without leaving the city limits. For anyone seeking an authentic nature experience in Seattle, Schmitz Preserve Park is a hidden treasure worth exploring.

▶ A sizable western hemlock tree put its roots down around another huge fallen tree known as a "nurse log."

FIELD TRIP 12

Lincoln Park

Get lost on a hike through the dense forest and then find yourself fawning over a sea star in the tide pools of this classic Seattle park hugging the Puget Sound shoreline.

Stretching across 135 acres along the shores of Puget Sound, Lincoln Park is one of West Seattle's most beloved natural spaces. Known for its breath-taking waterfront views, miles of trails, and dense canopy of towering trees, Lincoln Park offers a perfect blend of forest, beach, and recreational opportunities. Whether you're a hiker, birdwatcher, or just someone seeking solace by the water, Lincoln Park is a place where nature and urban life meet in beautiful harmony.

A Park with a View

Lincoln Park's location on the western edge of Seattle offers some of the city's most striking views of Puget Sound and the Olympic Mountains. On clear days, the snow-capped peaks of the Olympics rise dramatically across the water, providing a stunning backdrop for a walk along the park's beaches

▼ A standup paddleboarder plies Puget Sound's icy waters off of Lincoln Park on a classic Seattle fall evening.

or a quiet picnic on the bluffs. At sunset, the sky often bursts into shades of orange and pink, casting a warm glow over the Sound and offering a perfect end to a day spent outdoors.

The park's waterfront is easily accessible via a network of trails that wind down through the forested bluffs to the rocky beaches below. Here, you can stroll along the shore, comb the beach for driftwood, or simply sit and watch the ferries as they glide across the water to Vashon Island. The salty breeze, the sound of waves gently lapping at the shore, and the sight of boats passing by all contribute to the tranquil, coastal atmosphere that makes Lincoln Park so special.

Forest Trails and Wildlife-Watching

While Lincoln Park's beaches are a big draw, the park's expansive forested areas offer an equally inviting escape into nature. The park's trail network, which includes about 5 miles of paths, weaves through dense groves of Douglas fir, western red cedar, and Pacific madrone trees. These trails range from easy, flat routes suitable for casual walkers to more challenging, hilly paths that wind through the ravines and bluffs.

For those who enjoy birdwatching, Lincoln Park is a paradise. The mix of forest, shoreline, and open spaces attracts a wide variety of birds, making it a prime spot for both casual observers and serious birders. In the trees, you might spot the chestnut-backed chickadee or hear the drumming of a pileated woodpecker echoing through the forest. Along the shoreline, watch for great blue herons, cormorants, and gulls, and if you're lucky, you might catch sight of a bald eagle soaring overhead.

Migratory birds also pass through the park during spring and fall, with species like warblers, flycatchers, and sparrows making seasonal appearances. The park's blend of habitats provides food and shelter for these birds, making it a year-round destination for birdwatchers hoping to spot something special.

Exploring the Beach and Tide Pools

Lincoln Park's waterfront stretches for about a mile, offering a dynamic shoreline that's perfect for beachcombing, tide-pooling, and watching marine life. At low tide, the exposed rocks and tide pools are teeming with life, including sea stars, anemones, crabs, and small fish. It's a fantastic spot for kids and adults alike to explore the wonders of the intertidal zone.

The beach itself is a mix of sand and pebbles, with driftwood scattered along the shore, providing natural benches where you can sit and take in the view. The beach is also a popular spot for launching kayaks or paddleboards, allowing adventurous visitors to get out on the water and experience the beauty of Puget Sound from a different perspective.

For those looking to relax, there's no shortage of scenic spots along the water's edge. Whether you're sitting on a bench near the south beach, enjoying a picnic with friends, or just lying on the grass by the waterfront, the park's coastal vibe is hard to resist.

Fauntleroy Cove and Colman Pool

One of Lincoln Park's most distinctive features is the historic Colman Pool, a saltwater swimming pool located right on the shore of Fauntleroy Cove. Open during the summer months, Colman Pool offers a unique swimming experience, with its location giving swimmers the sensation of being right next to Puget Sound. The pool, which was constructed in 1928 on the site of a natural lagoon known as the "Old Mudhole," is filled with salt water pumped directly from the Sound, offering a refreshing dip unlike that of any other swimming pool in the city.

Tidal currents and the estuarine habitat make this point a great spot for seeing marine mammals. The most famous are orca whales, which are most often seen offshore here in fall and winter when they cross between Blake and Vashon islands. Sometimes they get close enough to shore that you can hear their blows. Gray whales are less frequent but can sometimes be spotted from here in spring, when they are migrating through. Also keep an

▼ A Turkish towel seaweed fragment alights on some sea-polished beach rocks.

eye out for harbor porpoises, with their chocolate-chip shaped dorsal fins, as they speed through the water topping 8 miles per hour. Meanwhile, harbor seals, California sea lions, and river otters also ply these waters, attracted by schools of herring, salmon, and other prey.

The Fauntleroy Cove area, just south of the pool, is one of the quieter parts of the park, with fewer visitors and a more secluded feel. Here, you can take a peaceful walk along the beach or sit on one of the benches to watch the ferries as they come and go from the Fauntleroy ferry terminal. It's a perfect spot for those looking to enjoy the park's coastal beauty in a more tranquil setting.

◄ Pacific madrone trees are relatively picky about where they colonize, but no one doubts they love a forested bluff on the edge of Puget Sound, like here at Lincoln Park, where a healthy population of the red-and-yellow, peeling-bark trees have set up shop.

Recreation and Relaxation

Lincoln Park is not just a place for nature lovers—it's also one of West Seattle's top destinations for outdoor recreation. The park's grassy lawns and open meadows provide plenty of space for picnicking, playing frisbee, or simply relaxing in the sun. There are numerous picnic tables scattered throughout the park, many of which are in scenic spots with views of the water or shaded by tall trees.

For families, the park's playgrounds are a big draw, offering fun and safe play areas for kids to burn off some energy. There are tennis courts and open fields that are perfect for informal games of soccer or catch. The park's blend of recreational amenities and natural beauty makes it an ideal spot for gatherings, whether it's a quiet afternoon with a book or a lively family barbecue.

Lincoln Park's Legacy of Preservation

Like many of Seattle's parks, Lincoln Park has a rich history of conservation and community involvement. Originally designated as a public park in 1922, Lincoln Park was named in honor of President Abraham Lincoln and has since become a cherished green space for West Seattle residents. Over the decades, the park has been carefully maintained and preserved, ensuring that future generations can continue to enjoy its natural beauty.

The park is actively managed to protect its diverse ecosystems, with ongoing efforts to remove invasive species and restore native plants. Community groups and volunteers play a key role in these efforts, regularly participating in restoration projects that keep the park's forests and shoreline healthy. It's this commitment to stewardship that has helped preserve Lincoln Park as a thriving natural area in the heart of the city.

A West Seattle Treasure

Lincoln Park is more than just a city park—it's a place where the wild beauty of the Pacific Northwest can be experienced in all its forms, from the towering trees of its forests to the pebbled shores of its beaches. Whether you're hiking the trails, exploring the tide pools, or simply sitting on a bench watching the ferries, Lincoln Park offers something for everyone.

For West Seattleites, Lincoln Park is a beloved sanctuary, offering a place to escape the hustle of city life and reconnect with nature. It's a park that invites exploration, relaxation, and reflection, with each visit offering new opportunities to experience its natural beauty.

Seward Park

Seward Park is a beloved green space in southeast Seattle, offering a serene escape from the urban hustle. Nestled on a forested peninsula that juts into Lake Washington, Seward Park encompasses 300 acres of lush, old-growth forest, vibrant wildlife, and panoramic lake views. As one of the city's most treasured parks, it provides a perfect destination for hikers, birdwatchers, swimmers, and anyone seeking to connect with nature without venturing far from the city.

The park's natural beauty, combined with its extensive trail system, beaches, and picnic areas, make Seward Park an ideal spot for families, outdoor enthusiasts, and those simply looking to unwind by the water. Whether you're strolling along the shore or exploring its dense woods, the park offers a peaceful, nature-filled retreat in the heart of Seattle.

A Glimpse into History

Seward Park's history stretches back thousands of years, long before it became a public park. The area was originally home to the Duwamish people, who fished in Lake Washington and used the forest for food, medicine, and shelter. In 1899, the City of Seattle purchased the land to create what is now known as Seward Park, naming it after William H. Seward, who negotiated the purchase of Alaska from Russia.

The park is known for its old-growth forest, one of the few remaining in the Seattle area. Some of the towering Douglas firs and western red cedars in the park are more than 250 years old, providing a glimpse of the region's natural history. Over the years, Seward Park has evolved into a cherished urban sanctuary, where visitors can experience the beauty of both the forest and the lake.

Exploring the Old-Growth Forest

One of Seward Park's greatest treasures is its old-growth forest, a rare feature in a city park. The park's 2.4-mile perimeter trail offers a scenic and easy walk along the water, but for those looking to venture deeper into the woods, several interior trails meander through the towering trees. As you step into the forest, you'll be enveloped by the quiet majesty of nature, with moss-covered logs, ferns, and understory plants carpeting the ground beneath the ancient trees.

The sound of birdsong fills the air, and the dense canopy above filters the sunlight, casting a soft glow on the forest floor. It's easy to forget you're in the middle of a major city as you wander these trails. The park's 120 acres of old-growth forest provide a peaceful, secluded experience that feels worlds away from urban life.

The Magnolia Trail and Crest Trail offer great opportunities to explore this forested landscape. Along the way, you'll come across interpretive signs that provide information about the park's flora and fauna, making it a wonderful learning experience for visitors of all ages.

◄ This western hemlock tree snag (otherwise known as "standing dead") provides important environmental services to the local ecosystem, including serving as a habitat for cavity-nesting birds like woodpeckers and chickadees, providing a home for insects that support local food webs, storing carbon, and slowly decomposing to enrich the soil with nutrients that sustain understory plants and fungi. Additionally, its structure offers perches for hawks and eagles and serves as a nursery for mosses and lichens, which further contribute to the park's biodiversity.

Birdwatching and Wildlife

Seward Park is a haven for wildlife, particularly birds. Birdwatchers flock to the park for a chance to see some of the area's most iconic species. The park's diverse habitats, from dense forests to open lakeshore, support a wide variety of birdlife. Bring your binoculars and keep an eye out for bald eagles, which nest in the tall trees along the water's edge. The sight of one of these majestic birds soaring over the lake is an unforgettable experience.

The park is also home to great blue herons, osprey, red-tailed hawks, and barred owls, making it an excellent destination for raptor enthusiasts. In the early mornings, you may hear the distinctive call of the belted kingfisher as it swoops over the water in search of fish. Other common species include chestnut-backed chickadees, American crows, and woodpeckers. Migratory birds also pass through in spring and fall, adding even more variety to the birdwatching experience.

In addition to birds, Seward Park is home to a variety of other wildlife. Squirrels, raccoons, and the occasional deer can be spotted in the forest, while turtles and frogs inhabit the wetlands near the shore. The park's natural areas provide a thriving ecosystem for many species, making it a great destination for anyone interested in local wildlife.

A Day by the Water

One of the most appealing aspects of Seward Park is its location along the shores of Lake Washington. The park's beaches and swimming areas are popular during the summer months, offering a perfect spot to cool off and enjoy the beauty of the lake. The calm waters of Andrews Bay provide a safe and family-friendly place to swim, and the park's scenic beaches are perfect for picnics, sunbathing, or simply watching the waves lap against the shore.

For those who prefer to explore the water, kayaking, canoeing, and paddleboarding are popular activities at Seward Park. The park's boat launch makes it easy to get out on the lake and enjoy a day of paddling. From the water, you'll have stunning views of Mount Rainier to the south and the Seattle skyline to the north, making it a picturesque setting for any water-based adventure.

If you'd rather stay on land, the park's 2.4-mile perimeter trail offers a beautiful walk or bike ride along the lakeshore. The wide, paved path is accessible and perfect for all ages, providing stunning views of the water, forest, and surrounding hills.

The Seward Park Audubon Center

Located in the park's historic bathhouse, the Seward Park Audubon Center is a hub for environmental education and community programs. The center offers a variety of programs and events for people of all ages, including guided nature walks, birdwatching tours, and family-friendly activities that explore the natural world. The center's mission is to inspire and cultivate a connection to nature through education and conservation efforts.

The Audubon Center is a great resource for those looking to learn more about the park's ecology, history, and wildlife. Whether you're interested in joining a birdwatching walk, attending a lecture on local ecosystems, or participating in a volunteer restoration project, the center provides many opportunities to engage with the park in a meaningful way.

Seasonal Beauty and Year-Round Exploration

Seward Park's natural beauty shines year-round, making it a destination worth visiting in every season. In spring, the park comes alive with blossoming wildflowers, new growth in the forest, and the return of migratory birds. The forest is particularly vibrant during this time, with bursts of color from flowering plants like salmonberry and trillium.

Summer is the park's busiest season, with visitors flocking to the beaches, trails, and picnic areas to enjoy the warm weather and lakeside views. Autumn brings a quieter atmosphere, as the park's trees turn brilliant shades of red, orange, and yellow. The crisp air and changing leaves make fall an ideal time for hiking and photography.

Even in winter, Seward Park remains a peaceful retreat. The forest takes on a mystical quality, with mist rising from the lake and the bare branches of trees creating a stark yet beautiful landscape. It's a time to appreciate the park's tranquility and the quiet beauty of nature in its more subdued form.

A Natural Sanctuary in the City

Seward Park is more than just a park—it's a sanctuary for nature and for people. Its old-growth forest, lakeside views, and abundant wildlife provide a space where visitors can reconnect with the natural world, find peace, and explore the beauty of Seattle's landscapes. Whether you're visiting for an afternoon hike, a swim in the lake, or a morning of birdwatching, Seward Park offers an unforgettable experience in one of the city's most cherished green spaces.

A visit to Seward Park is a reminder that nature is always close at hand, even in the midst of a bustling city. It's a place to slow down, breathe in the fresh air, and appreciate the beauty of the natural world that surrounds us.

▲ The two kings of the Pacific Northwest temperate rainforest, the Douglas fir and western red cedar, stand side by side in all their old-growth glory at Seward Park.

► A hemlock varnish shelf mushroom adorns its favorite substrate, the bark of a western hemlock tree.

Kubota Garden

Wander serene trails past waterfalls, intricate stonework, and seasonal blooms amid a harmonious blend of Japanese design and Pacific Northwest beauty.

Tucked away in Seattle's Rainier Beach neighborhood, Kubota Garden is a hidden gem that offers a serene escape into lush greenery, artful landscaping, and the beauty of Japanese garden design. Spanning 20 acres, Kubota Garden is a living testament to the vision of Fujitaro Kubota, a Japanese immigrant and self-taught gardener who transformed this space over the course of decades. It combines traditional Japanese design principles with the native plants of the Pacific Northwest, creating a peaceful haven where nature and artistry intertwine.

Whether you're drawn to the intricate stone pathways and peaceful ponds, or you simply want to explore the harmonious blend of native and exotic plants, Kubota Garden is a place that invites reflection, contemplation, and a deeper connection to the natural world. For nature lovers, history buffs, or anyone seeking a moment of tranquility, this garden offers a truly unique experience in the heart of South Seattle.

A Rich History Rooted in Tradition

The story of Kubota Garden begins with Fujitaro Kubota, who immigrated to the United States from Japan in 1907. In 1923, he founded the Kubota Gardening Company which eventually offered landscaping services that brought Japanese garden design to the Pacific Northwest. Over time, Kubota's reputation grew, and his work can still be seen in notable projects around Seattle, including the gardens of the Bloedel Reserve and the Japanese American Remembrance Garden at Seattle University.

Kubota Garden, however, was his personal masterpiece. In 1927, Kubota purchased 5 acres of land in Rainier Beach, where he began to experiment with blending Japanese design elements and the local flora of the Pacific Northwest. Over the next several decades, he expanded the garden to its current size and continued to refine its design. During World War II, the

◀ The serene setting of Kubota Garden belies its location smack-dab in the middle of urban South Seattle.

► The elaborate stonework throughout Kubota Garden even extends to footbridges crossing over Mapes Creek.

Kubota family was interned, like many Japanese Americans, but upon their return, they resumed their work on the garden. In 1987, the City of Seattle purchased the garden to preserve it as a public park, recognizing both its beauty and its cultural significance.

Today, Kubota Garden remains a beloved space for visitors to experience the unique fusion of Japanese gardening traditions and the natural beauty of the Pacific Northwest.

Exploring the Garden's Delicate Balance of Nature and Art

The moment you step into Kubota Garden, it's clear that this is no ordinary park. The garden is designed to take visitors on a journey, with winding paths that lead through a series of carefully crafted landscapes, each with its own distinct character. From tranquil ponds to artfully placed stones, every element of the garden feels intentional, drawing the eye and inviting contemplation.

The Heart of the Garden: Pond and Waterfall

At the heart of Kubota Garden lies a series of ponds and waterfalls, which serve as focal points for the garden's design. Water plays an essential role in Japanese garden philosophy, symbolizing renewal, tranquility, and the flow of life. As you walk around the ponds, you'll notice how the sound of cascading water adds a calming backdrop to the experience, making it easy to lose yourself in the moment.

The bridges that span the ponds provide scenic viewpoints, where you can stop and take in the reflections of trees and sky in the still water. In summer, the ponds are dotted with water lilies, adding splashes of color to the greenery.

▶ This pair of trees, a native bigtooth maple up top and an "exotic" Japanese maple on the bottom, showcases what's so special about Kubota Garden: it mixes traditional native plants with introduced species from Japan and elsewhere in a way that makes them look like they were meant to go together.

Stonework and Pathways: A Journey through the Garden

One of the most striking features of Kubota Garden is its stonework. Large boulders and carefully placed stones are used to create pathways, steps, and borders that guide visitors through the garden. In Japanese garden design, stones are considered the "bones" of the landscape, providing structure and balance. At Kubota Garden, this philosophy is beautifully evident in the way stones are integrated into the landscape, whether as part of a stepping-stone path across a stream or as the foundation for a graceful bridge.

FIELD TRIP 15

The garden's paths are designed to encourage exploration, with winding trails that lead to hidden corners and quiet spaces. As you wander, you'll encounter stone lanterns, bridges, and waterfalls, each placed to create a harmonious balance between natural beauty and human craftsmanship.

The Mountains and the Forest: A Pacific Northwest Touch

While Kubota Garden follows traditional Japanese garden design principles, it also celebrates the native plants and natural landscapes of the Pacific Northwest. Towering Douglas firs, western red cedars, and maples are a key part of the garden's landscape, their presence grounding the garden in its Seattle setting. Fujitaro Kubota believed in blending the beauty of Japanese design with the unique character of the local environment, and the result is a garden that feels deeply connected to both its cultural roots and its natural surroundings.

One of the highlights of a visit to Kubota Garden is climbing the small hill that offers panoramic views of the garden below. From this vantage point, you can see the way the garden is nestled into the forest, with the peaks of trees rising above the ponds and pathways. It's a reminder that while the garden is carefully designed, it remains in harmony with the wild landscapes that surround it.

Seasonal Beauty and Changing Moods

One of the joys of visiting Kubota Garden is experiencing how the landscape changes with the seasons. In spring, the garden bursts into color as azaleas, rhododendrons, and cherry blossoms bloom, creating a vivid tapestry of

▼ The spider flower, native to South America, is one of many cultivated wildflowers adding splashes of color throughout the Kubota Garden landscape.

pinks, reds, and whites. Spring is a particularly popular time to visit, as the cherry trees in the garden are reminiscent of traditional Japanese *hanami* (flower-viewing) celebrations.

Summer brings lush greenery with the garden's ponds surrounded by ferns and lilies. The shade provided by the towering trees offers a cool, refreshing retreat during the warm months. In fall, the garden transforms once again as the maples turn brilliant shades of red and orange, contrasting beautifully with the evergreens. Even in winter, the garden's beauty endures, with the bare branches and moss-covered stones creating a peaceful, contemplative atmosphere.

Wildlife and Birdwatching

Kubota Garden is also a haven for birds and wildlife. The ponds attract a variety of bird species, including ducks, great blue herons, and songbirds. In the quieter parts of the garden, you may spot squirrels darting between the trees or hear the calls of woodpeckers. The diversity of plant life provides food and shelter for many species, making the garden a lively place for birdwatching, especially in the early morning.

A Community Effort

The preservation and maintenance of Kubota Garden is made possible by a dedicated group of volunteers and the Kubota Garden Foundation, which works closely with the City of Seattle to care for this special place. Regular community work parties help keep the garden healthy, and the foundation offers educational programs and tours to share the garden's history and significance with visitors. This collaborative effort ensures that Kubota Garden will continue to thrive as a public space for generations to come.

A Place of Reflection and Beauty

Kubota Garden is more than just a park; it's a place of reflection, where nature and human artistry come together in perfect harmony. Whether you're wandering along the stone pathways, pausing by the waterfall, or admiring the seasonal blooms, a visit to this garden offers a peaceful retreat from the noise and busyness of the city. It's a place to reconnect with nature, reflect on the beauty of thoughtful design, and experience the quiet joy of being surrounded by greenery.

For anyone looking to slow down and appreciate the finer details of the natural world, Kubota Garden is a must-visit destination. Its blend of Japanese tradition and Pacific Northwest landscapes creates an environment that feels both timeless and uniquely Seattle. Whether it's your first visit or your fiftieth, Kubota Garden never fails to inspire a sense of wonder and tranquility.

Duwamish Hill Preserve

Hike in the footsteps of Native American ancestors at this remnant nature preserve overlooking the historic Duwamish River Valley.

Perched above the Duwamish River in Tukwila, Duwamish Hill Preserve is a place where nature, history, and culture intersect in a meaningful and beautiful way. This 10.5-acre park may be modest in size, but it holds immense significance both ecologically and culturally. For thousands of years, it has been a sacred site for the Duwamish people, serving as a cultural landmark and a place for gathering, storytelling, and ceremony. Today, it is preserved not only as a green space in the city but also as a living reminder of the region's deep Indigenous roots. With sweeping views of the Duwamish River Valley, engaging trails, native plant restoration projects, and interpretive signs that tell the story of the land, Duwamish Hill Preserve is a destination that invites visitors to connect with both the natural environment and the cultural heritage of the region. Whether you come for a peaceful walk, to learn more about local history, or simply to enjoy a quiet spot in nature, Duwamish Hill Preserve offers a uniquely enriching experience.

A Sacred Site for the Duwamish People

For the Duwamish people, the land known today as Duwamish Hill is a place of great spiritual significance. This hill has long been associated with the creation stories and cultural heritage of the tribe. According to Duwamish tradition, it is a place where the landscape itself tells the stories of the people who have lived in the region for thousands of years. Oral histories and cultural practices were passed down through generations on this land, and the hill was a place for ceremonies and gatherings that connected the Duwamish people to the earth, water, and sky.

Today, the Duwamish Hill Preserve stands as a tribute to that cultural heritage, with interpretive signs and public art pieces that help visitors

▲ An Anna's hummingbird nest made of plant down, moss, spiderweb, and lichen contains two eggs.

understand its importance. The preservation of this site in 2004, after decades of industrial development threatened its existence, was the result of a collaborative effort between the local community, conservation groups, and the Duwamish people. Now, Duwamish Hill is a protected space where both the natural environment and cultural legacy of the Duwamish tribe can be honored and shared with future generations.

Exploring the Landscape

Duwamish Hill's landscape is a blend of rocky outcrops, native plants, and open fields that offer a peaceful escape in the middle of an urban area. Though it is a relatively small preserve, its elevated position gives visitors panoramic views of the Duwamish River, Tukwila, and the surrounding mountains. The trails that wind through the preserve are designed to highlight both the natural beauty of the hill and the cultural significance of its location.

As you walk the trails, you'll encounter a variety of habitats, from open meadows to restored native-plant gardens. The trails are well-maintained and offer easy, gradual hikes that are accessible to most visitors. Along the way, interpretive signs provide insights into the ecology of the area, the cultural stories of the Duwamish people, and the importance of protecting this unique landscape.

Restoring Native Plants and Habitats

One of the central goals of the Duwamish Hill Preserve is to restore the native vegetation that once thrived in the region. Over the years, volunteers and community groups have worked hard to remove invasive species and replant native plants that are crucial to the local ecosystem. Today, the preserve is home to a variety of native trees, shrubs, and wildflowers that not only enhance the beauty of the landscape but also provide important habitat for local wildlife.

Among the native plants you'll find here are western red cedar, Oregon grape, snowberry, and wild rose. These plants have been used by the Duwamish people for food, medicine, and cultural practices for centuries, and their presence in the preserve helps reconnect the landscape with its Indigenous roots. In spring, wildflowers such as camas and yarrow bloom, adding splashes of color to the meadows and attracting pollinators like bees and butterflies.

The restoration efforts at Duwamish Hill are ongoing, with community work parties regularly held to continue the work of planting, weeding, and maintaining the health of the ecosystem. For visitors, the restored native gardens are a beautiful and educational feature of the preserve, offering a glimpse into what the landscape might have looked like before European settlement and industrial development transformed the area.

Birdwatching and Wildlife

Despite its urban surroundings—don't be put off by the sounds of planes taking off overhead from nearby Sea-Tac Airport and Boeing Field or gunfire from a nearby shooting range—Duwamish Hill Preserve is a surprisingly good spot for birdwatching and observing local wildlife. The variety of native plants and the preserve's proximity to the Duwamish River make it an attractive habitat for a range of bird species. Throughout the year, you can spot birds like red-tailed hawks, black-capped chickadees, and Anna's hummingbirds, and seasonal visitors like warblers and swallows make their appearance during migration periods.

In the early morning or late afternoon, it's not uncommon to see birds of prey soaring overhead, taking advantage of the open skies and elevated vantage point of the hill. The meadows and shrubs provide food and shelter for smaller birds, and the restored plantings help create a rich environment for both resident and migratory species. Whether you're an avid birder or just enjoy spotting wildlife, Duwamish Hill offers a quiet space to observe the rhythms of nature.

▲ The bark and roots of Oregon grape were used by Coast Salish tribes in traditional remedies for a variety of ailments, and its berries were an important food staple.

Public Art and Interpretation

One of the most distinctive features of Duwamish Hill Preserve is its integration of public art and interpretive elements that highlight the cultural and ecological significance of the site. Throughout the preserve, you'll find sculptures, murals, and other art installations that celebrate the history of the Duwamish people and their connection to the land. These pieces, created by local artists in collaboration with the Duwamish Tribe, help tell the story of the preserve in a way that is both visually engaging and deeply meaningful.

In addition to the art, the interpretive signs scattered along the trails provide context for the history of the site, the cultural practices of the Duwamish people, and the ongoing restoration efforts. The signs also offer information about the native plants and animals that call the preserve home, making a walk through the preserve both an educational and reflective experience.

A Place of Reflection and Learning

For many visitors, Duwamish Hill Preserve is more than just a park—it's a place of reflection, where the natural and cultural history of the region come together in a way that invites contemplation and learning. Whether you come to hike the trails, take in the views, or learn about the Duwamish people and their deep connection to the land, the preserve offers a peaceful, thought-provoking space that feels far removed from the urban world that surrounds it.

A Community-Driven Preserve

The story of Duwamish Hill Preserve is one of community action and collaboration. After years of industrial use and the threat of further development, it was the combined efforts of local residents, conservation organizations, and the Duwamish Tribe that saved the hill from destruction. Today, the preserve stands as a testament to what can be achieved when communities come together to protect and restore natural and cultural heritage.

The ongoing stewardship of the preserve relies heavily on volunteer involvement, with regular work parties, educational programs, and events that engage the community in the care of the land. For those interested in getting involved, Duwamish Hill offers many opportunities to contribute to the preservation of this important site.

A Unique Urban Oasis

Duwamish Hill Preserve is a rare and special place, where the natural beauty of the Pacific Northwest and the rich cultural history of the Duwamish people are intertwined in a meaningful way. Whether you're exploring the trails, learning about native plants, or reflecting on the stories of the land, a visit to Duwamish Hill is an experience that connects you to both the past and the present in a profound way. It's a reminder of the resilience of the land and the people who have cared for it for generations and an invitation to be part of its future.

▼ It's worth hoofing it up the quarter-mile to the high point of Duwamish Hill Preserve not just for the panoramic view but also to see the profusion of Pacific madrone trees making themselves at home up there.

Black River Riparian Forest and Wetland

Trade a concrete jungle for a seemingly real one at this unique urban wetland in the heart of Renton, where you can walk, look for birds, and contemplate the glory of nature along the twisting creek.

Hidden within the bustling City of Renton, just south of Seattle, the Black River Riparian Forest and Wetland is a sanctuary for wildlife and a tranquil escape for nature lovers. This unique natural area, which spans over 100 acres, is one of the last remaining urban wetlands in the region, offering a blend of riparian forest, marshes, and waterways that are teeming with life. Despite being surrounded by development, the Black River Riparian Forest feels worlds away, providing a rare opportunity to explore an ecosystem that plays a vital role in supporting local biodiversity.

For birdwatchers, hikers, and anyone interested in wetlands ecology, the Black River Riparian Forest and Wetland is a place where you can observe the dynamic interplay between land and water while experiencing the wild side of the Pacific Northwest just minutes from the city.

A Vital Ecosystem on the Black River

The Black River, once part of the Cedar River before it was diverted, is now a quiet waterway that flows through the forest and wetlands. This river

provides the lifeblood for the riparian ecosystem that surrounds it, creating a diverse habitat that supports an abundance of plants and animals. The wetland is a crucial link in the health of the local environment, helping filter water, reduce flooding, and provide a home for countless species of birds, mammals, amphibians, and insects.

The forested sections of the riparian area are dominated by native trees such as black cottonwood, red alder, and bigleaf maple, which provide shade and habitat for birds and mammals. Beneath the canopy, dense thickets of salmonberry, snowberry, and horsetail create a lush understory that supports everything from nesting birds to small mammals and insects. The combination of forest, wetland, and open water makes the Black River Riparian Forest one of the most ecologically rich urban habitats in the Puget Sound region.

▲ The Black River Riparian Forest is an oasis amid Renton's highways and tarmacs.

A Birdwatcher's Paradise

For bird enthusiasts, the Black River Riparian Forest and Wetland is a dream come true. This area is designated as an Important Bird Area (IBA) by the Audubon Society, due to the high concentration of birds that rely on its diverse habitats. The wetlands and forests here are home to more than 100 species of birds, making it one of the best birdwatching spots in the Seattle area.

Great blue herons are perhaps the most iconic residents of the Black River Riparian Forest. The heron rookery here is one of the largest in the region, with over 100 active nests. Each spring, these majestic birds can be seen flying over the wetlands, gathering nesting materials, and fishing in the shallow waters of the Black River. During the breeding season, the sight of these tall, elegant birds flying overhead or perched in the trees is a highlight for visitors.

In addition to great blue herons, the riparian area attracts a wide variety of other bird species, including wood ducks, northern flickers, red-winged blackbirds, and song sparrows. Migratory birds, such as warblers and sandpipers, also use the wetland as a stopover during their long journeys. Whether you're an experienced birder or just starting out, the Black River Riparian Forest is a place where you can expect to see something exciting.

Exploring the Trails and Wetlands

The Black River Riparian Forest and Wetland features a network of trails that wind through the diverse habitats, offering opportunities for both leisurely walks and more in-depth exploration of the ecosystem. The main trail, which runs along the edge of the wetland and through the forest, is an easy, flat path that makes the area accessible to visitors of all ages and fitness levels.

As you walk along the trails, you'll pass through dense stands of trees and open marshlands, with views of the Black River peeking through the vegetation. Interpretive signs along the way provide information about the importance of wetlands, the species that live here, and the conservation efforts that are helping protect this vital area.

▼ A female wood duck is right at home resting in South Seattle's Black River wetlands.

The wetland itself is a dynamic environment, with changing water levels depending on the season. In spring, the marshes are filled with water, and the sounds of frogs, insects, and birds create a vibrant symphony of life. As summer progresses, parts of the wetland may dry out, revealing muddy areas where you can spot tracks of wildlife like raccoons, deer, and even the occasional coyote.

A Refuge for Wildlife

The Black River Riparian Forest is more than just a birdwatching destination—it's also home to a wide range of other wildlife. Small mammals like beavers, river otters, and muskrats can often be seen in or near the water, particularly at dawn or dusk when they are most active. Beavers, in particular, play an important role in shaping the landscape, creating ponds and wetlands that benefit many other species.

Amphibians, such as Pacific chorus frogs and long-toed salamanders, thrive in the wetland areas, while the forest provides shelter for small mammals like squirrels, raccoons, and bats. The mix of open water, wetlands, and dense forest creates a complex food web that supports a rich variety of life.

Even predators such as coyotes and red-tailed hawks are known to frequent the area, taking advantage of the abundant prey.

For those with an eye for smaller creatures, the wetland is also home to a variety of insects, including dragonflies, damselflies, and butterflies. These insects are not only fascinating to watch, but they also play a critical role in the ecosystem, serving as food for birds, amphibians, and fish.

Conservation and Restoration Efforts

The Black River Riparian Forest and Wetland is a prime example of urban conservation in action. Over the years, efforts to protect and restore this area have been crucial in maintaining its ecological integrity. Invasive species like Himalayan blackberry and reed canary grass, which threaten native plants and wildlife, are regularly removed by volunteers and city staff, and ongoing restoration projects aim to reintroduce native vegetation and improve water quality.

Community involvement is a key part of the success of these conservation efforts. Local groups and volunteers participate in restoration activities, planting native species and removing invasive plants to help ensure that the wetland remains a healthy habitat for wildlife. Educational programs and guided nature walks also help raise awareness about the importance of wetlands and encourage visitors to become stewards of this special place.

A Peaceful Escape

Despite its proximity to urban areas, the Black River Riparian Forest and Wetland feels like a world apart. The sounds of birds, the rustle of leaves in the wind, and the gentle flow of the river create a peaceful atmosphere that invites visitors to slow down and connect with nature. Whether you're looking to observe wildlife, take a quiet walk through the woods, or simply sit by the water and enjoy the serenity of the wetland, this natural area offers a restorative escape from the busy pace of city life.

A Hidden Gem in Renton

The Black River Riparian Forest and Wetland is a hidden gem, offering a rare glimpse of an urban ecosystem that is both beautiful and vital to the health of the environment. For nature lovers, birdwatchers, and anyone interested in wetlands conservation, it's a place where you can experience the richness of the Pacific Northwest's natural world up close, while also playing a role in its preservation.

With its diverse habitats, abundant wildlife, and opportunities for quiet exploration, the Black River Riparian Forest is a destination that reminds us of the importance of protecting our natural spaces—especially those that exist right in our own backyard.

Coal Creek Natural Area

Walk for miles through stunning second-growth forest primeval—it's hard to believe it used to be coal-mining central—just outside of downtown Bellevue.

▼ Coal Creek is the lifeblood of Bellevue's biggest greenbelt.

Just east of downtown Bellevue lies Coal Creek Natural Area, a 500-acre landscape of dense forest, rugged ravines, and a flowing creek that offers a true Pacific Northwest experience. This sprawling natural area is a haven for local wildlife and nature lovers alike, where verdant greenery, vibrant wildflowers, and a network of trails create an immersive environment. Coal Creek Natural Area is more than just a park; it's a window into Bellevue's past, rich in history, biodiversity, and scenic beauty, making it a treasured escape from the surrounding urban landscape.

Tracing the Trails of Coal Creek

The trail network within Coal Creek Natural Area spans around 7 miles, with pathways that lead hikers through an evolving tapestry of nature. The Coal Creek Trail is the main pathway, a moderately challenging trail that follows the creek's course for about 3.7 miles. The trail features rustic bridges, steep inclines, and forested segments that range from shaded, dense woodlands to clearings where sun filters through. As you venture deeper into the area, you'll encounter remnants of the historic coal-mining operations that give the park its name, adding a touch of history to the natural beauty surrounding you.

◄ In classic temperate rainforest style, a western hemlock tree grows out of the stump of an old-growth western red cedar stump. Note the springboard notches in the stump where loggers a century ago would balance on boards and team up to fell huge trees by pulling back and forth on two-man band saws.

The Rippling Waters of Coal Creek

Coal Creek is the park's central feature, a stream that starts in the foothills of the Cascades and meanders through Bellevue, eventually emptying into Lake Washington. The creek's cool, clear waters provide essential habitat for native fish, including cutthroat trout and salmon. Each fall, salmon return to the creek to spawn, a phenomenon that attracts both human visitors and local wildlife, including herons and the occasional bald eagle. These seasonal migrations are vital to the creek's ecosystem, helping sustain the park's rich web of life.

The creek side offers countless opportunities for nature observation. Ferns, mosses, and horsetails line its banks, thriving in the moist environment and adding layers of green to the forest floor. Fallen logs, often covered with lichens and fungi, create a complex habitat for amphibians and insects. Coal Creek's gentle babble is a soothing backdrop, enhancing the sense of peace that pervades the park's trails.

A Forested Tapestry: Flora of Coal Creek Natural Area

The dense canopy of Coal Creek Natural Area showcases the Pacific Northwest's classic temperate rainforests. Douglas firs, western red cedars, and bigleaf maples dominate the forest, their tall trunks stretching toward the sky and their branches forming a lush shade canopy. In spring, the bright green leaves of vine maple trees and the delicate white blooms of the Pacific dogwood create beautiful accents among the evergreens.

The understory is alive with diverse vegetation. Swordferns unfurl along the trails, their long, fronded leaves adding a prehistoric charm to the forest floor. Salal, Oregon grape, and red huckleberry grow thick in the shadier parts of the forest, their berries providing food for local wildlife. Wildflowers like trillium and bleeding heart bloom in the early spring, while bright pink salmonberry flowers add pops of color along the trails. In late summer, blackberries ripen along sunnier sections, offering a sweet treat to passersby and animals alike.

Wildlife Watching: Birds and Animals

Coal Creek Natural Area is home to a variety of birds, mammals, and amphibians. Birdwatchers will find an abundance of avian life in the park, from common species like chickadees, nuthatches, and robins to more elusive inhabitants like the pileated woodpecker, whose loud, rhythmic drumming can often be heard echoing through the trees. Great blue herons are sometimes spotted along the creek, particularly when salmon are running, and bald eagles occasionally soar overhead, their sharp eyes scanning for prey below.

The forest's resident mammals include black-tailed deer, raccoons, and coyotes, though sightings are often brief. The dense underbrush provides hiding places for these shy animals, making Coal Creek a true wildlife sanctuary. If you're lucky, you may spot river otters playing in the creek or catch a glimpse of a red fox darting through the ferns. In wetter months, keep an eye out for Pacific tree frogs and salamanders near the creek, where the humid environment supports their life cycles.

Seasonal Shifts in the Landscape

Coal Creek Natural Area offers a different experience with each season. Spring brings the forest to life with vibrant greens and blooming wildflowers, while the creek swells with snowmelt from the mountains. In summer, the canopy provides a cool respite from the heat, and the trails are lined with flowering plants and ripening berries.

Fall is perhaps the most spectacular season, as the maples turn shades of gold and crimson, contrasting beautifully with the evergreens. Fallen leaves create a rustling carpet along the trails, and the air carries the rich scent of damp earth. The cooler temperatures and changing colors make fall one of the best times to explore the park. Winter brings a quieter beauty, with moss and ferns taking on an even deeper green, and the occasional frost adding a sparkling touch to the landscape.

A Glimpse into History

Coal Creek Natural Area is steeped in history, dating back to Bellevue's early days as a coal-mining town. In the late 19th century, miners extracted coal from this area, leaving behind remnants that can still be seen along the trail. Interpretive signs throughout the park share the story of these early settlers, who carved out a livelihood amid the forests and hills. Abandoned mine shafts, rusting machinery, and old rail ties are subtle reminders of this past, now reclaimed by nature.

These relics are a fascinating aspect of Coal Creek Natural Area, offering a tangible connection to the area's industrial heritage and a reminder of how the landscape has transformed over the years. Bellevue has taken care to preserve this history, blending education with conservation so visitors can learn about the park's origins while appreciating its natural beauty.

Protecting Coal Creek's Ecosystem

As an ecologically significant area, Coal Creek Natural Area is actively managed to protect its diverse habitats. Conservation efforts focus on maintaining water quality in Coal Creek, controlling invasive plant species, and restoring native vegetation. These actions are critical for sustaining the park's ecosystem, which provides habitat for salmon, songbirds, and mammals.

Volunteer programs and community events offer Bellevue residents the chance to contribute to the park's upkeep, whether through invasive plant removal, native planting, or trail maintenance. By participating in these programs, visitors can connect with the area on a deeper level and help ensure that Coal Creek Natural Area remains a thriving green space for generations to come.

An Urban Wilderness Awaits

Coal Creek Natural Area is more than just a hiking destination; it's a sanctuary of natural beauty and historical significance right in the heart of Bellevue. From its meandering trails and serene creek to its towering trees and vibrant wildlife, the park offers a perfect retreat for those seeking solace in nature. Each visit brings new sights, sounds, and experiences, whether you're marveling at a woodpecker's call, spotting a trout in the creek, or simply savoring the quiet rustle of the forest.

For anyone who wants to explore the wonders of the Pacific Northwest without venturing far from the city, Coal Creek Natural Area offers an unforgettable escape into a world where history, nature, and tranquility converge.

► A bigleaf maple and a whole lot of licorice ferns grow out of an old-growth fallen "nurse log" near Coal Creek.

Mercer Slough Nature Park

Paddle or hoof it through one of the largest freshwater wetlands (and its mosaic of wildlife habitats) anywhere in greater Puget Sound.

In the heart of Bellevue lies Mercer Slough Nature Park, a sprawling 320-acre wetland that feels like a world apart from the bustling city. Just minutes from downtown, this tranquil refuge is a haven for plants, wildlife, and humans seeking solace in nature. The slough's marshes, meadows, and waterways form one of the largest freshwater wetlands in the Puget Sound region, offering a glimpse into a vibrant ecosystem that's both beautiful and vital to the health of the environment.

For visitors, Mercer Slough provides a chance to connect with the rhythms of the natural world, whether by walking its trails, paddling its waterways, or simply observing its diverse wildlife. The park offers a perfect blend of serene beauty and ecological significance, making it a treasure for nature lovers and conservationists alike.

▼ Mercer Slough is an urban wetland wonderland and plays host to a riot of plant and animal diversity.

◄ Looking up at a humongous Douglas fir tree and the canopy over Mercer Slough, a vine maple photobombs the view.

A Diverse Ecosystem in the Heart of the City

Mercer Slough is a living mosaic of habitats, each supporting its own unique community of plants and animals. Marshes and sedges line the waterways, their tall grasses swaying in the breeze and providing cover for frogs, birds, and small mammals. In the wetter areas, skunk cabbage bursts forth in early spring, its bright yellow spathes heralding the season's arrival.

Surrounding the marshes are forested wetlands dominated by black cottonwoods and red alders. These trees form a dense canopy that shades the ground below, where mosses, ferns, and salmonberry bushes thrive. The understory provides shelter for countless creatures, from birds to insects to the occasional raccoon foraging for food.

Open meadows intersperse the wetlands, blooming with wildflowers like yarrow and goldenrod in the warmer months. These areas are alive with the hum of bees and the flutter of butterflies, including painted ladies and western tiger swallowtails. The meadows also provide critical habitat for ground-nesting birds and pollinators that play an essential role in the park's ecosystem.

At the heart of Mercer Slough lies its namesake waterway—a slow-moving channel that connects the wetland to Lake Washington. This aquatic habitat supports an array of fish, amphibians, and aquatic plants. Its quiet waters offer a serene backdrop for wildlife-watching and paddling, drawing both humans and animals to its banks.

A Haven for Wildlife

Mercer Slough is teeming with life, making it a paradise for wildlife enthusiasts. The park is home to over 170 bird species, from the iconic great blue heron to the lively red-winged blackbird. Herons are a common sight, standing still in the shallows as they hunt for fish or flying gracefully overhead with their long legs trailing behind them. Their presence is a reminder of the delicate balance that wetlands maintain in supporting both predator and prey.

Birdwatchers might also spot ospreys and bald eagles soaring above the park, scanning the waters for fish. In spring, songbirds like yellow warblers and common yellowthroats flit among the shrubs, their bright plumage adding splashes of color to the greenery. During migration seasons, Mercer Slough becomes a stopover for waterfowl such as mallards, wood ducks, and green-winged teal.

The park's wetlands are also alive with amphibians, particularly in spring when Pacific tree frogs fill the air with their distinctive calls. These small frogs are a vital part of the food web, feeding on insects and in turn serving as prey for larger animals. Rough-skinned newts can sometimes be seen swimming in the slough's waters, their movements slow and deliberate.

Mercer Slough's mammals include river otters, muskrats, and beavers, all of which contribute to the health of the ecosystem. Beavers in particular are known as "ecosystem engineers" for their ability to create ponds and wetlands that benefit other species. Their lodges and dams can often be spotted along the water's edge, a testament to their industrious nature.

Exploring Mercer Slough

Visitors to Mercer Slough can explore its natural beauty through a variety of trails and water routes. The park features over 7 miles of walking paths, from

▶ A great blue heron glides through the air, no doubt en route to a favorite shallow-water stalking ground.

◀ The Bellefields Trailhead loop trail covers just under a mile and leads walkers through some of the most scenic spots in Mercer Slough via a network of boardwalks and footpaths.

gravel trails that wind through the forest to elevated boardwalks that cross the marshes. Each step reveals a new facet of the park's ecosystem, from the dense greenery of the forest to the open expanse of the meadows.

The Bellefields Trailhead is a favorite for its variety of scenery, offering a gentle walk through forested wetlands and meadowlands. Along the way, interpretive signs provide insights into the slough's plants, animals, and ecological importance.

For a unique perspective, paddling through the Mercer Slough is an unforgettable experience. The calm waters provide a window into the life of the wetland, from the fish swimming below to the dragonflies hovering above. Kayakers and canoeists often find themselves sharing the water with mallards, turtles, and the occasional muskrat. Rental kayaks and guided tours are available seasonally, making it easy for visitors to embark on this tranquil adventure.

Seasonal Beauty

Mercer Slough transforms with the seasons, offering something new to discover year-round. In spring, wildflowers bloom in the meadows, and pollinators return to the park in full force. Frogs emerge from hibernation, and migratory birds fill the air with their songs.

Summer brings long days and vibrant activity. Butterflies flit through the meadows, dragonflies dart over the waterways, and the shaded forest trails offer a cool respite from the heat. The wetlands are alive with the hum of insects and the rustling of leaves, creating a symphony of nature.

Autumn paints Mercer Slough in warm hues, as the trees' leaves turn gold and orange. The air grows crisp, and the park becomes quieter, save for the calls of waterfowl preparing for migration. Winter reveals a stark beauty, with frost-covered grasses and the bare silhouettes of trees reflected in the still waters.

Education and Conservation

Mercer Slough is not only a place to enjoy nature but also a center for education and conservation. The Mercer Slough Environmental Education Center, operated by the City of Bellevue and the Pacific Science Center, offers programs that connect visitors to the natural world. Guided nature walks, workshops, and school programs foster a deeper understanding of wetland ecosystems and their importance.

Conservation efforts are at the heart of the park's mission. Volunteers regularly remove invasive species and plant native vegetation to maintain the slough's ecological health. These efforts ensure that Mercer Slough continues to thrive as a sanctuary for wildlife and a resource for the community.

A Natural Retreat in Bellevue

Mercer Slough Nature Park is a reminder of the beauty and resilience of nature in an urban setting. Its wetlands, meadows, and forests offer a tranquil escape where visitors can slow down and reconnect with the natural world. Whether you're kayaking through its quiet waters, strolling along its trails, or simply listening to the croak of a frog, Mercer Slough invites you to immerse yourself in its wonders. It's not just a park—it's a living, breathing ecosystem that enriches the lives of all who visit.

Nearby Nature Connections: Yarrow Bay, Wetherill, and Fairweather Preserves

While Mercer Slough stands as one of the Eastside's most prominent natural areas, nearby Yarrow Bay Wetlands, Wetherill Nature Preserve, and Fairweather Nature Preserve create essential links in the region's green network. Together, these spaces provide critical habitat for wildlife and offer Eastside residents additional opportunities to connect with nature.

Yarrow Bay Wetlands, located just north of Mercer Slough along Lake Washington, is a thriving wetland ecosystem that supports a variety of waterfowl, amphibians, and plant species. Its marshes and ponds act as vital stopovers for migratory birds, making it a prime destination for birdwatchers. Visitors can explore the area through a series of trails and boardwalks that weave through this lush habitat.

Wetherill Nature Preserve, nestled in the nearby City of Hunts Point, offers a smaller but equally serene escape. This forested preserve is a haven for native plants like ferns and wildflowers, as well as songbirds that thrive in its quiet, wooded environment. It's an ideal spot for those seeking a peaceful retreat away from urban noise.

Fairweather Nature Preserve, located along the shores of Lake Washington in Medina, combines shoreline access with forested trails, creating a diverse environment where visitors can observe eagles, otters, and other wildlife. Its proximity to the lake makes it an important corridor for species that depend on aquatic and terrestrial habitats.

These interconnected preserves enhance the Eastside's natural landscape, ensuring that both wildlife and people benefit from protected green spaces within the rapidly growing Puget Sound region. Together with Mercer Slough, they highlight the importance of preserving urban nature for future generations.

Bellevue Botanical Garden, Wilburton Hill Park, and Kelsey Creek Park

Explore these showcases for native plants and the pastoral and forested hiking trails all around them.

In the bustling heart of Bellevue, Washington, three nearby parks—Bellevue Botanical Garden, Wilburton Hill Park, and Kelsey Creek Park—offer an extraordinary opportunity to immerse yourself in nature without leaving the city. These green spaces each have their own character and charm, from meticulously maintained gardens to native forest trails and pastoral farm scenes. Together, they create a trifecta of diverse ecosystems, attracting visitors from all walks of life who come to experience the lush greenery, seasonal blooms, native wildlife, and peaceful landscapes.

◄ A massive western red cedar tree is visible through the window at the Tateuchi Pavilion.

Bellevue Botanical Garden: A World of Flora and Beauty

Bellevue Botanical Garden, a 53-acre oasis, is a living showcase of horticultural artistry and Pacific Northwest flora. Since its establishment in 1992, this botanical garden has grown to encompass themed gardens and woodland trails that captivate plant enthusiasts, wildlife watchers, and casual visitors alike. The garden's blend of cultivated spaces and natural forest areas creates an atmosphere of discovery, inspiring ideas for gardeners and a serene experience for nature lovers.

The Native Discovery Garden and Woodlands

The Native Discovery Garden highlights the Pacific Northwest's rich plant diversity and sustainable gardening techniques, featuring native species like red-flowering currant, vine maple, and Oregon grape. These plants not only create a landscape that celebrates regional ecology but also attract pollinators like bumblebees and hummingbirds, offering a valuable habitat in an urban setting. Interpretive signs throughout the area provide insights into the role native plants play in local ecosystems, making this garden an educational highlight.

Adjacent to the Native Discovery Garden is a trail that leads into a forested section of Bellevue Botanical Garden. Here, towering Douglas fir, western red cedar, and bigleaf maple create a lush canopy, while the understory teems with swordferns, salal, and moss. The damp, shaded environment is perfect for observing local birdlife, from the black-capped chickadee and red-breasted nuthatch to spotted towhees scratching among the leaves.

Seasonal Gardens and the Ravine Experience

Bellevue Botanical Garden's seasonal displays include the colorful Perennial Border, which reaches its peak in summer with vibrant flowers like coneflowers, daisies, and asters that attract butterflies. The Dahlia Display also dazzles in late summer and early autumn, with large blooms in shades from soft pinks to deep purples, creating a feast for the senses.

One of the unique features of the Bellevue Botanical Garden is the Ravine Experience—a pathway that crosses a 150-foot suspension bridge over a deep, wooded ravine. Below, a seasonal stream nurtures a lush ecosystem where ferns, skunk cabbage, and mosses thrive in the cool, moist air. The suspension bridge offers a bird's-eye view of this mini-ecosystem, providing visitors with a memorable nature immersion in the heart of Bellevue.

Wilburton Hill Park: Trails and Towering Trees

Adjacent to Bellevue Botanical Garden, Wilburton Hill Park expands the green space with over 100 acres of forested trails and sports fields, making it Bellevue's largest park. With its accessible trails winding through dense woodlands, Wilburton Hill Park attracts hikers, runners, and anyone looking for a peaceful walk under the trees.

Trails through Dense Forest

The forest trails at Wilburton Hill Park provide a serene escape into Bellevue's native woodlands. Walking along these paths, you'll encounter old-growth trees such as Douglas fir, western hemlock, and red alder, interspersed with younger understory growth. Swordferns, bracken, and salal line the trails, creating a lush green floor that's beautiful in every season. The park's proximity to Bellevue Botanical Garden means visitors can seamlessly move from cultivated garden spaces into a wilder setting.

Wilburton Hill's trails are ideal for birdwatching. Keep an eye out for flickers, woodpeckers, and songbirds like the Pacific wren and chickadees flitting among the trees. In the warmer months, dragonflies dart along sunlit clearings, while squirrels and rabbits make occasional appearances, adding to the park's quiet charm.

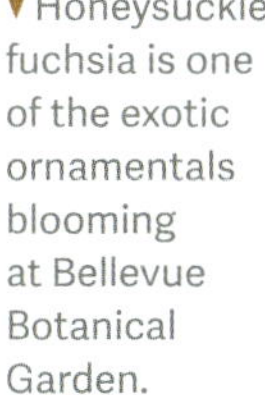

▼ Honeysuckle fuchsia is one of the exotic ornamentals blooming at Bellevue Botanical Garden.

The Viewpoint and Open Fields

One of the highlights of Wilburton Hill Park is its hilltop viewpoint. On clear days, visitors can see the distant peaks of the Cascade Mountains framed by the evergreen treetops. The park's open fields near the viewpoint are excellent for picnicking or simply relaxing and enjoying the view. These meadows also attract local wildlife, especially in early morning or late afternoon when deer sometimes venture out from the forest edge.

▲ A network of hiking trails leads up and around Wilburton Hill.

Kelsey Creek Park: Farm Life, Forests, and Wildlife

Kelsey Creek Park, a few miles south of Bellevue Botanical Garden and Wilburton Hill Park, adds another dimension to Bellevue's natural offerings with its combination of forest trails, open fields, and a working farm. The park spans 150 acres, incorporating everything from shaded creek-side paths to a picturesque farm setting that appeals to families and nature enthusiasts.

Kelsey Creek and Forest Trails

The park's namesake, Kelsey Creek, winds through the property, creating a habitat rich with plant and animal life. The trails meander along the creek through a damp forest, where the towering canopy of Douglas fir and western hemlock gives way to a rich understory of ferns, thimbleberry, and salmonberry. The bubbling sound of the creek and the soft light filtering through the trees create a tranquil atmosphere perfect for nature walks.

Along the creek, you may spot tree frogs and salamanders in the wetter months. The creek also provides essential habitat for local birdlife. Belted kingfishers, herons, and mallards are often seen along the water while woodpeckers tap away at the trees above. Salmon have been known to spawn in Kelsey Creek, a testament to the park's ongoing conservation efforts to maintain this valuable urban waterway.

The Farm and Pastoral Fields

Kelsey Creek Park is perhaps best known for its working farm, where resident animals—goats, sheep, chickens, and rabbits—make it a popular spot for families. The farm hearkens back to Bellevue's agricultural roots and offers educational opportunities through classes and events. In summer, children's camps let young visitors connect with animals and learn about sustainable farming practices.

The fields surrounding the farm add to the park's appeal, attracting wild visitors like rabbits, deer, and birds of prey. In late summer and fall, the fields come alive with wildflowers, which in turn attract butterflies and bees. Red-tailed hawks and bald eagles are sometimes seen circling overhead, scanning the fields for small animals, while swallows swoop and dive, feeding on insects.

A Year-Round Sanctuary

Kelsey Creek Park is a true year-round destination. In spring, forest trails are lined with blooming Indian plum and salmonberry flowers, while the fields around the farm burst with fresh greenery. Summer is perfect for picnics, with the open fields and shaded trails providing ample spots to relax. In fall, the park's deciduous trees turn vibrant shades of yellow and orange, creating a picturesque landscape, and winter's quieter months bring a calm beauty to the forest and creek.

A Green Connection in Bellevue

Together, Bellevue Botanical Garden, Wilburton Hill Park, and Kelsey Creek Park create a diverse natural experience in the heart of Bellevue. From cultivated gardens showcasing the beauty of native plants to forest trails and fields brimming with wildlife, each of these parks offers its own unique way to connect with nature. Whether you're admiring seasonal blooms, exploring forested paths, or simply sitting by a quiet creek, these spaces provide a valuable refuge from urban life and an opportunity to appreciate Bellevue's commitment to preserving green spaces.

With their varied habitats and recreational offerings, these parks invite exploration, education, and a renewed appreciation for the Pacific Northwest's natural beauty.

Saint Edward State Park

Immerse yourself in towering forests, wildlife-rich meadows, and vibrant wetlands along the shore of Lake Washington.

Nestled on the northeastern shore of Lake Washington, Saint Edward State Park offers visitors an escape into nature within the greater Seattle area. This 326-acre park, known for its verdant forests, sweeping lake views, and abundant wildlife, is home to a rich array of native flora and fauna. Once the site of a seminary, the park is now a sanctuary for nature lovers, hikers, birdwatchers, and anyone seeking a peaceful retreat among towering trees and vibrant ecosystems.

A Living Forest

One of the park's greatest treasures is its ancient forest, which holds a mix of coniferous and deciduous trees. Towering Douglas firs, western red cedars, and western hemlocks create a canopy of green, providing a habitat that is rare in the surrounding urban landscape. These giants can reach up to 200 feet tall and serve as essential components of the park's ecosystem, offering food, shelter, and nesting sites for countless species.

Beneath these towering trees, a dense understory flourishes, filled with vine maple, bigleaf maple, and red alder. In autumn, the vine maples turn brilliant shades of orange and red, adding a splash of color that contrasts beautifully against the evergreens. Swordferns blanket the forest floor, creating a thick, verdant ground cover, while the delicate maidenhair ferns add a soft, feathery touch to shady areas. These ferns are well-adapted to the moist conditions of the Pacific Northwest and are crucial in preventing soil erosion on the steep slopes.

In spring and early summer, the forest floor comes alive with native wildflowers. You might spot trillium, with its characteristic three-petaled white flowers, blooming in early spring before the tree canopy fully leafs

◄ Massive old-growth Douglas fir trees are among the natural wonders on display throughout the heavily wooded Saint Edward State Park.

out. Other wildflowers, such as yellow violets, bleeding hearts, and salmonberry blossoms, add subtle bursts of color, attracting bees, butterflies, and other pollinators.

A Rich Habitat for Wildlife

Saint Edward State Park is a sanctuary for wildlife, offering a variety of habitats that support many species of mammals, birds, amphibians, and insects. In the forested areas, black-tailed deer are sometimes seen foraging on vegetation, and in quieter moments, you may even catch a glimpse of a bobcat. Squirrels, chipmunks, and other small mammals are also abundant, often spotted darting between trees or gathering food along the trails.

One of the highlights of the park is its bird population. The forest's dense canopy and abundant undergrowth provide a perfect habitat for resident and migratory bird species. Bald eagles and red-tailed hawks are frequently seen soaring over the forest, while barred owls make their home in the park's older trees, filling the evening air with their haunting calls. Birdwatchers can enjoy sightings of Pacific wrens, downy woodpeckers, and pileated woodpeckers, whose distinct drumming echoes through the forest as they search for insects beneath tree bark.

◀ This Saint Edward State Park "still life" features shelf fungi and a big-ole bigleaf maple leaf.

▶ A Pacific yew tree grows out of a bigleaf maple trunk.

FIELD TRIP 21

In the spring and summer months, listen for the melodic songs of warblers, thrushes, and sparrows as they fill the air. Along the lake's edge, you might spot great blue herons stalking the shallows for fish, while mallards, wood ducks, and mergansers paddle in the water. Lake Washington's proximity also makes the park an excellent location for spotting migratory waterfowl during the winter months, when species like buffleheads and goldeneyes arrive to escape colder climates.

Exploring Wetlands and Streams

In addition to its forested areas, Saint Edward State Park contains wetlands and streams that contribute to the park's biodiversity. The wetlands, which can be found in lower-lying areas of the park, are teeming with cattails, skunk cabbage, and sedges. These water-loving plants provide essential habitat for amphibians, such as Pacific chorus frogs and long-toed salamanders, which rely on these areas for breeding and shelter. Listen closely, and you may hear the chorus of frogs in spring, their calls echoing through the wetland.

Stream corridors also wind their way through the park, carrying nutrient-rich water down to Lake Washington. These streams are important for the overall health of the watershed, acting as natural filters for stormwater and offering habitats for insects, small fish, and other aquatic species. These waterways support a unique ecosystem and connect the forest to the lake, creating corridors that allow wildlife to move freely across the park.

Meadow Habitat

One of the lesser-known gems of Saint Edward State Park is its meadow area. In spring and summer, these meadows burst into a vibrant display of wildflowers, attracting bees, butterflies, and other pollinators. Look for plants like yarrow, lupine, and common camas, which produce shades of blue and purple as they bloom. These open meadows provide a different kind of habitat within the park, ideal for species that prefer open, sunny spaces. Here, you might spot butterflies like the western tiger swallowtail or the painted lady, as well as dragonflies that patrol the meadow edges hunting for smaller insects.

In the evening, these meadows become feeding grounds for the park's resident bats, which emerge at dusk to feast on insects, contributing to natural pest control. If you stay late enough, you may also catch the silhouettes of deer as they venture out from the forest to graze on the meadow grasses.

Conservation and Restoration Efforts

Over the years, conservation efforts have played a vital role in preserving Saint Edward State Park's ecological richness. Volunteers and local environmental groups have worked tirelessly to remove invasive species like English ivy and Himalayan blackberry, which threaten the native plants that form the foundation of the park's ecosystem. Restoration projects are also in place to maintain the health of the wetlands and enhance the habitat for wildlife.

Interpretive signs throughout the park educate visitors on the importance of native plants and the role they play in supporting local wildlife. The park also encourages visitors to "leave no trace" to help protect sensitive habitats and to respect seasonal closures that allow wildlife to thrive undisturbed.

A Perfect Day Immersed in Nature

A day spent at Saint Edward State Park offers a glimpse into the stunning biodiversity of the Pacific Northwest. Whether you're hiking through towering forests, birdwatching along the lakeshore, or simply relaxing on a quiet bench, the park's natural beauty is ever-present. The changing seasons bring new colors and sounds, ensuring that each visit offers a unique experience.

From the enchanting calls of the barred owls at dusk to the sight of delicate wildflowers blooming in spring, Saint Edward State Park is a reminder of the quiet magic that nature holds. For those seeking a connection with the natural world, this state park is a priceless haven, offering a peaceful escape into the beauty of the Pacific Northwest's forests, meadows, and wetlands.

Swamp Creek—Where the Herons Are

Just a mile north of Saint Edward State Park as the crow flies, Swamp Creek is home to one of the largest great blue heron rookeries in western Washington. During nesting season, from mid-February to late July, dozens of nests can be observed in the spindly trees of the marsh.

The City of Kenmore has taken significant steps to protect this essential wetland habitat. In 2022, the city accepted a donation of a 6-acre tract in the Swamp Creek wetlands, enhancing its stewardship of the area and ensuring the preservation of the heron rookery for future generations.

Visitors are encouraged to experience the lively community of herons during the nesting season and to respect the natural environment to help maintain the sanctuary's tranquility and ecological balance. For optimal viewing, bring binoculars and observe the herons from outside the Kenmore Park and Ride, which is situated one block east of 73rd Avenue NE, at 7346 NE Bothell Way.

Kruckeberg Botanic Garden

Discover a backyard biodiversity hotspot, with Northwest natives and hardy exotics providing rich wildlife habitat amid the sprawl of Seattle's northern suburb.

Founded in 1958 by University of Washington botany professor Art Kruckeberg and his wife, Mareen, the Kruckeberg Botanic Garden began as a personal project on a 4-acre wooded lot in Shoreline. The site already hosted towering old-growth Douglas fir and western red cedar trees, but over five decades, the Kruckebergs transformed it into a lush garden filled with native and exotic plants. Each plant was carefully grown from seed or cuttings under Mareen's skilled direction. In 2007, the Kruckebergs sold the property to the City of Shoreline to preserve it for public enjoyment, ensuring that this oasis of biodiversity would continue to educate and inspire visitors for generations.

A Walk through Natural and Sustainable Design

◄ Pacific madrone, salal, and a Douglas fir make for a perfect Northwest forest scene in this Shoreline backyard.

Kruckeberg Botanic Garden is more than a scenic retreat; it is a model of sustainable landscaping. Many of the garden's plantings are drought-tolerant and arranged to mimic natural ecosystems, encouraging symbiotic relationships between flora and fauna. As visitors walk the meandering trails, they encounter a variety of sections showcasing different ecological themes. The spruce collection features species from around the world, while the climate resilience garden highlights plants adapted to thrive in warmer regional

temperatures. Nearby, the native plant demonstration garden focuses on the rich diversity of Pacific Northwest flora, blending seamlessly with other areas like the serpentine bed, meadow, and oak collection.

Highlights of the Garden Trail

The garden's compact trail system, totaling less than 0.3 miles, is perfect for both quick visits and leisurely exploration. The short but scenic walk includes remarkable sections like the spruce collection and the Pacific Northwest native garden. Visitors will also find the serpentine bed and the oak collection, which showcase a mix of native and exotic species arranged with an emphasis on harmony and sustainability.

Northwest Natives and Rare Finds

The garden's extensive collection of Pacific Northwest native plants includes iconic species like Douglas fir, vine maple, salal, and Nootka rose. One of the most notable residents is the Pacific yew, a sinewy tree thriving in the shade of the evergreen canopy. Known for its medicinal properties, the Pacific yew is "near threatened" on the International Union for Conservation of Nature's Red List. Visitors can also spot carefully selected exotic species such as Himalayan white pine, giant sequoia, and Cornelian cherry, which complement the garden's native flora without overwhelming it.

▼ Silver birch is one of many exotic trees that seem to fit right into the landscape at Kruckeberg Botanic Garden.

▲ Japanese spiraea's pink flowers brighten up an otherwise drab Northwest color palette of greens and browns.

Lichens: Tiny Ecosystems Everywhere

Lichens, fascinating composite organisms formed from fungi, algae, and cyanobacteria, thrive throughout the garden. These resilient life-forms cling to rock faces along the trails and derive nutrients from the air, creating self-contained ecosystems. Their quiet presence adds a layer of natural wonder, reflecting the intricate relationships that define the garden's ecosystem.

The garden's diverse habitats attract an impressive array of wildlife. Bird enthusiasts can spot more than 45 species, including Steller's jays, pileated woodpeckers, and Anna's hummingbirds. Mammals such as raccoons and coyotes frequent the area, often in pursuit of eastern gray squirrels and eastern cottontail rabbits—introduced species that have flourished in the region. These interactions, alongside sightings of native amphibians and insects, highlight the vibrant biodiversity thriving within the garden's boundaries.

Kruckeberg Botanic Garden is a sanctuary for more than 2000 plant species, offering an immersive escape into nature amid the suburban sprawl north of Seattle. With its seamless blend of native and exotic plants, the garden serves as both a tranquil retreat and an educational resource. It stands as a testament to thoughtful design and ecological stewardship, making it an inspiring destination for visitors seeking to connect with the natural world in any season.

Richmond Beach Saltwater Park

Enjoy the tide pools, salt marshes, forested trails, and breathtaking views from this iconic coastal park along Puget Sound in Shoreline, Seattle's northern neighbor.

Richmond Beach Saltwater Park, located in Shoreline, just north of Seattle, offers a mix of coastal beauty, sweeping mountain views, and diverse eco-systems that make it a true hidden gem for nature enthusiasts. With sandy beaches, rocky intertidal zones, grassy meadows, and forested trails, this 40-acre park attracts a wide variety of plants, wildlife, and marine life, all while offering stunning vistas over Puget Sound and toward the Olympic Mountains.

From beachcombing and birdwatching to hiking and picnicking, Richmond Beach Saltwater Park provides a variety of opportunities for connecting with nature in all its forms, making it a perfect spot to unwind and explore.

Coastal Beach and Marine Life

▼ Huge driftwood logs and salt marsh intermingle at Richmond Beach.

◄ A tale of two seaweeds: Turkish towel rests atop a bed of splendid iridescent at Richmond Beach.

One of the most compelling features of Richmond Beach Saltwater Park is its wide beach and intertidal zones. At low tide, the rocky and sandy areas are uncovered, revealing a fascinating world of marine life. Tide pools emerge between stones, harboring vibrant sea anemones, barnacles, and small crabs. If you look closely, you might spot ochre sea stars clinging to rocks, their bright orange or purple arms adding a pop of color to the muted tones of the shore.

The intertidal zone is also home to marine mollusks like limpets and per-iwinkles, which thrive in the dynamic environment where salt water and air meet. These organisms play a critical role in the ecosystem, as they are both

grazers and food sources for larger species. During summer months, look out for colorful nudibranchs, or sea slugs, that can sometimes be spotted grazing on algae—a special find for any amateur marine biologist.

The sandy stretches of beach invite shorebirds, which hunt in the shallows for small invertebrates and fish. You'll see sandpipers, killdeer, and even great blue herons as they stalk the water's edge. Occasionally, harbor seals swim just offshore, their dark heads bobbing above the water. This beach area is an ideal place for witnessing marine ecosystems up close, while learning about the relationships between different species and the tide's rhythmic influence.

Salt Marsh and Birdwatching

Just above the beach lies a small salt marsh, where fresh water from upland areas mingles with salt water from Puget Sound. This unique brackish habitat attracts a variety of bird species that use the marsh for feeding and nesting. Red-winged blackbirds are a common sight, with their distinctive call and bright red shoulder patches that stand out against the green of the grasses. In spring, look for mallards and other ducks nesting among the vegetation.

Songbirds such as sparrows and wrens can often be spotted flitting among the reeds and cattails, especially in the early morning, when they're most active. The marsh also attracts occasional visits from shorebirds during migration periods, including sandpipers and plovers, making it a rewarding spot for birdwatchers. For those with a keen eye, bald eagles and osprey are frequently seen soaring above, drawn by the abundance of fish in the nearby waters.

The salt marsh's plant life is specially adapted to handle both salt water and fresh water, with species like pickleweed, saltgrass, and cattails creating a rich habitat for birds, insects, and amphibians. In spring and summer, the grasses take on a vibrant green hue, contrasting beautifully with the blues and grays of Puget Sound just beyond.

Upland Meadows and Forested Trails

Beyond the beach and marsh areas, Richmond Beach Saltwater Park's upland meadows and forested trails provide a completely different kind of ecosystem, adding to the park's diversity. The grassy meadows are filled with wildflowers in the warmer months, including daisies, lupines, and yarrow. These blooms attract bees and butterflies, creating a lively display of color and movement.

The forested areas of the park feature trees like Douglas fir, western red cedar, and Pacific madrone, whose twisting red bark stands out sharply against the green canopy. This mix of native trees supports various bird species, including robins, nuthatches, and chickadees, whose calls fill the air in

▲ Like many bird species, osprey pairs tend to stick together as monogamous couples for their entire lives.

► Nootka rose hips dot the edge of the salt marsh with spots of red.

the early morning and late afternoon. Woodpeckers, including the northern flicker, can often be heard tapping away as they forage for insects within the tree bark.

The trails here meander through shaded woods and open grassy patches, offering plenty of opportunities to observe the natural surroundings. Look out for native understory plants like salal, Oregon grape, and swordferns, which form thick green carpets on the forest floor. The diversity of plant life provides food and shelter for small mammals like squirrels and rabbits, while coyotes are sometimes spotted in the quieter parts of the park at dusk.

Seasonal Changes and Local Wildlife

Each season at Richmond Beach Saltwater Park brings unique beauty and opportunities for wildlife watching. Spring is a vibrant time when wildflowers bloom and migratory birds return to the salt marsh and shoreline. Summer brings warmer weather and an increase in marine life activity, as crabs, fish, and sea stars are more easily spotted in the shallow tidal pools.

In autumn, the park's foliage transforms into a tapestry of gold, red, and green as the trees prepare for winter. This season is particularly exciting for birdwatchers, as migrating waterfowl and shorebirds use the park as a stop-over, and resident species become more visible against the bare branches. Winter at Richmond Beach is quieter but offers an entirely new experience. Snow-capped Olympic Mountains are visible across the Sound on clear days, and eagles and other raptors are more active along the shoreline.

Conserving Richmond Beach's Natural Beauty

Efforts to conserve Richmond Beach Saltwater Park's ecosystems include community-based projects aimed at removing invasive species and promoting the growth of native plants. The park's salt marsh and intertidal zones are especially sensitive, requiring ongoing conservation to maintain their delicate balance. Community volunteers frequently work on habitat-restoration projects, which help protect the marsh and improve the health of Piper's Creek, a small stream that winds through the park.

Educational signage placed along the trails and beach provides insights into the ecology of the area, encouraging visitors to appreciate and respect the park's natural spaces. Programs and events hosted by local environmental organizations often engage the public in understanding the park's ecological importance and learning about sustainable ways to enjoy the beach without disrupting marine life.

A Day at Richmond Beach Saltwater Park

A visit to Richmond Beach Saltwater Park offers a refreshing immersion into coastal nature, with diverse habitats, serene views, and abundant wildlife. Whether you're combing the beach for sea life, exploring the salt marsh, hiking through forested trails, or simply taking in the views from the bluff overlooking Puget Sound, this park provides a perfect slice of the Pacific Northwest's natural beauty.

With each visit, you're likely to discover something new—a blooming wildflower, a hunting osprey, or a tide-pool creature you hadn't noticed before. Richmond Beach Saltwater Park is more than just a beautiful landscape; it's a place where visitors can experience the quiet yet powerful rhythms of nature right on Seattle's doorstep. For those looking to connect with the rich biodiversity of the area, this park is a true treasure worth exploring year-round.

▼ Silver burr ragweed pops up where it can in its native territory along Pacific Ocean beachfronts from Alaska to Mexico (including right here at Richmond Beach).

Golden Gardens Park

Dip your toes into the sand and stroll the intertidal zone at Seattle's western edge and watch the sun go down over the Pacific.

Golden Gardens Park in Seattle's Ballard neighborhood is a place where the beauty of the Pacific Northwest meets the stunning coastline of Puget Sound. Known for its sandy beaches, salty sea breezes, and panoramic views, Golden Gardens offers more than just a place to relax by the shore—it's a dynamic landscape where wetlands, forested trails, and intertidal zones come together in a coastal sanctuary bustling with wildlife. From the shores to the forests, Golden Gardens immerses visitors in Seattle's diverse ecosystems and makes for a rewarding exploration into coastal nature.

Coastal Wetlands and Marshlands

▼ Golden Gardens is one of only a few spots in and around Seattle where you can truly put your toes in the sand—and take a dip or swim in the ocean.

The wetlands at Golden Gardens, nestled just behind the beach, are a hidden gem often overlooked by visitors focused on the ocean views. These wetlands play a vital role in supporting local wildlife and filtering stormwater runoff before it reaches Puget Sound. Coastal wetlands are essential for biodiversity, and the marsh at Golden Gardens is no exception. It's home to cattails, sedges, and bulrushes, all of which thrive in these watery conditions and provide habitat for insects, amphibians, and small mammals.

During spring and early summer, you might spot bright yellow blooms from skunk cabbage along the wetland's edges. This native plant, known for its pungent scent, is a favorite among pollinators. Dragonflies and damselflies flit over the water, feeding on smaller insects and providing a mesmerizing dance as they dart through the air. The marshy habitat also attracts tree frogs whose chirping fills the air in the evenings, creating a natural symphony that blends with the gentle rustle of reeds and grasses.

Intertidal Zone: A Dynamic Habitat

Golden Gardens' rocky and sandy intertidal zone is a microcosm of life, where each low tide reveals a thriving ecosystem. This area between the high- and low-tide marks is teeming with marine life, making it a favorite spot for tide-pooling and marine exploration. The barnacle-encrusted rocks and clusters of mussels provide a habitat for many species, and with a careful eye, you can often find sea stars, hermit crabs, and anemones clinging to the rocks.

A highlight of the intertidal zone is the array of green and purple sea stars, which have made a notable comeback in recent years after declines due to sea star wasting disease. Watching these slow-moving creatures cling to rocks and scavenge for food is a unique experience that demonstrates the resilience of marine ecosystems.

In the shallows, small fish and scuttling crabs thrive, drawing the attention of shorebirds, which flock to the intertidal area in search of food. Species like sandpipers and great blue herons are common visitors, while gulls patrol the shoreline, scanning for shellfish or other easy meals. The intertidal zone at Golden Gardens offers an accessible way to observe marine life and learn about the delicate balance of these coastal ecosystems.

Forested Trails and Native Flora

Beyond the beach and wetlands, Golden Gardens has a network of forested trails that wind up the bluff, offering shaded paths and a change of scenery from the sunny shoreline. These trails are lined with native flora, including towering bigleaf maples, western red cedar, and Douglas fir trees. Beneath the canopy, the understory is rich with swordferns, salal, and Oregon grape, creating a lush green corridor that feels worlds away from the bustling beach below.

Spring and early summer are excellent times to explore these trails, as native wildflowers like trillium and bleeding heart bloom alongside the paths, adding vibrant bursts of color to the forest floor. Huckleberry bushes also dot the trails, attracting small birds and animals eager to snack on their seasonal berries. Golden Gardens' forested trails provide an escape from the open beach, offering a quieter and more intimate experience of the park's natural elements.

The forested bluffs are also home to a variety of birds, from the charismatic song sparrows to the bold red-breasted nuthatch. Birdwatchers can spot hawks soaring above, scanning for small mammals, while smaller forest birds like chickadees and towhees dart through the foliage. Golden Gardens' trees and shrubs provide critical cover and nesting sites for these species, making the area an ideal location for bird enthusiasts.

Coastal Wildlife and Birdwatching

Golden Gardens is a hotspot for birdwatchers and nature photographers, with a diversity of birds that changes with the seasons. Seagulls and cormorants are year-round residents, often seen drying their wings on the pilings or diving into Puget Sound. During migration seasons, flocks of ducks and grebes appear along the shore, adding to the variety of avian life visible from the beach. Winter brings in species like buffleheads and common goldeneyes, while spring and fall attract migratory shorebirds stopping over to rest and refuel.

Golden Gardens' beachside logs are popular perches for bald eagles, which can be seen scanning the water for fish. Watching these majestic birds against the backdrop of the Sound is an unforgettable experience, and their presence is a testament to the richness of this coastal habitat. In the early morning or late afternoon, harbor seals are sometimes spotted swimming along the shore, their round heads bobbing above the water before they disappear back into the depths.

A Landscape Rich in Natural and Cultural History

Beyond its natural appeal, Golden Gardens holds a significant place in the history of Seattle. Originally a recreation destination developed in the early 1900s, the park has evolved into a preserved natural area that combines public beach access with conservation. Today, restoration efforts focus on maintaining native plant communities, reducing erosion along trails, and removing invasive species like Himalayan blackberry and English ivy that threaten the natural balance.

The park's significance extends beyond conservation, as it also serves as an educational space where local residents can learn about native ecosystems and wildlife. Interpretive signs placed throughout the park detail its flora and fauna, as well as the history of the area, offering visitors a chance to deepen their appreciation of Golden Gardens' unique landscape.

A Day Immersed in Seattle's Coastal Wilderness

Golden Gardens Park offers an ideal blend of beachside relaxation and nature exploration, making it a beloved destination for Seattleites and visitors alike. Whether you're walking the shore, exploring the wetlands, or hiking through forested trails, there's something for every nature lover at Golden Gardens. The park's diverse habitats—the intertidal zone, wetlands, forested bluffs, and Puget Sound—are teeming with life and offer a window into the beauty of the Pacific Northwest's coastal ecosystems.

As you leave the park, you're likely to carry with you the lingering scents of salt water and cedar, the memory of seabirds against a bright horizon, and the serene feeling that comes from connecting with nature. In a city known for its urban vibe, Golden Gardens remains a cherished escape to the coast, where the wild meets the water and visitors can experience the rich tapestry of Seattle's natural world.

▼ Nighttime bonfires on the beach are a long-standing summertime tradition at Golden Gardens.

Bloedel Reserve

Make the journey to Bainbridge Island to revel in the serene blend of outdoor art and nature in the extensive gardens on this formerly private estate.

Tucked away on Bainbridge Island, the Bloedel Reserve offers a serene escape into nature that transports visitors far from the hustle and bustle of nearby Seattle. Covering 150 acres of meticulously curated gardens, forests, and meadows, this former private estate is a sanctuary of tranquility where both native and exotic plants come together in a carefully orchestrated celebration of the natural world.

The Bloedel Reserve is the legacy of Prentice and Virginia Bloedel, who purchased the property in the 1950s. Prentice, a timber magnate with a passion for conservation, sought to create a landscape that blended the wild beauty of the Pacific Northwest with the elegance of formal garden design. Under the Bloedels' stewardship, the land was transformed into a living work of art, balancing natural ecosystems with cultivated gardens in perfect harmony. In 1986, the Bloedels gifted the property to the public, ensuring that future generations could enjoy and be inspired by its beauty.

Landscape Diversity = More Biodiversity

Visitors to the Bloedel Reserve can explore a wide variety of landscapes, from the fern-filled forests of towering Douglas fir and western red cedar to the reflective quietude of a Japanese garden. Meandering paths guide you through environments both wild and tamed, each thoughtfully designed to highlight the natural splendor of the land. Whether you're a passionate botanist, a casual nature lover, or simply seeking a peaceful retreat, the reserve's winding trails offer endless opportunities for discovery.

One of the Reserve's signature features is the Moss Garden, a verdant expanse where soft, spongy moss blankets the forest floor. Walking through this tranquil space feels almost like stepping into a fairytale—the air is cool

▲ Getting to Bainbridge Island on the ferry—and getting great views of downtown Seattle from the water along the way—is the cherry on top of any visit to Bloedel Reserve.

and damp, the canopy above is dense with ancient trees, and the moss underfoot creates a hushed, otherworldly atmosphere. The Moss Garden is a living testament to the Pacific Northwest's unique ability to sustain lush, green plant life even in the shadiest and dampest corners of the forest.

Intermingling Exotics

While the Bloedel Reserve places a strong emphasis on native plants, it also incorporates exotic species that have been carefully selected to complement the local flora. The Rhododendron Glen, for example, is home to an impressive collection of rhododendrons and azaleas, many of which hail from the Himalayas and Southeast Asia. In spring, this glen bursts into a kaleidoscope of color, with blossoms in shades of pink, purple, and white creating a dazzling contrast against the deep green of the surrounding trees.

Serenity Now

Another highlight is the Reflection Pool, a serene water feature framed by manicured hedges and towering evergreens. The stillness of the water perfectly mirrors the sky and trees above, creating a breathtaking visual effect that invites quiet contemplation. Nearby, the Buxton Bird Marsh and Meadow offer a more open, sunlit environment that attracts a wide variety of bird species, from great blue herons and red-winged blackbirds to swallows and woodpeckers. Birdwatchers will find this area particularly rewarding, as the reserve is home to more than 80 species of birds that make their nests in the diverse habitats across the property.

The Japanese Garden is perhaps the most tranquil part of the reserve, offering visitors a space for quiet reflection and meditation. Designed in the traditional style, the garden features a koi pond, stone lanterns, and meticulously pruned trees. A graceful teahouse overlooks the water, offering the perfect vantage point to appreciate the garden's symmetry and simplicity. This garden, like many other areas of the reserve, draws on the principle of *wabi-sabi*, an aesthetic that finds beauty in imperfection and the natural cycle of growth and decay.

A Legacy of Conservation and Education

While the Bloedel Reserve is undoubtedly a place of beauty, it is also a place of learning. The Bloedels' vision was not just to create a beautiful garden, but to foster an appreciation for the natural world and the importance of conservation. Throughout the reserve, you'll find interpretive signs that offer insight into the history of the landscape, the ecology of the plants and animals that live there, and the sustainable practices used to maintain the grounds. The reserve also offers educational programs, workshops, and guided tours that delve deeper into topics such as native plant gardening, habitat restoration, and forest ecology.

▶ Bloedel Reserve has its own Japanese garden with colorful plantings year-round.

▼ A wild Columbian black-tailed deer "hikes" the Bloedel Reserve Loop.

In keeping with its conservation ethos, the Bloedel Reserve has also been involved in restoration projects aimed at preserving and enhancing the health of its ecosystems. One such project is the rehabilitation of the wetlands that surround the bird marsh. By removing invasive species and planting native wetland vegetation, the reserve has helped restore this critical habitat, which provides food and shelter for birds, amphibians, and other wildlife. These efforts underscore the reserve's commitment to not just preserving its beauty, but also ensuring that it remains a thriving ecosystem for generations to come.

Outdoor Art Decorates Wild Nature

For those who appreciate a blend of art and nature, the Bloedel Reserve also offers a series of outdoor art installations that change with the seasons. These works of art, often made from natural materials, are integrated into the landscape in such a way that they seem to emerge organically from the surroundings. These installations add an element of surprise and delight to the visitor experience, inviting you to look at the natural world in new and unexpected ways.

No visit to the Bloedel Reserve would be complete without a stop at the estate's former residence, the Bloedel mansion. The house, designed in the French château style, now serves as a visitor center where guests can learn more about the history of the reserve and its founders. The mansion's formal gardens, with their geometric hedges and classical statuary, provide a striking contrast to the wilder, more naturalistic areas of the reserve.

◄ The unassuming yet beautiful flower of the vanilla-leaf plant, a hardy West Coast native, has decorated the forest floor here since time immemorial.

Engendering Wonder and Love for Nature

In all, the Bloedel Reserve is more than just a garden—it is a living testament to the beauty and diversity of the natural world. Whether you spend an hour or an entire day exploring its trails, you'll come away with a deeper appreciation for the delicate balance between nature and human design and a renewed sense of wonder for the world around you.

▲ The Residence at Bloedel Reserve is tastefully sited to not overshadow the beauty of the natural landscape.

ACKNOWLEDGMENTS

What a pleasure it has been to create *Wild Seattle*! I couldn't have and wouldn't have done it if not for Ryan Harrington at Timber Press asking me if I was ready for another project after finishing up three other titles in as many years for him. Luckily I was ready, and this one didn't require any travel as I live smack-dab in the middle of Seattle itself. That said, researching and photographing for the book introduced me to many a new corner of this fabulous urban center on Puget Sound than I would have discovered on my own. After all, I have lived in Seattle for almost three decades, so it took a project like this to get me off the couch and out the door to find new ways to experience the wild even within city limits. I hope the book will do the same for you. Thanks also go out to Matthew Burnett, Timber's senior production editor, who shepherded the book from soup to nuts, and Ellen Foreman, Timber's copy editor par excellence, for her attention to detail in reviewing and fact-checking the manuscript. Also deserving of a shout-out is Timber assistant editor Nick Dysinger, for his diligent work tracking down suggested stock photos from some obscure sources. As always, creating books with Timber Press is a joy; stay tuned for more Roddy Scheer titles in the future.

PHOTO & ILLUSTRATION CREDITS

All photos are by the author, except for the following:

Courtesy of the Seattle Municipal Archives;
    [31004], 17; [390], 19
University of Washington Libraries,
    Special Collections; [POR857], 2;
    [SOC20266] 13 (top)

Alamy
Cliff LeSergent/Alamy Stock Photo, 131
Doug Wilson/Alamy Stock Photo, 139, 143
Laura Romin & Larry Dalton/Alamy Stock
    Photo, 140

DanitaDelimont.com/All rights reserved
Adam Jones, 13 (bottom), 65, 73, 81
Cathy & Gordon Illg/Jaynes Gallery, 79
David Northcott, 109
Daybreak Imagery, 107
Emily Wilson, 93
Gary Luhm, 4, 49, 40, 43, 44, 46, 52, 53, 61, 74,
    104, 163, 269
Gavriel Jecan, 113
Jamie and Judy Wild, 95, 119, 135, 158, 166, 226,
    238–239
Janet Horton, 84, 86, 101
Jaynes Gallery, 89
Jim Engelbrecht, 12
Ken Archer, 35, 37, 51 (top), 68, 77
Michel Hersen, 71
Savanah Plank, 141
Steven Kazlowski, 8, 118, 124, 126, 240 (top)
Trish Drury, 59, 60, 90, 105
William Perry, 132–133, 193
William Sutton, 96

Dreamstime
400tmax, 13
Wim Verhagen, 29–30

Flickr
CC BY 2.0
Andy Reago & Chrissy McClarren, 45
Backbone Campaign, 31
James Johnstone, 82
CC BY ND 2.0
Jonathan Hover, 69

iStock
GarysFRP, 108
gkuchera, 99
Henk Wallays, 112
MarvVandehey, 47
Radomir Jovanovic, 137
Randimal, 111, 123
RPFerreira, 170
Siur, 159
SolomonCrowe, 114
Wirestock, 115, 121

Shutterstock
Holger Kirk, 100

Wikimedia/Public Domain
Marjef07, Jeffrey Marsten, 117

All illustrations by Stevie Shao.

INDEX

Roddy Scheer is a journalist and photographer specializing in environmental issues, the outdoors, and travel. When he is not out in the field taking pictures, Roddy produces EarthTalk, a weekly environmental Q and A column syndicated to more than 1000 news outlets reaching more than six million readers. He has served as a regular contributor to *E—The Environmental Magazine*, *Seattle Magazine*, *Northwest Travel & Life*, *American Photo*, *PhotoMedia*, *Wildflower*, and others. His books include *Oregon and Washington's Roadside Ecology*, *Yellowstone and Grand Teton's Best Nature Walks*, and *Southwest Canyon Country's Best Nature Walks*. He is a three-time Society of Professional Journalists' "Excellence in Journalism" winner.